LAKOTA PERFORMERS IN EUROPE

The William F. Cody Series on the History and Culture of the American West

LAKOTA PERFORMERS IN EUROPE

THEIR CULTURE AND THE ARTIFACTS THEY LEFT BEHIND

STEVE FRIESEN WITH FRANÇOIS CHLADIUK

LETTER TO THE AUTHORS FROM WALTER LITTLEMOON

UNIVERSITY OF OKLAHOMA PRESS : NORMAN

ALSO BY STEVE FRIESEN

A Modest Mennonite Home: The Story of the 1719 Hans Herr House, an Early Colonial Landmark (Intercourse, Pa., 1990)

Buffalo Bill: Scout, Showman, Visionary (Golden, Colo., 2010)

Buffalo Bill Center of the West sponsorship of The William F. Cody Series on the History and Culture of the American West is generously funded by the Geraldine W. & Robert J. Dellenback Foundation, Inc.

LIBRARY OF CONGRESS CATALOGING-IN-PUBLICATION DATA

Names: Friesen, Steve, 1953– author. | Chladiuk, François, author.
Title: Lakota performers in Europe : their culture and the artifacts they left behind / Steve Friesen, with François Chladiuk ; letter to the authors from Walter Littlemoon.
Description: First edition. | Norman, OK : University of Oklahoma Press, [2017] | Series: William F. Cody Series on the history and culture of the American West ; volume 3 | Includes bibliographical references and index.
Identifiers: LCCN 2016049902 | ISBN 978-0-8061-5696-5 (hardcover) ISBN 978-0-8061-9608-4 (paper)
Subjects: LCSH: Exposition universelle et internationale (1935 : Brussels, Belgium) | Lakota Indians—Material culture—Catalogs. | Lakota Indians—Biography. | Indians of North America—Material culture—Catalogs.
Classification: LCC T468.G1 I63 2017 | DDC 978.004/9752440074493—dc23
LC record available at https://lccn.loc.gov/2016049902

Lakota Performers in Europe: Their Culture and the Artifacts They Left Behind is Volume 3 in the William F. Cody Series on the History and Culture of the American West.

The paper in this book meets the guidelines for permanence and durability of the Committee on Production Guidelines for Book Longevity of the Council on Library Resources, Inc. ∞

The manufacturer's authorized representative in the EU for product safety is Mare Nostrum Group B.V., Mauritskade 21D, 1091 Amsterdam, The Netherlands, email: gpsr@mare-nostrum.co.uk

CONTENTS

SERIES EDITORS' FOREWORD

In 1887 Buffalo Bill's Wild West traveled to Europe to perform in London, England, marking the first of three overseas tours that reintroduced Europeans to the American frontier experience. While the overall performance emphasized conquest of the American West through the military defeat of American Indians, the exhibition also introduced a new generation of Europeans to American Indian cultures. In the arena, Lakota performers from the Pine Ridge reservation, under contract with Buffalo Bill's Wild West, re-created their defeats on the Great Plains, but outside of the arena, within the Plains Indian encampment, they interpreted their culture to curious European spectators. In the decades to come, many other traveling shows would follow, enacting the very themes popularized by Buffalo Bill throughout Europe.

The experiences of these American Indian performers traveling Europe have been represented in various forms, most notably in John G. Neihardt's recounting of his interviews with Black Elk, which appear in the now classic *Black Elk Speaks*. In the stunningly illustrated volume before you, Steve Friesen, with François Chladiuk, examines the cultural influence of Lakota performers such as Black Elk on Europe by highlighting a recently recovered collection of Lakota performers' artifacts, used in Brussels in 1935, that had been acquired by August Hermans, a Belgian butcher fascinated by the indigenous peoples of North America. This book, or "biography of artifacts," as Friesen and Chladiuk term it, showcases artistic objects used by Charles High Hawk, Sam Lone Bear, White Buffalo Man, and other Lakota performers, and suggests the lasting impact Wild West tours had upon European spectators.

Lakota Performers in Europe: Their Culture and the Artifacts They Left Behind provides an intriguingly intimate view of the American Indian performers' contribution to public impressions of the mythical American West on an international stage. The artifacts highlighted in this volume offer cultural insights into Lakota performers and their work during the Brussels International Exposition and reveal European fascination with American Indian cultures, a phenomenon that persists to the present day. The use of these American Indian artifacts by Lakota actors and European reenactors offers a unique perspective not only on the transnational impact of Wild West shows and American Indian performers, but also on the ways that Nazism, World War II, and the Cold War affected European perceptions of American Indians.

The William F. Cody Series on the History and Culture of the American West is pleased to offer this visual study of American Indian influence on European culture. *Lakota Performers in Europe: Their Culture and the Artifacts They Left Behind*, by Steve Friesen, with François Chladiuk, provides readers a rare glimpse of the Wild West exhibition's legacy as embodied by Lakota performers, a Belgian family, and their material record of transatlantic cultural exchange.

JEREMY JOHNSTON
FRANK CHRISTIANSON
DOUGLAS SEEFELDT

A LETTER TO THE AUTHORS

My friends François and Steve,

Thank you for preserving a most positive event in our tribal history and, in particular, my family's history. I am so grateful for all your dedication and hard work.

There have been so many negative memories for our people, beginning in the mid-1800s, during my grandparents' lives and continuing on through mine. So much of who we are has been lost and destroyed. Wars and broken treaties have greatly reduced our land base. Living under restrictive laws on reservation lands and being subjected to acculturation through "Indian" boarding schools destroyed much of our culture as well as our identity and our understanding of what it means to be tribal people. In fact, there are days in which I fear we are on the verge of extinction. The old time people used to say, "It's hard to be Indian." I agree. The life we have been born into has been confusing, and it has been hard to hold to who we are.

The preservation of artifacts and physical things by caring individuals is so important for the survival of all tribal people because those acts of kindness remind us and encourage us during hard times that we are human beings. We are a part of the brotherhood of life.

Pilamaye,
WALTER LITTLEMOON
Wounded Knee, South Dakota
April 17, 2016

ACKNOWLEDGMENTS

Those American Indians who performed in wild west shows were neither savages nor naïve victims. Faced with extinction or assimilation, they chose a third way. In this effort they found an unexpected ally in a remarkable man who had been their enemy and had made his reputation as an Indian fighter. William F. "Buffalo Bill" Cody changed his mind about his former enemies, forging friendships with them, employing them, and advocating on behalf of their rights. Buffalo Bill's Wild West was not a tool for exploitation of the Indians, as the politically correct but historically confused argue today. Those who criticize his and other wild west shows are simply voicing a modern version of the paternalism that was so prevalent in the late nineteenth and early twentieth centuries. The show represented not exploitation but opportunity. As Black Heart said in 1890, "We were raised on horseback; that is the way we had to work. These men furnished us the same work we were raised to; that is the reason we want to work for these kind of men." So the first acknowledgments in this book must be to those who performed, the Lakotas themselves, and to the people who enabled those performances, the foremost being Buffalo Bill Cody.

In 2006 I was alerted by the front desk at the Buffalo Bill Museum and Grave that a tall Belgian man was wandering around the museum with a film crew. He wanted to meet the director. I emerged from my office to meet François Chladiuk, who immediately launched into a story about a group of Lakota artifacts in his possession. He was on his way to Pine Ridge but wanted to see what information the museum might have that would be useful in his efforts to document the materials. François was so effusive and passionate about the subject that I was drawn into his story like a tree uprooted by a tornado. As we talked, the crew videotaped the conversation, adding footage to a documentary that would be aired on Belgian television later that year. Two years later we exhibited some of his collection at the Buffalo Bill Museum, in a special exhibit called *Found in a Belgian Basement*. Thus began a friendship that would be renewed at least twice annually with François' visits to Denver. The visits involved lengthy conversations about the artifacts and western history as well as special gifts of Belgian chocolates for my wife, Monta Lee. In 2011 Monta Lee and I traveled to Brussels to visit François and his Western Shop, where she purchased a pair of cowboy boots (a rather unique souvenir of our trip to Europe). There we also saw the artifacts in a special exhibit area he had created for them. A year later we visited Florence, Italy, with François to see one of the headdresses on exhibit at the Pitti Palace. By then my conversations with François included his desire to have a book written about the collection. A small catalog had been produced about the collection when it was on exhibit in the Royal Museums of Art and History, but François felt something more comprehensive was needed. By the time we left Florence, we had a plan: I would write a book about the collection. François would provide me with the research he had done so far as well as gather other materials from Brussels as I needed them. I would dig deeper into the stories of those who performed, starting with Buffalo Bill's Wild West.

In addition to François, who also provided the color images of the items in his collection, a number of people provided invaluable assistance with this book. The catalog created by Sergio Purini and Marc Lauwens for the exhibit at the Royal Museums of Art and History provided useful initial information. Freddy Thielemans, mayor of Brussels and a mutual friend, helped François find important local records about August Hermans. Walter Littlemoon, whose family had performed in Belgium, and his wife, Jane Ridgeway, provided helpful information and advice from Pine Ridge. At Fort Robinson in Nebraska, during a symposium on the Indian Wars, I had a chance to discuss the project at some length with Jerome Greene and Paul Hedren, who continue to be valuable sources of ideas and information. At the symposium I also met Patsy LaPointe, who directed my attention toward her great-grandmother Jennie LaPoint, a most remarkable woman who had performed in Wild West shows in the early twentieth century. These were just some of the many conversations at gatherings with fellow researchers, western history enthusiasts, and descendants of the Lakota performers that inspired and informed me during this project.

Several trips to the National Archives in Kansas City yielded a great deal of information, provided by Jake Erslund and other staff members. On one of those trips, my good friends Bill Carle and Herbert Garmaier (who helped me wade through some of the German documents) provided excellent research assistance, reducing a four-day process to two. And, as always, visits to the Western History Collection of the Denver Public Library and to the library at History Colorado (formerly Colorado Historical Society) yielded several gems. Despite our disagreements over Buffalo Bill's choice of a burial site (Lookout Mountain rather than Cody, Wyoming), the folks at the Buffalo Bill Center of the West have always been the best of friends, bending over backwards in their efforts to help me on my research visits to Cody, Wyoming. They include Mary Robinson and Charlotte Gdula at the McCracken Library as well as the folks involved with the "The Papers of William F. Cody" project, notably Jeremy Johnston, Linda Clark, and Deborah Adams. Shelley Buffalo Calf, assistant registrar at the Center of the West, also pointed me in some good directions.

Just as I was concluding my work on my manuscript, I took a trip to Germany and stopped at the Munich Cowboy Club. There I spent some wonderful hours with club members Billy Kopf and Andi Schneider, looking at early club scrapbooks and artifacts in the club's collection. Hartmut Reitschel, an expert on American Indian performers in Germany, drove down from Dresden to join us that evening. Hartmut helps maintain Edward Two Two's grave near Dresden and has provided me with important information regarding Indian hobbyists over the past five years.

L. G. Moses deserves a great deal of credit for his seminal work of 1996, *Wild West Shows and the Images of American Indians: 1883–1933.* At a time when many scholars were making their paternalistic claims that Buffalo Bill and other show operators had exploited their Indian performers, he provided solid evidence that the shows were a bulwark against the destruction of native culture.

My own institution, the Buffalo Bill Museum and Grave outside Golden, Colorado, must be mentioned. This comparatively small institution is a treasure trove of information about wild west shows and those who performed in them, thanks to the vision of Johnny Baker, foster son of Buffalo Bill and founder of the museum in 1921. In my role as director for the past twenty-plus years, it has been my pleasure to continue Baker's vision. As I worked on this book, I found myself returning repeatedly to the museum's archival and photographic collections.

Finally, I quite happily acknowledge the support of my wife, Monta Lee Dakin. That support ranged from assisting me on research trips to providing me with critical input and ideas during conversations on our daily walks. A fellow historian and intellectual companion, she is my guiding light in both calm and troubled waters.

LAKOTA PERFORMERS IN EUROPE

PROLOGUE

The artifacts slumbered for years, carefully preserved in steel boxes. One hundred and fifty-seven pieces of Lakota culture, carefully stored and labeled . . . awaiting discovery. Like the objects in a time capsule, these artifacts would become the keys to unlocking a story of the past, a story interrupted and then resumed in the twenty-first century.

That story is of a people who were not "savages" at all, though they were often given that label, but a people who had a distinctive and vibrant culture—a culture they struggled to practice and preserve against tremendous odds.

"François, I just ran across a very interesting collection of American Indian materials. I thought you might be interested." This telephone call from an antique dealer in 2004 began a quest that would take François Chladiuk from Brussels, Belgium, to Wounded Knee, South Dakota, and on to Buffalo Bill's grave on Lookout Mountain outside Denver, Colorado. It would send this Belgian collector back in time, as he researched more than one hundred years into the past to learn about Buffalo Bill's Wild West, and forward to the troubled present of Pine Ridge, where he would learn about the damage done by the boarding schools to the very descendants of the Lakotas who had used the artifacts that interested him.

After François acquired the collection and began exploring its history, he learned how truly unique it was. Never before had he seen such a large group of American Indian artifacts, all of which had remained together since 1935. Of the 157 artifacts, 145 pieces composed a nearly complete collection of materials used by a group of Lakota performers who had traveled to the 1935 Brussels International Exposition on the eve of a world war. The materials had been acquired from the Lakotas by August Hermans, a butcher in Brussels. Hermans' documentation was thorough, with paper labels for more than half of the artifacts, naming them and the performers they had served. François Chladiuk began combing Belgium and the rest of Europe for more information about the exposition. The search paid off, as he found postcards and photographs of the Lakotas posing and performing, wearing the artifacts that were in his collection. The more he searched, the more he realized that he had acquired one of the most thoroughly documented collections of American Indian artifacts in Europe, and possibly the world. As he reviewed the materials, it became clear that he indeed had before him a time capsule from the past, a time capsule that preserved an era that began with Buffalo Bill's Wild West and ended with the world at war.

This book is a biography—a biography of the artifacts and their people. Artifacts gain their significance from the people who made them, used them, and possessed them, whether these are all the same people or not. So this book includes the stories of those who were involved with the artifacts discovered by François Chladiuk. Within these pages are the stories of Sam Lone Bear and others like him, who made careers as performers, and of the Little Moon family, who spent nearly a year in Europe, then returned to the reservation for the rest of their lives. There is the story of the butcher August Hermans, who had originally collected the American Indian artifacts, and the story of collector François Chladiuk himself, whose interest in the American West led him to the butcher's collection and eventually to Pine Ridge, where he became friends with the Little Moons. Overlying these stories are the larger stories of the wild west shows and Buffalo Bill; of the Indians' experience of acculturation and the attempts to assimilate them through the Indian schools; of the impact of Lakota performance on Europeans' interest in the American West; and of ongoing change in the culture of the Lakotas. Uniting these stories are the artifacts, transplanted from one continent to another.

For more than four hundred years, American Indians had been visiting Europe as curiosities, at first unwillingly as colonial captives, then as ambassadors of the American West with the wild west shows. When the 1935 exposition took place in Brussels, it provided Europeans with a snapshot of a Lakota culture and lifestyle that had nearly been destroyed. It was a snapshot taken at a time just before Belgium, and all of Europe, would be altered drastically by the rise of the Nazis and the arrival of World War II. Over the course of one decade, everything would be different. American Indians, some of whom had first visited Europe wearing strange and colorful costumes, would return later that decade as American GIs, wearing the clothing of modern warfare. And their return would not be as representatives of a suppressed culture but as allies and liberators. Just as the war transformed Europe, uniting its nations against a common enemy, American Indian nations too were transformed.

Following World War II, some of the things that had separated the tribes for centuries were placed aside. The powwow, a pan-Indian movement that both celebrated and blended the cultures of the tribes, rose to prominence. Today the powwow continues to be strong, accompanied by fresh attention to the unique tribal cultures of the United States. After years of suppression of their tribal cultures, American Indians are revitalizing not just their clothing, foods, and arts, but also their languages. Just as museum exhibits in the United States have focused on the cultures and arts of Europe, now there are exhibits of the distinctive cultures and arts of the United States in Europe. European attention to the American West and its people has moved beyond the wild west shows of the past to become more thoughtful and profound. One manifestation of this change was a 2012 exhibit at the Medici Pitti Palace in Florence, Italy, where the arts of American Indians were exhibited nearly side by side with those of the Renaissance masters. The stories in this book are not about a "savage" and "ignorant" people; they are about a people who were able to preserve their cultural heritage despite suppression and adversity.

Buffalo Bill saw that the American West and its peoples were changing. Through his show, he sought to present the West that he had known before that version of the West vanished altogether.
Buffalo Bill Museum and Grave

CHAPTER 1

RISE OF THE WILD WEST SHOWS

The arena was packed, and Buffalo Bill was confident that the show would continue drawing crowds from New York City to the grounds at Erastina. But the Wild West show had been touring the United States for nearly four years, and it was time to conquer new territories. Mark Twain had told him it was time to take a truly authentic show about the American West to Europe. Twain was right. They would all go, cowboys and cowgirls, Annie Oakley, vaqueros, the Deadwood Stage, the buffalo, and of course, the Lakotas.

Buffalo Bill was not the first to think about taking representatives from America to Europe. The first Indians were taken from home unwillingly by Columbus and later explorers. By the 1700s, some Indians visited of their free will, seeking to intercede with the colonial powers of England and France on behalf of their peoples. Even those who adopted the European style of dress were regarded as curiosities during their visits. Small groups of American Indians continued to visit Europe into the 1800s, as diplomats or tourists.

They would not visit as performers until 1819, when a group of seven Senecas and Oneidas visited England to "exhibit interesting Performances." The exhibition was described as "a natural and simple Illustration of the Native Manners and Customs of a Nation totally uncivilized."[1]

In 1827, a group of Osage Indians traveled to Paris, where they were exhibited as novelties, with an admission paid to see both them and a balloon ascension. Then they traveled to Brussels, Belgium, for the Christmas and New Year holidays, where they were treated more like visiting dignitaries.[2]

Later, in the 1840s, artist George Catlin took American Indians to Europe to dance, sing, and demonstrate their culture during his lectures. These real-life exhibitions made Catlin's lectures, which included his portraits of American Indians, instantly popular in Britain and France. Catlin took one group to Brussels in 1846, where several died of smallpox. Because of this incident, Catlin decided to no longer transport American Indians to Europe and even spoke out against doing so.[3]

At the same time that Catlin was touring with Indians in Europe, there was a growing interest in the United States in Indians and the

American West. This interest, fueled by news stories of true events as well as dime novels and their fictional events, led to the growth of a variety of performances. P. T. Barnum staged a "Grand Buffalo Hunt" near New York City in 1843. A buffalo hunt was also incorporated with a skit about Pocahontas and an exhibition of Indian culture in Tyler's Indian Exhibition in the 1850s. Around this same time, cowboys were beginning to show off their skills in competitions that would become known as rodeos many years later. By the 1870s the interest in the frontier had also spawned various stage shows, including plays about the West. Those performed by the Buffalo Bill Combination included high-profile frontiersmen like William F. "Buffalo Bill" Cody, adding celebrity to their drama.[4]

The year 1883 was a watershed in show business. That year Buffalo Bill moved beyond the limitations of the indoor stage to a larger venue, the great outdoors. With the outdoor arena, Buffalo Bill's Wild West brought cowboy skills, reenactments of frontier scenes, buffalo and other animals from the West, and the peoples of the West together to create an extravaganza. Combining elements of what had been done before and yet unlike anything that had preceded it, Buffalo Bill's Wild West initiated an era of show business that lasted fifty years. Its influence on the entertainment industry would continue after its demise and the demise of the other wild west shows. The reach of Buffalo Bill's Wild West would touch everything from the circus to the rodeo to the movies.

Central to Buffalo Bill's Wild West exhibition, intended to be not a show but an educational experience, were American Indians. They took part in re-creations of battles, danced, showed off their horsemanship, and demonstrated their cultures to audiences. With the inclusion of Indians, exotic to many in the eastern United States, as was the entire collection of other people and animals from the West, Buffalo Bill's Wild West soon became immensely popular. It gained acclaim from such notables as Mark Twain, who wrote Cody in 1884, encouraging him to take Buffalo Bill's Wild West to Europe, where it would have the advantage of being the first distinctively American exhibition to visit the continent.[5]

Following the unfortunate demise of Catlin's lectures in the 1840s, American Indians did not travel to Europe in any numbers to demonstrate their cultures until forty years later. In 1883 a group of Chippewas traveled to Berlin as purported examples of the Indians who were in James Fenimore Cooper's books, capitalizing on the books' popularity in Europe. Then in 1886 a group of fifteen men, women, and children from the Lakota tribe visited Europe, where they spent a month in a zoological garden in Budapest, then traveled on to Vienna. They demonstrated aspects of their tribal life, including marksmanship with bows and arrows, horsemanship, and dances. The program finished with a re-creation of an attack on white settlers in the West. Perhaps inspired in part by Buffalo Bill's Wild West, which had been touring the United States for three years, the show at the zoo was a first effort to introduce the Lakotas to Europe. But this introduction was minor. Buffalo Bill and his large cast, including ninety American Indians, would most effectively introduce Lakotas and other peoples of the American West to Europe, beginning with Buffalo Bill's Wild West traveling to London in 1887 for the golden jubilee of Queen Victoria's rule.[6]

William Cody realized that the American frontier and its peoples were changing, the frontier even disappearing, and he wanted to show the West as he had experienced it. He had first met an Indian at the age of eight, when his family moved to Kansas, and he would come to know Indians as both friends and enemies. He understood the fascination with Plains Indian cultures among many people in the eastern United States, a fascination due in part to the many news reports from the Indian Wars and in part to depictions of Indians in dime novels. When he took his Wild West to London four years after creating the show, he was well aware that this fascination would also exist in Europe, where people were even less acquainted with American Indian cultures. He also did something that none of his predecessors, not even Catlin, had done. He introduced American Indians to the general population, not just to the aristocracy or the intellectual elite. He referred to his Wild West as America's entertainment, and he aimed to make it Europe's entertainment too.

The Lakotas demonstrate breaking camp during the Wild West's appearance in Brussels in 1891.
Buffalo Bill Museum and Grave

Building on the show's successes in America, Cody offered a two-pronged approach, largely unprecedented in Europe, to interpreting American Indian life and culture. Central to the show was the arena, with re-creations of western life and skill, including reenactments of battles from the Indian Wars. But Cody was interested in showing more than battles in the arena. Plains Indian performers demonstrated tepee raising, showed off their horsemanship, and illustrated other aspects of their lives. Away from the arena, Cody felt it important for visitors to meet and even photograph the peoples of the West. During the show's appearance at Erastina on Staten Island, New York, in 1886, advertising emphasized that "every representative of the world from this cosmopolitan city linger[s] about the tepees of the red man, the tents of the white men and the marquees of the leaders." This was the Wild West's encampment, where visitors could see the peoples of the West outside of the arena context. A reporter from the Brooklyn Daily Eagle remarked on the Erastina setup: "The genius who laid out the encampment proper falls only a little short of being a veritable artist. The grouping of nationalities, of the lodges of the several tribes of Indians, the quarters of the frontiersmen, the natives of the land of the Incas and the temporary abiding places of the representatives of advanced civilization, constitutes a picture which may at once be pleasurably and profitably studied."[7]

Cody offered a "Picturesque Western Camp" while his show was in New Orleans in 1884–1885, at Erastina on Staten Island in 1886, at the American Exhibition at Earl's Court in London in 1887, and in Paris near the Bois de Boulogne during the 1889 Exposition Universelle. Certainly critical to the success of these encampments was the American Indian "village," where visitors could see the warriors relaxing with their families, observe their cultures up close, and even get photographs. The 1887 encampment in London included seventeen tepees. Years later, George Dull Knife would tell his grandchildren about performing with Buffalo Bill's Wild West. His grandson remembered, "When they traveled overseas, the Indians all lived together. Shortly after arriving in England, France, Germany, Italy or Spain, their camps soon began to resemble the camps they had always lived in on the plains. A village of tipis clustered in traditional fashion emerged

American Indians performing in Buffalo Bill's Wild West arena at Erastina on Staten Island in 1886.
Buffalo Bill Museum and Grave

In this stereocard, Lakota performers with Buffalo Bill's Wild West pose in front of a tepee during the show's appearance in Brussels in 1891. *Buffalo Bill Museum and Grave*

near the show grounds." Luther Standing Bear noted that in 1902, after the conclusion of the show, British visitors to Buffalo Bill's Wild West then went to the village, where they "had a chance to see how we lived."

Cody was not alone in creating such encampments at expositions. As early as 1883, Joe Miller of the 101 Ranch in Oklahoma had presented an Indian village to visitors to the Alabama State Fair. The success of this model in both the United States and Europe laid the groundwork for all wild west shows, which used both reenactments and encampments through the rest of the nineteenth century and into the twentieth. The Indian village concept was later copied by traveling circuses and offered, often without any reenactments, by expositions and fairs.[8]

The Wild West was a hit in Europe. Although Buffalo Bill and other performers, like Annie Oakley, were mentioned in the news, the people of Europe were most fascinated by the Indians. Red Shirt, a Lakota chief, was good looking and well spoken; he became the focus of many newspaper articles as the show traveled Europe. He was even a special guest of the British Parliament. The publicity for Buffalo Bill's Wild West emphasized the presence of charismatic chiefs like Red Shirt, but to re-create battles and village life, many more Indian performers were needed than had ever been part of a traveling show before. With Wild West's first European visit in 1887, the show included 90 Indian performers. By the show's European tour of 1904, the number had swelled to 110.[9]

The Indians who traveled with Buffalo Bill's Wild West were from the Great Plains. There were representatives of other tribes in the show, but the majority of the performers were Lakota. Outside of reading accounts of visits to the Great Plains and seeing artifacts brought back by those visitors,

European visitors to Buffalo Bill's Wild West were fascinated by the living representation of a culture they had only read about. The travois used by Indians to transport their goods were completely alien in countries that had used the wheel for centuries. *Buffalo Bill Museum and Grave*

the people of Europe had little exposure to the culture of the Plains Indians. The first visits by Buffalo Bill's Wild West as well as subsequent visits by various traveling shows, most of whom employed members of Plains tribes, had an indelible impact on the Europeans, who were impressed by Plains Indian tepees, dances, and lifestyles. The year 1887 was thus pivotal, marking the beginning of many trips to Europe by the Lakotas as well as the beginning of Europeans' fascination with the Indians of the Plains.

CHAPTER 2

OSKATE WICASA
ONE WHO PERFORMS

Fast as the wind, the Lakota warriors rode around the arena, chasing the stagecoach. As they rode they smiled, shouting and waving their rifles. They knew that after they overtook the coach, they would be driven away by Buffalo Bill and the cowboys. But they didn't care. This was a life worth living, so much better than being on the reservation where they were forced to dig in the dirt or starve.

Whooping for joy, Lakota warriors race through the arena in Buffalo Bill's Wild West. Black Heart testified about the show organizers: "These men furnished us the same work we were raised to; that is the reason we want to work for these kind of men." Quoted in Moses, *Wild West Shows*, 103. *Buffalo Bill Museum and Grave*

Known as the Sioux by their enemies, Lakotas were a logical choice for the arena. There were performers from other tribes, such as Arapahos, Pawnees, and Crows, but Lakotas dominated Buffalo Bill's Wild West and the other wild west shows—just as they had dominated the Great Plains. They were the preeminent warriors of the northern plains, fierce in their battles and proud in their culture. Referred to by those professional soldiers who encountered them as "the finest light cavalry in the world," Lakotas were ferocious in battle and feared by their enemies. They had held out the longest against the encroachment of the U.S. Army, settlers, and American culture. Even before Buffalo Bill's Wild West started touring Lakotas around the country, they had been a source of fascination to the American people. They were the subject of numerous news articles, dime novels, and plays, long after other tribes had faded from the limelight. Lakotas were the tribe with the celebrities, like Red Cloud, Sitting Bull, and Crazy Horse. It was mainly Lakotas who had defeated Custer at Little Bighorn, and they remained independent long after other tribes had begun assimilating.[1]

Buffalo Bill flanked by Pawnee warriors on the left and Lakota warriors on the right during the show's engagement at Erastina on Long Island in 1886. During the first visit of Buffalo Bill's Wild West to Europe the following year, the show employed primarily Lakota performers. *Buffalo Bill Museum and Grave*

Lakotas' reputation as fierce fighters translated into crowd-pleasing action on the arena floor. They brought a zeal to the performance that was hard to match. A writer for the *New York Times* observed in 1886 that even though they suffered defeat time after time in the arena, "they seemed to have become used to it and entered the contest with no less spirit on that account." One Lakota performer, Short Boy, remarked in 1911 that they took great pleasure in going up against the U.S. Army in the arena, even if they had to use blank ammunition. When it came to re-creating battles in the arena, even those they had lost, Lakotas were perfect performers. When they performed, there was a very thin line between re-creation and reality, giving their re-creations an authenticity remarked on by those in the military who attended the shows and had actually opposed them in battle.[2]

The name Lakota comes from the language used by seven different bands known as the Tetonwans who were scattered around the northern plains. Best known among these bands are the Oglalas, Brulés, Miniconjous, and Hunkpapas. While Tetonwans were previously referred to as Sioux, a name given them by their enemies, today they are more frequently referred to as Lakotas. After their final defeat at the conclusion of the Great Sioux War in 1877, they were forced onto reservations in the Dakotas and Nebraska. The largest of those reservations was the Pine Ridge Reservation in South Dakota, populated primarily by Oglala Lakotas. Although performers were recruited from other reservations, Pine Ridge was not only the largest reservation, it was also readily accessible by rail. No wonder, then, that recruiters for Buffalo Bill's Wild West and the other shows that would follow beat a path to Pine Ridge Reservation to assemble their performers. The Lakotas of Pine Ridge coined the phrase *oskate wicasa*, "one who performs," as a designation and point of pride for those who were selected for the wild west shows.

After the initial visit to England in 1887, Cody and his Wild West returned to Europe and traveled across the continent from 1889 to 1892, passing through Brussels and making other stops in Belgium. In 1891 he and many of the Lakota warriors in his group visited the Waterloo monument outside Brussels. There, on the site of Napoleon's defeat, they posed for photographs and had their names recorded on the guest register: "Warriors of the Ogallala and Brule Sioux, Buffalo Bill's Wild West Co., June 2nd, 1891." Buffalo Bill's Wild West returned to Europe between 1902 and 1906, once again performing in Brussels. These visits helped create an interest in the American West that made

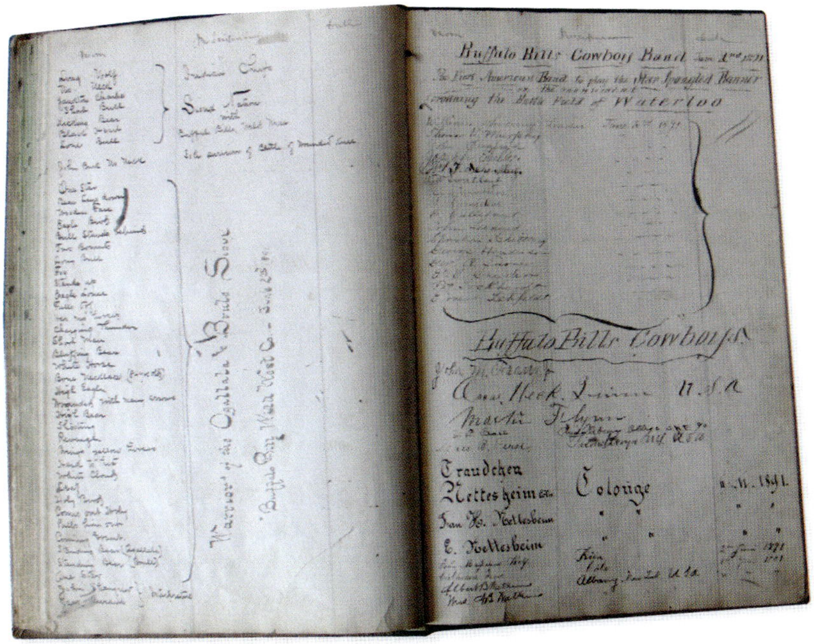

On June 2, 1891, Buffalo Bill and a group of performers visited the Waterloo monument near Brussels. The group included forty-one Lakotas, listed in the guest register kept at the monument. In addition to signing the guest register they all posed for a photograph on the monument's steps. *Buffalo Bill Museum and Grave*

Brussels an important stop for other wild west shows, in addition to laying the groundwork for a Lakota presence at expositions such as the Brussels International Exposition in 1935.[3]

Buffalo Bill was certainly not the only person to take a wild west show to Europe. His success spawned many imitators, more than one hundred in the thirty years following 1887. Most of the shows confined their travels to the United States, but some did cross the Atlantic to play Europe. Two of the more successful show organizers got their start with Buffalo Bill's Wild West: Doc Carver, a former partner of Cody's, and Gordon "Pawnee Bill" Lillie, who had learned show business while a part of Cody's show. Doc Carver took his show to Europe in 1889, and Pawnee Bill toured Europe several times. After Buffalo Bill's return to the United States in 1892, Pawnee Bill took his show to Antwerp, Belgium, for the 1894 Exposition Universelle d'Anvers, where it appeared for five months. With the exception of Carver and Lillie, most of the imitators' shows were short lived and of dubious quality, often playing one season and folding. Buffalo Bill's Wild West was arguably the best of the shows and exhibitions that toured Europe during the 1890s and during the first part of the next century.[4]

The rise of the wild west shows, even the short-lived ones, provided opportunities for Lakotas. Life on the reservation was difficult. After years of problems, the government made considerable effort to ensure that Indians got their promised rations and payments, but by the late 1880s and early 1890s, instances of corruption by Indian agents and suppliers meant that food and other promised materials were often in short supply. As late as 1895, Buffalo Bill arranged a meeting between Indians with his show and the commissioner of Indian affairs, to whom they complained that the treaties had been violated and that they were short on rations, blankets, and clothing on the reservations. Additionally, the Plains Indian tribes, who were nomadic hunters in tradition and skills, were expected to become sedentary farmers, yet the land on the reservation had little agricultural potential and would have challenged experienced farmers. The result was a bleak existence of malnutrition and little opportunity. Once Buffalo Bill's Wild West and other shows started hiring, the Indians jumped at the opportunity. Black Heart, a member of the Wild West cast, said, "We were raised on horseback; that is the way we had to work. These men furnished us the same work we were raised to; that is the reason we want to work for these kind of men." After Luther Standing Bear's first season with the Wild West in 1902–1903, he returned for the next season. He traveled to Rushville, Nebraska, to meet show representatives, and, he wrote, "when I arrived there I was surprised to see all the Indians from my reservation there, waiting. They had a big camp. It seems they had found out in some manner that I was again to be in charge and when I entered the camp I was besieged on all sides from those who wanted to go out with the show."[5]

Program from Pawnee Bill's Wild West, during its visit to Antwerp (Anvers) for the 1894 Exposition Universelle d'Anvers. *François Chladiuk Collection*

Lakota performers with Buffalo Bill's Wild West were as excited to see the sights in Wales as the gathered crowd was to see them.
Buffalo Bill Museum and Grave

Performing with wild west shows provided opportunities that were not only unavailable on the reservations but open to few other people in America. Luther Standing Bear wrote about his visit to London with Buffalo Bill's Wild West: "I was sorry to leave this city, because I had been given a chance to see many wonderful sights and visit many interesting places." Some performers, like Sam Lone Bear, traveled all over America and visited Europe several times. Years later Lone Bear wrote nostalgically about his visits to Europe, saying he would much prefer to be there rather than living at Pine Ridge. Others, like Thomas Stabber, established friendships with the people they met in Europe, corresponding with them on their return to the United States. These performers clearly established an affinity with Europe and Europeans, an affinity that led them to return to the continent. Those visits were frequently marked by meet-ups with friends they had made on previous visits.[6]

In the shows the Indians were also able to earn much better wages than they would have earned farming or doing other work on the reservations. In 1899 the commissioner of Indian affairs complained that even Indians who had attended schools and become "civilized" adopted the old garb and performed in order to make money. And why not? Forty-seven Lakotas traveled to Europe with Buffalo Bill's Wild West in 1888. The total payroll for the Indians was $27,200, averaging out to nearly $579 per performer. Those were very good wages for 1888.[7]

Some of the American Indians, predominantly Lakotas, returned again and again to Buffalo Bill's Wild West after their first season, adopting performing

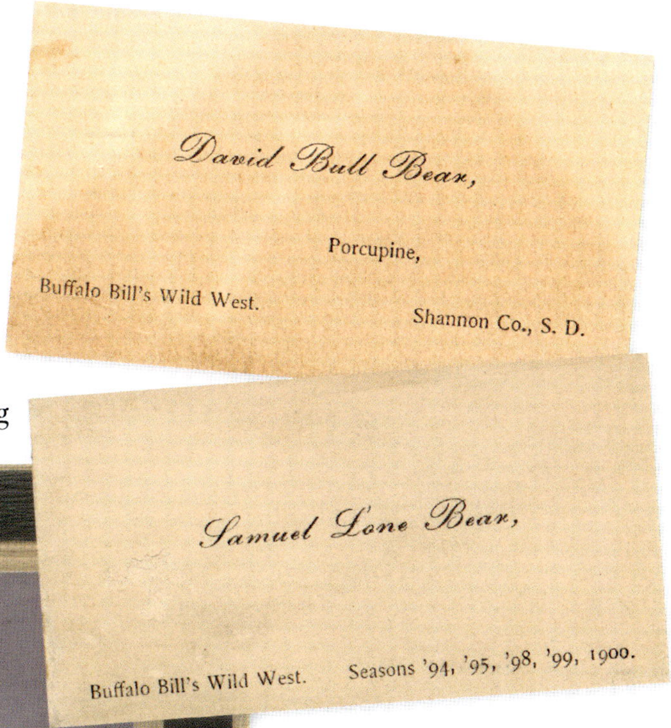

Business cards used by David Bull Bear, who was a Lakota translator for Buffalo Bill's Wild West in 1899, and Sam Lone Bear. Lone Bear later also became a translator for Buffalo Bill's Wild West. *Buffalo Bill Museum and Grave*

One of the most photographed performers with Buffalo Bill's Wild West, Sam Lone Bear posed for this professional image in a studio in Cardiff during the show's visit to Wales in 1903. *Buffalo Bill Museum and Grave*

as a profession. David Bull Bear acted as a Lakota translator in the 1899 season. Sam Lone Bear even had a business card showing he had performed with the Wild West in 1894, 1895, 1898, 1899, and 1900. He performed with the Wild West again in 1903–1904, 1907, 1908, 1910, 1911, and 1912. When Buffalo Bill's Wild West closed in 1913, he continued to be a performer for Wild West shows and circuses until 1935.

Some Lakota performers tried to maintain farms on the reservations, in an effort to meet government expectations. Nevertheless, the government agents barely tolerated their efforts as performers. Even after thirty-eight years of Lakotas leaving the reservation to perform in shows and expositions, Pine Ridge agent H. M. Tidwell wrote, in 1921, "I do not believe it to the best interest of the Indians that they participate in exhibitions where they show themselves as years ago. If it were possible for the Indian to go before the public either through shows or otherwise and demonstrate the progress of the Indian I would find no objection, however I do not approve of them going out before the public in their native garb and their teepes [*sic*]."[8]

Despite the efforts of some Indian agents to prevent the Lakotas from joining shows, they continued doing so and in large numbers well into the twentieth century. In 1928, E. W. Jermark, the agent at Pine Ridge, observed that there was a lot of demand for Indians to perform and that "[t]he Indians seem to be making quite a career for themselves." In 1920 Charles Black Horn had his own letterhead advertising that he could do "Riding, Roping and Rope Spinning. Also Broncho Riding." The letterhead included a brief biography, stating he had worked with Buffalo Bill, Pawnee Bill, and the 101 Ranch. The conscious choice to become a performer, like that made by Sam Lone Bear, is reflected in the 1927 passport for James Hawkins of Pine Ridge. It is stamped by a variety of municipalities in Germany, where he toured with a show. His occupations are listed as "farmer" and "showman."[9]

Performing was something Lakotas chose to do not only willingly but with pride. (That pride, and the dignity the performers brought to their work, is reflected in a series of images taken by noted Philadelphia photographer William H. Rau. The photographs were made of Jerome Little Elk, Sam Lone Bear, Whirling Horse, and other cast members during a visit to Philadelophia by the Wild West in 1900.) As Calvin Jumping Bull explained in 1981, "We Sioux use a term of honor that dates from Cody's day, *oskate wicasa*—one who performs." Special songs, *oskate olowan*, were also sung for those who were leaving the reservation to join a show. When frequent show performer Thomas Stabber, also known as White Buffalo Man, left to join a wild west show, an oskate olowan was sung for him: "White Buffalo Man, be brave! There's a big Wild West show coming for you. When you hear the sound of the boat your heart will beat faster." Stabber performed with Buffalo Bill's Wild West in 1899 and again in Europe with the Wild West in 1903. After the demise of Buffalo Bill's Wild West,

Opposite: Jerome Little Elk was one of ten Lakota performers who posed for photographer William Rau in Pennsylvania during the Wild West's visit there in 1900. During his time with the show, he also served as a member of the Wild West's Indian police. *Buffalo Bill Museum and Grave*

15.

he returned to Europe with the Circus Sarrasani in the 1920s and later performed at the 1935 exposition in Brussels.[10]

Though some Lakotas performed only once, others clearly embarked on a profession of performing as oskate wicasa. And they were kept busy. When Buffalo Bill wrote to Pine Ridge in 1914 about hiring Indians, he received this reply from the superintendent: "In regard to securing Indians for your Show and in reply, will say that it is very difficult to secure Indians for show purposes at the present time owing to the fact that an unusual number of this class of Indians have joined shows this season." That "class" was composed of oskate wicasa.[11]

Whether in the United States or in Europe, an oskate wicasa not only had an opportunity to make a living as a performer and leave the reservation, but also to serve as an ambassador for Lakota culture. Literally millions of persons met the Lakotas and saw the material manifestations of their culture. High-profile performers like Red Shirt, Luther Standing Bear, Lone Bear, and even Sitting Bull met with U.S. officials in Washington while traveling with Wild West shows. In Europe, they were introduced to heads of state, who treated them as representatives of their people. Luther Standing Bear's time with Buffalo Bill's Wild West launched him on a lifetime of activism, lecturing, and film appearances. He later wrote, "I determined that, if I could only get the right sort of people interested, I might be able to do more for my own race off the reservation than to remain there under the iron rule of the white agent."[12]

Being an oskate wicasa clearly offered many opportunities. For more than one hundred years, families from Pine Ridge have shared stories of ancestors who first performed as oskate wicasa with Buffalo Bill's Wild West. For some, like the Jumping Bull family, participation in the nineteenth-century Wild West began a tradition of performance that continued into the twenty-first century. It also offered an alternative to a hard life on the reservation and to acquiescing to the suppression of their culture.

CHAPTER 3

EXTERMINATION OR CIVILIZATION

THE REFORMERS

Luther Standing Bear faced a difficult choice. He had been the first Indian boy to enter the Carlisle Indian School. There he had been told he must learn to be like the white man, cut his hair, and give up his Lakota ways. Now he had returned to his people at Pine Ridge. He was like them but also like the white man. Perhaps if he joined Buffalo Bill's Wild West, he could be both.

On the face of it, one would expect that everyone would be happy with the situation; Buffalo Bill and the other showmen included a very popular component with their shows, and Lakota performers enjoyed an opportunity to make money and travel. With their meager reservation income supplemented, the Indians were able to better their lives. But not everyone was happy. In 1911 Richard Davis, a Cheyenne and a graduate of the Carlisle School, wrote Joe Miller of the Miller Brothers 101 Ranch Wild West, asking about joining for the season. By that time, he had worked with the Bureau of American Ethnology and had appeared in several wild west shows. In his letter he remarked that he had a home, eight farms, and plenty of money in the bank. Despite this apparent success, Richard Henry Pratt, founder of the Carlisle School, considered him a failure because of his participation in wild west shows. Pratt was not alone in his criticism of the shows; they were also condemned by others who considered themselves reformers.[1]

This postcard of Luther Standing Bear was sold during Buffalo Bill's Wild West tour of England in 1902. After his season with the Wild West, Standing Bear became an advocate for Lakota self-determination, including the choice to perform in show business.
Buffalo Bill Museum and Grave

The reformers' approach suggested that the United States had only two alternatives: either the Indians would be wiped out by the forward march of civilization or they would need to be civilized. Former secretary of the interior Carl Schurz put it bluntly in 1881 when he voiced the Indians' two choices as "extermination or civilization." The reformers rejected extermination as an inhumane and unacceptable alternative. But they also felt that the Indians' way of life and culture not only would, but should, end. In an effort to facilitate that process, they created several

Indian advocacy organizations in the 1880s: the Indian Rights Association, the Women's National Indian Association of Philadelphia, and the National Indian Defense Association. Where some had said during the Indian Wars that "the only good Indian is a dead Indian," they now embraced a different concept: "kill the Indian, save the man." It was a saying coined by Richard Henry Pratt, when he created the Carlisle Indian School in 1879. This was the approach Pratt used at Carlisle and the other schools where he was involved. The idea of these Indian schools was to remove individual Indians from their culture and the "bad" influence of their way of life. In this context, they could then become civilized.[2]

The paternalistic and so-called civilizing approach of the reformers was in direct opposition to the efforts of people like Buffalo Bill. Buffalo Bill and other wild west show organizers felt the Indians' cultures were unique, interesting, and therefore something to be shown off. They also took full advantage of the fact that the West was changing, as were all of its peoples, not just the Indians. Buffalo Bill's Wild West even drew parallels between the ways of the West and the dinosaurs in its advertising, pointing out that the Old West was also becoming extinct. "You would not miss a dancing dinosaur or sabre-toothed tiger. Then don't miss Buffalo Bill's Wild West." Buffalo Bill felt this phrase applied not only to the Indians but to life in the West in general. He repeatedly emphasized that he was not just producing a show but providing an educational exhibition. For this reason, Buffalo Bill and his partners rejected the term "show" as an inappropriate term for their form of entertainment. In so doing, they encouraged their performers to value and preserve their ways of life. This was unacceptable to the reformers like Pratt, who felt the wild west shows only encouraged what he saw as the Indians' uncivilized and savage ways. The more influence the reformers wielded over the Indian agencies and their superintendents, the more resistance there was to allowing the Indians to leave the reservations to perform.[3]

Buffalo Bill's Wild West was the most celebrated of the wild west shows, so it attracted most of the reformers' anger. Pratt's Carlisle School in particular led a campaign to undermine the Wild West, publishing highly critical articles in its newspaper *Indian Helper*. These articles contrasted the movement toward civilization that occurred at the school with the "savage" and "ignorant" performers in Buffalo Bill's Wild West. One article in 1898 criticized Buffalo Bill for "hiring the reservation wild man to dress in his most hideous costume of feathers, paint, moccasins, blanket, leggins, and scalp lock, and to display his savagery, by hair lifting war-whoops make those who pay to see him, think he is a blood-thirsty creature ready to devour people alive." The article went on to state, "It is this nature in our red brother that is better dead than alive, and when we agree with the oft-repeated sentiment that the only good Indian is a dead one, we mean this

These Lakota performers with Buffalo Bill's Wild West wear the "hideous costume of feathers, paint, moccasins, blanket, leggings" that was criticized by the Carlisle Indian School and other reformers. *Buffalo Bill Museum and Grave*

characteristic of the Indian. Carlisle's mission is to kill THIS Indian, as we build up the better man." It concluded "We do not like to keep alive the stories of his past, hence deal more with his present and his future."[4]

An *Indian Helper* article in 1897 poked fun at Iron Tail, one of the most prominent performers in Buffalo Bill's Wild West, calling him "weak and helpless in many ways" because he continued to dress in his traditional manner and performed instead of farming. It said he was unprepared for life outside his reservation and could be easily swindled. The article contrasted him with his son Philip, who was attending the Carlisle School, working on a farm, and becoming fit for "civilized, useful life." Ironically, Philip was killed in a railroad crash six years later, on his way to join Buffalo Bill's Wild West with his father, Luther Standing Bear, and other Lakota performers. Iron Tail, who continued on to join the show after the crash, wrote from England that he would save some of his earnings for his son's children. He also asked the Indian agent at Pine Ridge to hold on to Philip's money on his widow's behalf until Iron Tail's return, when he would help his daughter-in-law manage it. Iron Tail, as a professional performer with experience traveling the world by that time, not only had extra funds to help his family members but also had the knowledge to guide them. He was not naïve at all. The reformers, unable to see beyond their

Iron Tail, the most photographed Lakota performer, moved comfortably from re-creating Lakota life in the arena to interacting with other American and European cultures. *Buffalo Bill Museum and Grave*

own narrow views, refused to acknowledge the wisdom and abilities of those who were oskate wicasa and the valuable experiences in the larger world that they were acquiring.[5]

The reformers' paternalistic attitudes were based on an assumption of superiority, grounded in the idea that Indians were not only ignorant but not quite human. Commissioner of Indian affairs William Jones stated that educating the Indian to be civilized would "preserve him from extinction, not as an Indian, but as a human being." Buffalo Bill, Pawnee Bill, and other showmen from the frontier who had encountered and worked with Indians since they were youths had a different and much higher regard for them. There was no question in their minds that the Indians were indeed human beings and their equals. Some had encountered them as worthy opponents during the Indian Wars and spoke positively about them. For example, Buffalo Bill wrote about Sitting Bull, "In war his bitter opponent, in peace he won my friendship and sympathy; he impressed me as a deep thinker; conscientious as to the proper rights to the lands of their fathers." Cody knew full well that the Lakotas who joined his show were neither childlike nor naïve, both traits attributed to the Indians by reformers. In 1891 he wrote to a sympathetic Indian agent, "I have often found it that myself & Co. were under the Indian instead of us being the 'upper dog'—You can understand this from the Indian nature, but his philanthropic friends can't." In short Cody felt that the reformers underestimated the Indians, who were quite capable of standing up for themselves. His business partner Nate Salsbury stated that same year, "[W]e find that an Indian knows the value of a dollar quite as well as a white man."[6]

Following the lead of the reformers, the schools took paternalism to an aggressive level. Indian children were not just taught English and about the culture around them; they were forced to become like that culture. Their hair was cut short, and they were not allowed to wear their traditional clothing. Some of the schools used more draconian methods than others, employing beatings and other punishments when the children tried to use their own languages and ways. Vestiges of these methods would linger well into the twentieth century, as the Little Moon family later discovered at Pine Ridge. Despite the efforts of the reformers, it was not unusual for Indians attending Carlisle and the other Indian schools to leave and join Buffalo Bill's Wild West or one of the other wild west shows, returning to the culture that the reformers sought to eradicate. Sometimes they were motivated by a personal desire and sometimes by necessity. They graduated from places like the Carlisle School prepared to enter white society, but white society was not prepared for them.

Despite assurances from the schools and reformers that the newly educated Indians would be successful, Lakotas frequently encountered prejudice that prevented them from employing their new skills. On the other hand, they could find work with the Wild West shows. Because they spoke English and, in a sense, had feet planted in both their culture and the surrounding white culture, those who had been educated at the schools were very desirable as performers.

Luther Standing Bear was one Lakota who applied his schooling in ways that the reformers did not approve of. An early attendee of the Carlisle Indian School, he used the English language and other skills he had learned at the school to advocate for his culture. At the urging of his cousin Daniel Black Horn, he joined Buffalo Bill's Wild West in 1902 as an interpreter and a designated leader among the Indians performing with the show. His experience traveling to Europe with the Wild West launched Standing Bear on what became a career in show business that took him into the realm of film as the twentieth century progressed. He became involved with the American Indian Progressive Association, which advocated for Indian rights. He was also the oldest member of the Indian Actors Association.

The school in Pine Ridge, pictured here in the 1890s, would perpetuate efforts to eliminate Lakota culture well into the twentieth century. *Denver Public Library, Western History Collection, X-31655*

Screenland's First Americans, a booklet published by the Indian Actors Association around 1935, advocated for hiring real American Indians for film roles. The inside cover of the booklet gave tribute to Buffalo Bill as "The Indians Greatest Friend" because of his hiring of Indian performers.[7]

The wild west shows offered Lakotas an opportunity to demonstrate and to preserve a culture and way of life they had experienced before the Indian Wars. During a 1901 appearance of Buffalo Bill's Wild West, it was noted that "most of the Indian acts in the Wild West show were devised by the redskins themselves. Their dances are their own absolutely. Their

A booklet published by the Indian Actors Association around 1935. It promoted hiring American Indians for roles in western movies.
Buffalo Bill Museum and Grave

leaders realize that the purpose of Col. Cody and 'Nate' Salsbury is to present illustrative pictures of the real, historic life of these people, and the Indians enter fully into the spirit of the thing." Both Cody and his business partner Salsbury understood that the show's authenticity was based on the performers' participation in its creation. While this active encouragement of their culture served many of the performing Indians well, it was unacceptable to the reformers. It wasn't only that each individual Indian had to be civilized, the reformers and their allies in the Bureau of Indian Affairs felt that the entire culture must be killed. Accordingly, it was forbidden to behave like an Indian not only in the schools but also on the reservations. But in the wild west shows, the Indians were not only encouraged to dance and sing their songs, they were paid well to do it.[8]

It is no wonder that the reformers opposed the wild west shows. Commissioner Thomas Jefferson Morgan wrote in 1890 that "the schools encourage Indians to abandon their paint, blankets, feathers and savage customs, while the retention and exhibition of these is the chief attraction of the shows." The shows offered an opportunity for Indian cultures to not only survive but thrive. As long as the Indians were encouraged to re-create that culture, as far as the reformers were concerned, they would never become civilized.[9]

To advance their cause, the reformers went to Washington, mounting a direct attack on the wild west shows. Again, as the most successful of the shows, Buffalo Bill's Wild West was the focus of their offensive. Buffalo Bill and his partners were accused of abusing the Indians in their employ through poor living conditions, unfair business practices, and exposure to immoral situations. Fearing the loss of a major component of his show, Cody was forced to return from Europe in 1890 to reply to these accusations. By presenting evidence, along with the testimony of Indian performers with his show, he was able to successfully demonstrate that he and his partners did not mistreat the Indians in their employ. He would later tell Luther Standing Bear, "my Indians are the principal feature of this show and they are the one people I will not allow to be misused or neglected."[10]

Cody's words were reinforced by his actions, leading the Indians themselves to defend Buffalo Bill and his agents. The great Lakota leader Red Cloud remarked in 1890, "Major Burke and Buffalo Bill take my people among the whites and they travel and learn some things. I get letters from them and they bring me good news, for they tell me they are all well taken care of." Short Bull, defeated leader of the Ghost Dance, joined the Wild West for one season after Wounded Knee. In his account of that experience, he stated, "Ever since I have been with the Company I have been well treated and cared for, all of the promises made have been fulfilled. Col. Cody, Mr. Salsbury and Maj. Burke as well as the entire Company are our friends, and do all they can for us in every way." Despite such comments from his performers, Cody continued to be a lightning rod for the reformers' ire. In 1899 the Department of the Interior issued a statement that Indians would no longer be permitted to leave reservations "for Wild West Exhibitions purposes." Cody once again had to demonstrate that the Indians were fairly treated in his show to get the department to drop the policy.[11]

Concerns about abuses were not unfounded; they were just aimed at the wrong target. There had indeed been abuses by other showmen, who failed to pay the Indians as promised and even closed their shows prematurely, leaving performers, including the Indians, stranded somewhere in the United States, or, worse yet, in foreign countries. One positive result of the controversy initiated by the reformers was that more protections for Indian performers were put in place. Persons wishing to hire Indians for their shows or events were required to create contracts with each performer and post bonds to pay the Indians in the event show organizers defaulted on their contracts. The contracts always emphasized the requirements for both parties and were an effort to protect both the Indians from abuses by show organizers and the organizers from inappropriate employee behavior. It was an employer/employee situation, and there were inevitable complaints about treatment by management from Indians as well as other employees of the shows. There were also problems with employee behavior. As a result, some Indians were not rehired, and in several cases, Indians were sent back midseason because of misbehavior. For example, in 1903 Cody wrote from England to Pine Ridge agent John Brennan that he was returning three able-bodied men at the request of the other Indians in the show because "they were continually getting drunk and fighting with their own people." The contracts further enabled show organizers and Indian agents to assure the reformers that they had the best interests of the Indians in mind.[12]

The highly successful appearance of Buffalo Bill's Wild West during the 1893 World's Columbian Exposition in Chicago struck a decisive blow against the reformers' efforts to stop the shows. More than eighteen thousand people a day, several million through the entire period of the fair, visited the Wild West, situated just outside the exposition. Within the exposition itself, there was also an Indian village, which was highly popular. The World's Columbian Exposition and the Wild West each demonstrated that adding Indian performers to a fair setting could be both a crowd pleaser and lucrative. From that point on, both large-scale and small fairs in America sought out Indian performers.

After 1893, the reformers' efforts to stop wild west shows from hiring Indians diminished. Hiring Indians at reservations like Pine Ridge became more systematic, with show managers petitioning the agents for show Indians and then recruiting. Deals were finalized with contracts, signed by the Indians, a representative of the show, and the agent. Show operators used this to their advantage, emphasizing in their advertising that they had made arrangements with the government, at great difficulty, for Indians to leave their reservations and perform. Often it was indeed with great difficulty, as some agents did try to slow down the progress of hiring. They wanted to keep the Indians on the reservation as farmers, arguing that allowing them to perform with wild west shows both undermined efforts to domesticate the Indians and demonstrated that the attempts of the government to do so were a failure. Despite these efforts, the numbers of Indian performers increased.

It was also after 1893 that the term "show Indian" entered popular usage. At that time Indian Bureau personnel and the general public began recognizing tribal performances in shows as professional entertainment and show Indians as professionals. This roughly paralleled the rising use of the name oskate wicasa by Lakotas. Despite the objections of the reformers, the government's action signaled a grudging acknowledgment of the legitimacy of show business as an alternative career for reservation Indians.

In the twentieth century, opposition by Indian agents and commissioners to Indians performing in wild west shows, fueled by the belief that it encouraged their "savagery," was replaced with a more paternalistic approach. The agents were receiving as many as twenty requests per year for Indians to appear in Wild West shows and circuses, as well as at exhibitions. By then the Lakota had adopted the clothing and other aspects of the surrounding dominant culture, donning traditional outfits only for events on reservations and for performance in shows. Even if agents were personally opposed to allowing such travel, they were expected to entertain and approve these requests. But there was still concern that the Indians needed protection from the less desirable aspects of the dominant culture.[13]

Reservation agents' primary concerns were aimed at protecting the Indians from the bad influences they would encounter on their travels, particularly exposure to alcohol and "loose women." Some Indians did get drunk, and some also patronized loose women, as revealed in letters exchanged between the Indian agents and various show organizers. Other show performers were not subject to comparable restrictions. The diary of William House, an English lancer with Buffalo Bill's Wild West in 1898–99, contained entries about show personnel getting drunk and involved in fights. He remarked that at one stop in 1898, he and some of the other show personnel went into town to see "cooche-cooche dancers." The agents' double standard reflected the earlier paternalism of the reformers.[14]

It was in the best interests of show organizers like Buffalo Bill to ensure that order was maintained both within and outside their camps. Managing security was critical for the Wild West, which had as many as eight hundred employees in addition to thousands of spectators. The same problems applied to other large shows, such as Pawnee Bill's Wild West and the Miller Brothers 101 Ranch Real Wild West. Added security issues were created by the environs within which all wild west shows performed. In both U.S.

and European cities, the shows would attract pickpockets and con men of all kinds, who preyed on spectators and performers. Indians new to show business were particularly vulnerable to these criminal elements, since their culture left them unprepared for such behaviors. There was also outright prejudice against them in some places. One visitor to Buffalo Bill's Wild West wrote to a friend on a postcard showing Iron Tail that "'This' with his band and other 'animals' like himself were in Baltimore last week." In the smaller towns visited while the show was on tour, prejudices against show people in general led to occasional conflicts with locals. On June 24, 1899, performer William House noted in his diary that there had been a "fight in town between cavalry and town people."[15]

The prejudice confronted by some of the performers is illustrated by the handwritten message on this postcard of Iron Tail. It reads, "'This' with his band and other 'animals' like himself were in Baltimore last week." *Buffalo Bill Museum and Grave*

To minimize such incidents and provide for the safety of performers, Buffalo Bill's Wild West maintained tight security. While the show was in Paris during the Exposition Universelle in 1889, observers remarked that it was run like a military camp, requiring passes when members of the show left the premises. The pass system continued to be used in the Wild West at other times as well. While discipline among the rest of the personnel was maintained by management, the Wild West created a corps of Indian police to specifically oversee the Indian performers. Not only was this a way of accounting for significant language and cultural differences, it was another way of placating the Bureau of Indian Affairs and the reformers. The police were chosen from the ranks of the Indian performers by the performers themselves. John Burke, a manager for the Wild West, stated, "For every dozen Indians there is an Indian policeman. He wears a badge, and is paid $10 a month more than the rank and file. This policeman is elected by the twelve, and he can be deposed by them at any time." The head of the Indian police was usually appointed by Buffalo Bill and accountable to him.[16]

Buffalo Bill's Wild West and shows like it offered a third alternative to the two extremes of extermination or civilization posed by Secretary Schurz in 1881. The problem had been that civilization, as visualized by Schurz, the reformers, and the government, had merely offered extermination of a different kind . . . complete assimilation. Rather than assimilation, the Wild West shows offered accommodation. Through the device of show business, the Indians were able to represent themselves as themselves, not as unwilling replicates of the dominant culture. This representation happened

This unknown Lakota performer was elected by his peers to serve as a policeman with Buffalo Bill's Wild West in 1902. *Buffalo Bill Museum and Grave*

in the arena and in the Indian villages, both of which functioned as more than just curiosities for visitors. By creating village settings and encouraging performing warriors to bring their families, the shows helped maintain the family unit and the culture it fostered. Even when the shows involved financial and other risks to participants, they nevertheless provided an attractive alternative to existence on the reservation. That was one reason so many Lakotas showed up at Rushville when they learned that Buffalo Bill might be recruiting. It was a clear choice that provided opportunity and allowed them to maintain their traditions, even if in a theatrical setting. The shows offered a different path than the one advocated by the reformers and the government, a path that enabled the Indians to at least passively resist assimilation.

But it was still a path of accommodation. Many aspects of their involvement with the shows, from entering into an employee/employer relationship to learning to work side by side with former foes, involved compromise. Wild West performer Short Boy remarked during an interview in 1911, "There's no more hunting for the Indians and there's no use fighting against the hopeless odds, and so we take great pleasure in going up against a fair fight with the American soldiers even with blank cartridges. But even there we don't get a square deal; we are always licked . . . always licked." Lakotas like Short Boy reluctantly acknowledged that the past was indeed the past and could only be re-created in the paler form of show business . . . it would never return.[17]

As late as 1914, Chauncey Yellow Robe, a Lakota advocate of assimilation, wrote that through the Wild West shows, fairs, and moving pictures, the white man was "persistently perpetuating the tribal habits and customs." As transformed as those habits and customs were by show business, they persisted. And the vision of Schurz, Pratt, and the reformers of eliminating Lakota culture would not be realized. The young Indian men who attended the Carlisle School but later grew their hair long to perform in the shows did not abandon their past but found both cultural and monetary value in it. They, Luther Standing Bear, and even Phillip Iron Tail were all examples of the third alternative. They represented compromise and accommodation, not assimilation. This other way, begun by Catlin and taken to new levels by Buffalo Bill's Wild West and the other shows in the latter nineteenth century, enabled the Indians to avoid the path to cultural extermination that the government and the reformers had laid for them.[18]

CHAPTER 4

THE LAKOTAS IN EUROPE, 1902–1914

It was a big step for Jennie LaPoint, and she had every reason to be nervous. She would be leaving Pine Ridge to visit a foreign country for the first time. She wouldn't be with Buffalo Bill's Wild West, but if she enjoyed performing, she might go back for another season. Chief Red Shirt, who had been to England with Buffalo Bill, assured her there was nothing to fear.

In 1902, the beginning of a new century, Buffalo Bill's Wild West returned to Europe. It had been ten years since the show had been on the continent. Over the course of that decade, the Wild West had crossed the United States several times, playing in nearly every state, at towns large and small. Buffalo Bill's reputation, greatly assisted by his earlier appearances in Europe, had grown as well, with the engagement at the 1893 World's Columbian Exposition in Chicago and numerous appearances at Madison Square Garden in New York City.

Although Buffalo Bill's Wild West was the largest and best known of the Wild West shows, it was not alone: there had been more than twenty other shows performing in the States during that last decade of the nineteenth century. The combination of those other shows plus the continual touring of the Wild West itself had nearly satisfied the hunger for such shows in the United States. There was ongoing competition from circuses, which grew larger and more extravagant. The immensely successful Columbian Exposition had also stimulated American interest in fairs and expositions. Attendance numbers at Buffalo Bill's Wild West began to sag.

Buffalo Bill's Wild West returned to a Europe still eager for shows about the American West. The show also included the Congress of Rough Riders of the World, a review of horsemanship by a variety of groups from all over the globe. There were Cossacks, gauchos, Arabs, and others, but the central and most popular performers continued to be the Lakotas. Other shows had toured the continent since the Wild West's first appearance there in 1887, but the memories of the show from ten years earlier made the new visit a resounding success. The strength of Buffalo Bill's prestige was such that in France, some advertising posters and postcards simply depicted a running buffalo with Cody's head in an oval and the words "Je Viens," meaning "I am Coming."

All this postcard for Buffalo Bill's Wild West needed to say about the show's visit to France in 1905 was "Je viens" ("I am coming"). *Buffalo Bill Museum and Grave*

The new European tour began in Great Britain, as it had more than a decade earlier. During 1903 and 1904, the Wild West traveled throughout England, Wales, and Scotland. Then it crossed the channel to spend a full year in France. In 1906 several months in Italy were followed by a foray into new territory: the lands of modern-day Austria, Hungary, Romania, Ukraine, Serbia, Croatia, Slovakia, Slovenia, Poland, and the Czech Republic. The tour returned from eastern Europe to Germany in late 1906 and concluded its circuit of the continent with a return to Belgium.[1]

The twentieth-century incarnation of Buffalo Bill's Wild West was new, improved, and huge. It included eight hundred personnel and five hundred horses, as well as other livestock ranging in size from rabbits to buffalo. The performing rabbits were part of a series of sideshows: a snake charmer; "moss haired lady"; tattooed man; and other unusual offerings. The arena portion of the program included the Congress of Rough Riders of the World, with demonstrations of horsemanship by Arabs, Cossacks, gauchos, cowboys, and cowgirls. The show still had Indians "living exactly as they did many, many years ago," with reenactments and the grouping of tepees offering "all that pertains to an Indian village." The show took as many as three trains to transport and occupied much of the Champ de Mars during its encampment in Paris.[2]

As long as Buffalo Bill's Wild West toured Europe, it was difficult for competing shows to make a go of it. In 1905 J. T. McCaddon organized McCaddon's International Shows and Wild West, which he took to France. Following on the heels of the Wild West's two-month stand on the Champ de Mars and its subsequent tour of the provinces through the rest of 1905, the McCaddon show simply didn't draw enough visitors. By August 1906, McCaddon's show had folded. The fact that his show had fewer than ten Lakota performers, compared to Cody's fifty, certainly didn't help.[3]

Buffalo Bill's Wild West dominated the European scene during its four-year tour. But it proved to be the last time Buffalo Bill or his show would visit Europe. He returned to dwindling crowds in the United States as new tastes drove audiences to western movies offering cinematic re-creations of action as well as circuses featuring exotic acts from foreign lands. There were still plenty of small wild west shows touring, but they simply weren't drawing the audiences. In 1909 Buffalo Bill joined Pawnee Bill, a former employee and competitor whose show had also toured Europe. The combination, Buffalo Bill's Wild West and Pawnee Bill's Far East, was touted in the 1909 program as an ethnological exhibition where "the splendors of the Orient

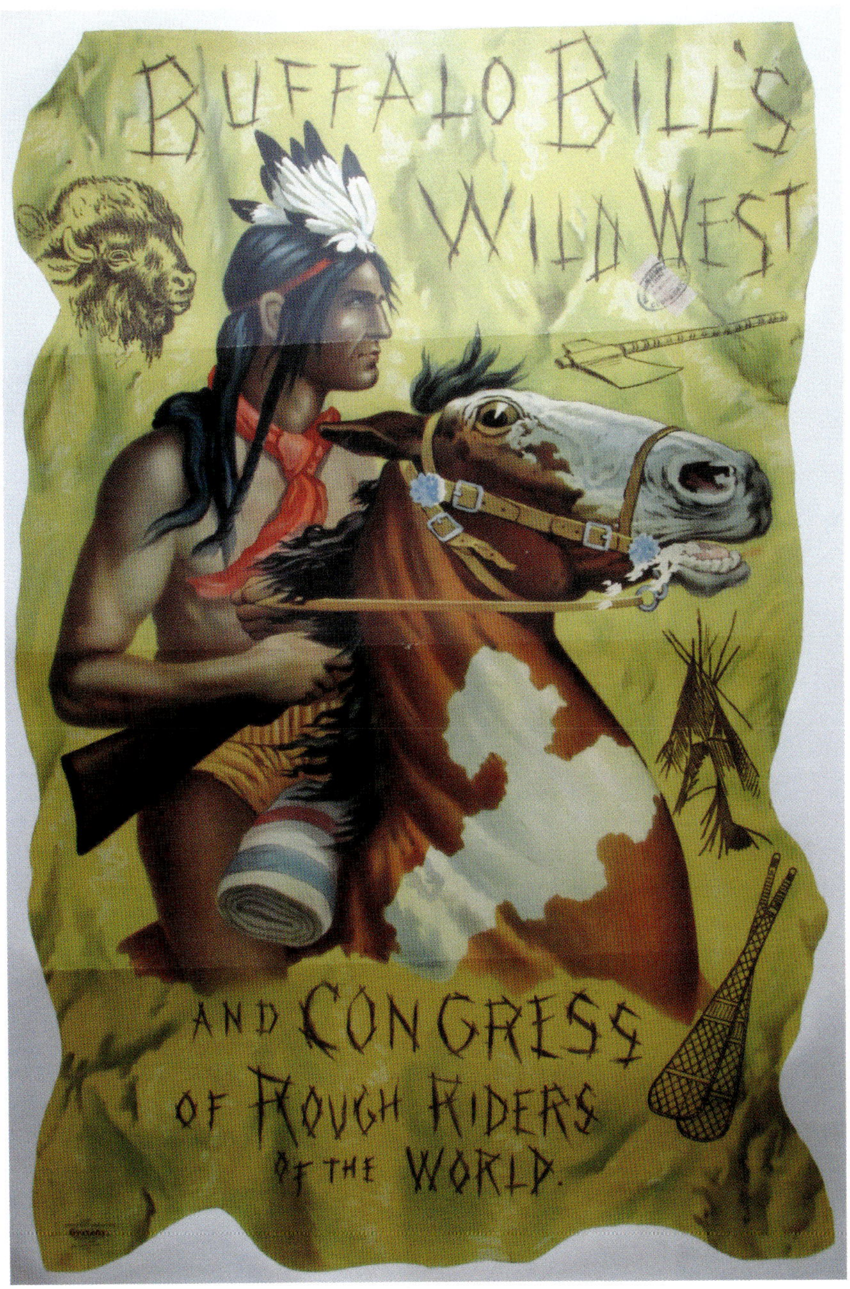

When Buffalo Bill's Wild West returned to Europe in 1902 for a four-year tour, it had expanded to include the Congress of Rough Riders of the World. The most popular rough riders were still the Lakotas, one of whom is shown in this Wild West poster. *François Chladiuk Collection*

are contrasted with the aboriginal feathers and finery of the American Indian." But even this did not draw enough audiences, and the show was lost to creditors, who dissolved it in 1913. It was the end of Buffalo Bill's Wild West. Sam Lone Bear, Thomas Stabber, and Iron Tail went on to perform with other shows. Iron Tail performed until his death two years later. Cody appeared briefly with the Sells-Floto Circus and then the Miller Brothers 101 Ranch Wild West before dying in 1917.

Buffalo Bill had said that the American Indians were the most important component of his show and that proved particularly true in Europe. Articles in European newspapers invariably focused on the Indians, who achieved a prominence nearly as great as Buffalo Bill himself. The American Indians represented that which was truly unique about the United States and its western territories. Even as the hunger for things wild west diminished in the United States in the early twentieth century, it remained strong in Europe, particularly where the Indians were concerned.

After the first successful presentation of the Lakotas by Buffalo Bill at Earl's Court in London, the venue continued to offer shows with American Indians. In 1905 the *Naval, Shipping and Fisheries Exhibition* included representatives from several Canadian tribes, including Ojibways. *Steve Friesen Collection*

As interest in Wild West shows faded, exhibitions provided an alternative. Building on the popularity of the cultural presentations at the Midway during the 1893 World's Columbian Exposition, Colonel Frederic T. Cummins organized an Indian Congress for the Trans-Mississippi exhibition in Omaha, Nebraska, in 1898. It was supported by the Indian Bureau and featured representatives from thirty-one tribes. Billed as "not a Wild West show, but a serious ethnological exhibition," Cummins' Indian Congress appeared at the Pan-American Exposition in Buffalo, New York, in 1901 and continued to tour the United States until 1906. Beginning in 1907, Cummins traveled Europe for four years, counting on the popularity of Indians with European audiences. Cummins' show included periodic appearances by well-known Lakotas, like Red Shirt and Alfred American Horse, who had made their first trip to Europe with Buffalo Bill back in 1887.[4]

The first appearance of Buffalo Bill's Wild West, as part of the American Exhibition commemorating Queen Victoria's rule in 1887, had been at Earl's Court in London. Earl's Court continued hosting various exhibitions into the first two decades of the twentieth century. Several of these included Indian villages.

In 1905 the *Naval, Shipping and Fisheries Exhibition* had a Canadian Indian village, which included members of the Iroquois, Ojibway, and Lakota tribes. Rather than emphasizing the cultural differences between these tribes, the village instead dressed them in stereotypical Plains Indian garb, echoing the wild west show approach established by Buffalo Bill. By this time the people of Europe had come to expect all American Indians to resemble Lakotas.[5]

In 1909 Earl's Court served as the site for the *Golden West and American Industries Exhibition*, which featured a wild west show with American Indians. Earle Gandy, an American living in London, was the "impresario" for the show, organized under the name Red Man's Syndicate.

The *Golden West and American Industries Exhibition* at Earl's Court in 1909 concentrated not only on showing progress in the United States but also on including Lakota performances and an Indian village. *Buffalo Bill Museum and Grave*

A souvenir guide from the *Golden West* exhibition at Earl's Court included a photograph of the Lakota performers at the Indian village. *Buffalo Bill Museum and Grave*

Earl Gandy organized the Red Man's Syndicate at Earl's Court as part of the 1909 *Golden West* exhibition. The following year he was in charge of the American Wild West Show at the 1910 Exposition Universelle et Internationale in Brussels. *Buffalo Bill Museum and Grave*

Gandy created contracts with thirty-seven Indians from Pine Ridge in late 1908 for a twenty-five-week performance in 1909. Among them were Red Shirt, who had appeared with Buffalo Bill's Wild West at Earl's Court in 1887 and had just completed touring Europe with Cummins. He was the "chief" of the group. But he was not the only person with experience in Buffalo Bill's Wild West. Spotted Weasel, Little Bull, William Owns Many Horses, William-Chases-the-Winter, James Red Horse, James White Bear Claws, Alfred American Horse, Charging Thunder, Oscar Two Dogs, Eagle Horn, Eagle Horse and Mrs. Eagle Horse, and Albert Running Bear had all performed at one time or another with the Wild West. They accounted for more than one-third of the performers. Each was an oskate wicasa, a professional performer. Among the new performers was Jennie LaPoint, the only single woman in the group. Frank C. Goings, a translator and the chief of the Indian police at Pine Ridge, was chaperone.[6]

The chaperone position was initiated by a series of letters between the commissioner of Indian affairs, the Pine Ridge Reservation superintendent, and the U.S. consulate in London. Consul General Robert Wynne wrote, "If you will permit me to offer my judgment, I do not believe your Indians would be properly placed at Earls Court." He was concerned about three matters: Earl's Court was mainly a series of side shows of a Coney Island nature, and Americans attending the exhibition would be disappointed; the Indians would be prey for loose women; and liquors of all kinds were sold on the grounds. His two main objections were the latter, both issues of paternal concern for the government.[7]

In response Commissioner Francis Leupp wrote to Superintendent John R. Brennan stating his personal feelings that "if an Indian wishes to go into the show business, he has just as much right to do that as to go into the blacksmithing business or harnessmaking business or anything else." Given the circumstances outlined by Wynne, however, Leupp advised, "[Y]ou can do a great deal in the way of discouraging him from entering into contracts with outside show-men" and recommended that Brennan make it difficult for both the showmen and the Indians to enter into agreements. He suggested, in addition to expecting the London showmen to put up money as a bond, that they also pay the salary and expenses of a government employee to go with the Indians. As a result Frank Goings was hired as chaperone, addressing Wynne's concern that, otherwise, the Indians "will have no greater protection than a board or rail fence to keep them from temptation." For Goings it was the beginning of a career that would last two decades and take him to Europe several times.[8]

Before the group left for England, Goings signed a contract with Superintendent Brennan agreeing to exert strict discipline over the thirty-seven Indians "in the prevention of whiskey or other intoxicating beverages being furnished them and especially in prevention of their visiting houses of prostitution or association with prostitutes and lewd women." Goings' wife and children joined the group and participated in the program, which included an Indian village and a show in the arena.[9]

Frank Goings earned his money that season. In May, just over a month after the group's arrival in London, he and several other performers wrote Gandy, "We, the undersigned, find we cannot rule or govern in any way Charley Yellow Wolf and Alfred Running Bear. As you know, they have been drunk for three days and nights and very insulting to the women of our party, and particularly our chief, Red Shirt. We therefore ask you, on behalf of all the Indians in your employ, to furnish them with transportation and send them home as early as possible." Gandy responded by sending both home in June. Some of the other less-seasoned performers also caused problems for the show. After the show's close, Gandy wrote Brennan with the names of seven persons whom he "could not defend on acc. of getting drunk, raising disturbances, fighting and immorality."[10]

The *Golden West and American Industries Exhibition* had a successful run from April through September 1909. Despite the problems, which Goings and Gandy had promptly solved, Superintendent Brennan was

A souvenir guide to the American Wild West Show at the 1910 Exposition Universelle et Internationale de Bruxelles featured Lakota warrior Red Shirt on its cover. *François Chladiuk Collection*

pleased with the care and monitoring the Indians had received. When Gandy asked if he could employ a group of Indians for the Exposition Universelle et Internationale de Bruxelles the next year, he had no difficulty receiving permission.[11]

The Red Man's Syndicate reorganized under a new name, The American Wild West Show Co., for the Brussels exposition. Gandy and his partners hoped to capitalize on the success of their showing at Earl's Court the year before, following roughly the same program. It featured all the dimensions of a wild west show: Indians, cowboys and cowgirls, skills of horsemanship, fancy shooting, a cowboy band, a re-creation of a battle, and the now increasingly familiar Indian village. The show was located in the Plaine des Attractions portion of the exposition. Entitled The American Wild West Show, it provided an eighty-minute spectacle. Visitors could purchase a souvenir program outlining the entire show, including descriptions of American Indian life and photographs of the show's performers. The photos showed Red Shirt and the other Indians, including Frank Goings' family, in their native costumes. As chaperone and translator, Goings was the only one not in Indian attire; he wore a vest, tie, and derby hat.[12]

Twenty-four of thirty-six Lakotas performing at the Exposition Universelle et Internationale de Bruxelles had been in London in 1909. Returnees included Red Shirt, Frank Goings, Spotted Weasel, Fred Standing Soldier, Painted Horse, Eagle Horse, Thomas Brown Eyes, Oscar Two Dogs, Charging Thunder, Little Bull, Henry Lone Bear, Phillip Returns from Scout, Charles Red Hawk, William Bear Shield, James Red Horse, Charles Yellow Wolf, Stephen Holy Pipe, William Owns Many Horses,

The Lakota women who appeared as part of the American Wild West Show in Brussels pictured in the souvenir guide to the show. *François Chladiuk Collection*

Above left: This page from the souvenir guide for the 1910 American Wild West Show in Brussels shows Frank Goings, chief of police at Pine Ridge, and his family. He was recruited to be a chaperone for Lakotas attending the *Golden West* exhibition in 1909, then visited Europe several times later in that capacity. *François Chladiuk Collection*

Above right: Red Shirt, who had appeared with Buffalo Bill's Wild West in 1887, acted as the "chief" of the Lakota performers at both the *Golden West* exhibition and the 1910 exposition in Brussels. Here he is pictured in the souvenir guide to the American Wild West Show in Brussels. *François Chladiuk Collection*

Albert Running Bear, and Little Wolf. Among the women were Mrs. Red Shirt, Jennie LaPoint, and Mrs. Eagle Horse. Not included in the thirty-six adults were the "enfants indiens": the Goings, Red Horse, and Eagle Horse children. There were as many Indians performing in Brussels as had performed the year before in Earl's Court.[13]

Earle Gandy had complained to Brennan in 1909 that Alfred American Horse, George Red Bear, Henry Lone Bear, Stephen Holy Pipe, Charles Yellow Wolf, Charging Thunder, and Mrs. Eagle Horse had caused disturbances at Earl's Court. They apparently got a second chance and were among those rehired to go to Belgium. In June 1910, Gandy did send eight of the performing Indians back to Pine Ridge, but not because of bad behavior. The show simply wasn't bringing in the expected proceeds, and he couldn't afford to keep them any longer. His show wasn't alone. Gandy wrote, "I would like to say that the business here is terrible not only for the Wild West Show but every attraction in the Brussels exhibition[;] they have never one day taken their running expenses money[,] and I am very much afraid that we will all have to close our shows and return people home during this month." The return of the eight did not save enough money. As the chaperone for the Indians, Goings was also concerned. He wrote Superintendent Brennan: "I have the honor to report to you that the Wild West Show Co. is in a bad condition and me on behalf of the Indians advise you to cash the $5000 check for Silver or Gold or Bills. . . . Bad weather and cold every day and they have cut down salarys on the cow boys and girls." When the show folded in July, Brennan cashed the check that Gandy and partners had put up as bond and used it to pay for the Indians' return. The cowboys and cowgirls were left to their own devices.[14]

The Indians left just in time. On August 14, not long after the American Wild West Show folded, the Exposition Universelle experienced a disastrous fire that destroyed many of its buildings. The exposition closed in November as intended, but it did so in debt. Nevertheless, millions had attended. Among them was August Hermans' father, who purchased artifacts from the Indians. His father's interest in the Indians would influence August. Twenty-five years later, he made numerous visits to the Indian village at the 1935 exposition in Brussels. There he would forge friendships with some of the performers and purchase more artifacts from them.[15]

Despite his rather bad experience in Brussels, Frank C. Goings was not ready to give up on show business. Fernand Akoun, a French promoter, had produced an attraction at the Brussels exposition in 1910. Perhaps he saw the American Wild West Show at that time and was inspired to create an Indian village of a different sort. The village would be staged at the Jardin d'Acclimatation, in the Bois de Boulogne in Paris, not far from where Buffalo Bill's Wild West had appeared in 1889. The Jardin was a zoo that included exhibitions of the cultures of foreign peoples in addition to animals. It was, in effect, a human zoo; by today's standards, demeaning and ultimately racist, but very popular in its time. Exhibitions of African cultures had been staged there, and Akoun felt an exhibition of American Indian culture would be appreciated by the people of Paris. In 1911 Akoun sent a representative, John D. Tippetts, to Pine Ridge to obtain some Indians for his show. Soon Goings had made an agreement with Fernand A. Akoun and Company through Tippetts to travel to Paris. Once again, at the behest of Superintendent Brennan and paid by Akoun, Goings would "look after the welfare of the Indians" and "exercise proper care over their conduct." This, of course, included preventing their imbibing of intoxicating beverages and associating with lewd women.[16]

As in the past, Goings took his wife and children. The Paris trip would be Goings' last to Europe; after 1911 he confined his career with wild west shows, circuses, and rodeos to the United States. Forty-seven adult Indians went to Paris, plus eighteen children. The group included Jennie LaPoint, returning to Europe for the third time and taking her grown son, Oliver, with her. Other performers returning for a third time included Spotted

Weasel and his wife, Eagle Horse and his wife and daughter, Fred Standing Soldier and his wife and child, and Thomas Brown Eyes. Red Shirt's name was not on the list. Perhaps he had no interest in appearing as part of a human zoo. He did continue to perform in other shows until 1915.[17]

Fernand Akoun's show opened on April 22, 1911, with the intent of operating for fifteen weeks. But it proved no more successful than the American Wild West Show had been in Brussels; the show closed before the fifteen weeks was over. Akoun told the U.S. consulate in Paris that the Indians were now their problem and that the government could use the bond money he had deposited with the Indian Bureau to ship the Indians home.[18]

The zeal for wild west presentations may have subsided in France and Brussels, but the Germans were still fascinated. Buffalo Bill's Wild West had toured extensively through Germany during its two European visits. The show's appearance in Dresden in 1890 during its first tour influenced Karl May, a writer who had already set his sights on the American West. When the Wild West returned to Germany in 1906, Karl May's popular novel *Winnetou* had been in publication for more than a decade. *Winnetou* featured an Apache warrior of the same name as its main protagonist. That novel and May's other stories generated a good deal of interest in the American West among Germans. Crowds flocked from the towns to see Buffalo Bill's Wild West, particularly curious about the Indian performers. The impact of the Wild West show, reinforced by May's writings, inspired the rise of the Indian hobbyist movement in Germany in the early twentieth century. Hobbyists dressed as Indians and reenacted their culture, not just in imitation but also in tribute. In the wake of Buffalo Bill's Wild West tours from 1902 to 1906, comparable groups sprang up all over Europe, but the movement was strongest in Germany. If twentieth-century depictions of the American West and the Indians were going to be successful anywhere in Europe, it would be in Germany.

While Gandy's American Wild West Show was failing in Brussels, a group of Lakotas were performing for crowds at a Volkerschau (people show or display of peoples) at Carl Hagenbeck's zoo near Hamburg, Germany. Hagenbeck was a pioneer in creating zoos that offered natural settings for their animal inhabitants. His zoo near Hamburg also offered exhibits of native peoples, as did the Jardin d'Acclimatation in Paris. Performers from Pine Ridge at the Volkerschau included Spotted Weasel, who had performed with Buffalo Bill's Wild West and the Miller Brothers 101 Ranch Real Wild West, and Edward Two Two, who would later die while on tour with the Sarrasani Circus and be buried near Dresden.[19]

Even though some of the Lakotas may have felt demeaned by being put on display at a Volkerschau, it did offer an alternative to conditions on the reservation, which in many cases were much more demeaning. On the reservation, official policy discouraged the practice of Lakota traditional culture, and life was difficult. Travel with shows and to exhibitions offered a chance to make money and travel. Iron Tail, a veteran performer with Buffalo Bill's Wild West, told a reporter in 1907 that he liked traveling and that being with the show gave him the opportunity to see the rest of America. Thus, even after the bad experience in Brussels, Goings and many of the other performers returned to Europe to participate in Akoun's "human zoo." Demeaning or not, it also offered a way to resist assimilation efforts back in the United States.[20]

Two shows were emerging as the leaders of the wild west business in the United States: the Sells-Floto Circus and the Miller Brothers 101 Ranch Real Wild West. The rise of wild west shows in the latter nineteenth century paralleled the rise of the circus. Wild west shows and the circuses were similar in presentation, even though their content was different. Over time each borrowed content from the other. In the early twentieth century, even Buffalo Bill's Wild West included side shows and elephant acts.[21]

When Buffalo Bill lost his Wild West in 1913, he joined Sells-Floto Circus as a featured act, with the circus trading on his celebrity. But he discovered the circus had little interest in

A souvenir postcard showed the 101 Ranch Real Wild West during its season at the Anglo-American Exposition. The season was cut short by British entry into World War I and the confiscation of these and other horses for the war effort. *Steve Friesen Collection*

Cooperation and conflict between cowboys and the Lakotas were emphasized in souvenir booklets at the 1914 Anglo-American Exposition. This added to "cowboys and Indians" stereotypes in European popular culture. *Buffalo Bill Museum and Grave*

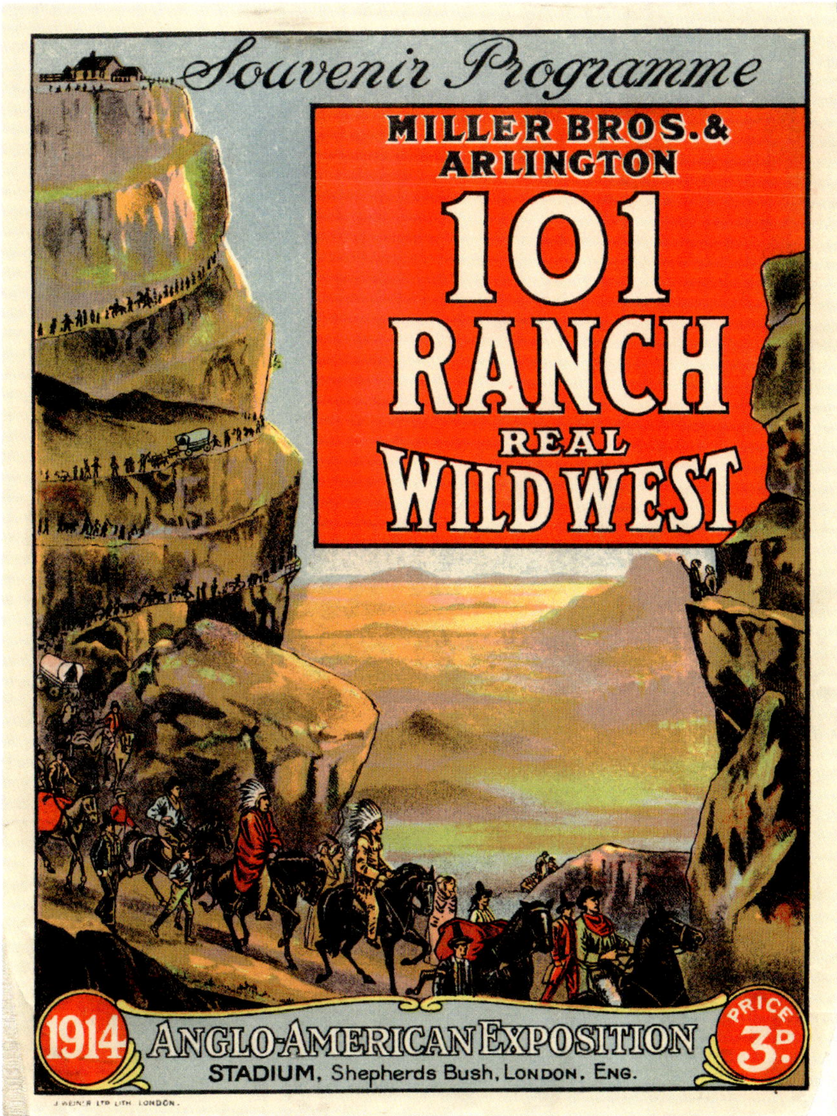

Souvenir program for the 101 Ranch Real Wild West show at the Anglo-American Exposition in 1914. *Buffalo Bill Museum and Grave*

presenting an authentic depiction of the West. The circus claimed to offer a wild west show and even used Buffalo Bill's name after his death and well into the 1920s, but the so-called wild west show was just another circus act. By 1923 the Sells-Floto Circus had only one wild west presentation: Indians performed skills of horsemanship in three rings while dances were demonstrated in the center of the big top.[22]

Buffalo Bill left Sells-Floto after two years, spending his last year of show business, and of his life, with a true wild west outfit, the 101 Ranch Real Wild West. The 101 Ranch show billed itself as offering "no circus but a real Wild West Show."[23]

The Miller Brothers 101 Ranch Real Wild West had its beginnings in 1905 and became one of the largest wild west shows by 1913. That year the show assisted Hans Stosch-Sarrasani in obtaining fifty Lakotas from Pine Ridge to appear with his circus, based out of Dresden, Germany. The

Lakotas were part of the Wild-West-Schau component of the circus, which began operation in 1902. The following year another group of Lakotas, including Jennie LaPoint and Edward Two Two, joined Sarrasani's circus on mainland Europe, while the Miller Brothers and Arlington 101 Ranch Real Wild West, with sixty-five Indians, appeared in London at the Anglo-American Exposition. With Buffalo Bill's Wild West gone, the Miller Brothers' London show included some of that show's performers, including Cody's foster son, Johnny Baker. Red Shirt also returned to London as a headliner with the Miller Brothers' show. It would be his last time in Europe. The program included an encampment with representations of Indian life by "genuine Warriors under the command of RED SHIRT, who were quite recently conquered by the United States Government, and by whose permission they are now allowed to leave their reservations." Thus the contractual restrictions placed on the show by the superintendent of Pine Ridge were once again used to an advertising advantage.[24]

During the Anglo-American Exposition, on June 28, 1914, World War I began, and chaos ensued for the 101 Ranch Real Wild West. The British government confiscated the show's horses and rolling stock for the war effort. The Cossacks who had been performing with the show returned to Russia. Communications ended with those Lakotas who were behind enemy lines with Sarrasani's circus. During the following month, Edward Two Two fell ill, died, and was buried in Dresden. Hans Stosch-Sarrasani arranged for the Lakotas to travel first to Scandinavia and then to England, where they were reunited with the rest of the 101 Ranch personnel and returned to the United States.[25]

Although the advent of World War I and the passing of Buffalo Bill Cody in 1917 did not signal the complete demise of wild west shows, they did mark significant changes. In the United States, wild west shows of various sizes continued to cross the country, offering acts that included Indian performances. But the appetite for that particular genre of entertainment had begun to wane in the early twentieth century, and that didn't change. Silent western movies, rodeos, circuses, and other diversions made inroads into the wild west shows' audience base. Over the next decades, the modern rodeo, itself a child of the wild west shows, would hasten the demise of the shows. Rodeos like the Pendleton Roundup and Cheyenne Frontier Days included the parades, Indian villages, and nostalgia for the past that made the wild west shows so popular. Plus, they incorporated the thrill of competition for prizes. Johnny Baker and other members of the Cody family organized the Buffalo Bill Wild West Show and Circus after his death in 1917, but it lasted only one season. Even adding the term "circus" was not sufficient to draw the necessary crowds. The golden era of the wild west show, begun in 1883, had drawn to a close.[26]

CHAPTER 5

DELEGATIONS AND CIRCUS ACTS, 1918–1934

White Buffalo Man cleared his throat, then addressed the crowd gathered around Father De Smet's statue. They listened attentively and respectfully as he told them the story of Pierre-Jean De Smet's concern for the well-being of the Lakotas and other Indians of the Plains. Then young Stanley Adams performed a dance, which received a great deal of applause. The boy had a mischievous streak, which had caused the troupe some trouble, but he certainly could dance.

When World War I finally ended in 1918, American shows could once again travel to Europe. But the Miller Brothers 101 Ranch Real Wild West did not return. Those wild west acts that were successful were within the domain of the circuses, something both Sells-Floto and Circus Sarrasani had foreshadowed. When the Sells-Floto Circus traveled to Europe in 1927 and 1928, it took its solitary wild west act with it. But it couldn't compete with the Circus Sarrasani, which dominated the wild west scene from the 1920s until 1935. Sarrasani emphasized the American West in advertising, show programs, posters, and souvenir postcards, nearly always with images of Indians. While there were other circus acts, the Indian performances in the Wild-West-Schau, such as dances, stagecoach holdups, and skills such as tomahawk throwing, were clearly critical to the circus.[1]

But wild west shows, circuses, and even expositions encountered a new obstacle after the war. Where Pine Ridge superintendents like Brennan had grudgingly allowed the Indians to join shows, the new superintendent, H. M. Tidwell, was opposed to the very idea of show Indians. When D. V. Tantlinger, who had previously worked with the 101 Ranch for nine years, contacted Tidwell in 1919 about hiring five Lakotas to appear in a show he was organizing, Tidwell wrote to the commissioner of Indian affairs:

> The matter of entertaining the public along these lines should not be tolerated as it is detrimental to the Indians as a whole. People who see the exhibition of these war dances and other habits of the Indians, as shown in these Wild West shows, labor under the impression that no progress is being made by the Government of the United States in the advancement of the Indians and it is my opinion that our Department

should take proper steps to discontinue the practice of allowing these Indians to travel with these shows.

Even though Tidwell clung to this attitude for the next five years, the position advanced by Commissioner Leupp in his 1909 letter to Superintendent Brennan, that an Indian had as much right to go into show business as into any other business, still remained a policy reluctantly observed.[2]

The Lakotas' right to go into show business, however, did not stop Tidwell from raising as many obstacles to leaving the reservation as possible. When, in 1922, Colonel W. F. Fleming asked about hiring twenty-eight Indians for a show, Tidwell replied, "As a general thing the Department does not favor the encouragement of Indians to take up such employment." He added that it was preferred that the Indians take up stock raising, farming, or some other occupation. He concluded, "For these reasons the number of Indians permitted to go on such occasions are limited to those who have no home or occupation." In 1923, Tidwell wrote commissioner of Indian affairs Charles H. Burke complaining of his difficulty in keeping the Lakotas from performing at "every fair within a radius of one hundred miles of the Reservation." In 1924 Tidwell was replaced as Pine Ridge superintendent by Ernest W. Jermark. After a few months, Jermark wrote Burke that the practice of allowing the Indians to perform in shows had been observed at the agency for the past twenty-five years, and he was not in favor of it. According to Jermark, "[T]he practice of encouraging an Indian to exhibit himself as a freak should not be permitted." He asked what rulings or policies Burke had to offer on the practice. While acknowledging that the Lakotas had a right to go into show business, Burke agreed with Tidwell's and Jermark's feelings that being on the road doing demonstrations of earlier life interfered with their improvement. Although these men had no authority to stop the Indians, Burke wrote Jermark, "[W]e should and do object by the strongest moral influence, at least, to this waste of time and neglect of home and industrial welfare by wild west performances."[3]

In 1925 Jermark joined superintendents from seven other reservations in the Dakotas and Montana in a letter to fair associations in the region. The letter emphasized that they, and Commissioner Burke, felt the Indians had to conform to being successful farmers if they were to become "capable citizens." They stated that when the Indians participate in fairs, rodeos, and traveling shows, they neglected their farming duties. The letter said that some had traveled the entire year of 1925 performing their "old time dancing" in "their old time costumes" rather than farming. An example was given of one Indian "addicted to this practice" who neglected his crops, resulting in their complete loss. The goal of the superintendents was clearly to turn all of the Indians into farmers. This rather short-sighted goal failed to recognize that not everyone, whether white or Indian, was interested in or cut out for farming. It also ignored the fact that the Indians were being expected to farm some of the least arable soil on the Great Plains. The superintendents' other objective was to prevent the Indian from taking part in shows and parades "in paint and feathers while he goes back two generations and dances the old savage dances."[4]

The government's desire to suppress dancing had become less important than it had been, when policies sought to force the Indians to give up their traditional cultures. In 1924 P. H. Marshall wrote Commissioner Burke proposing to create a traveling "Inter-tribal Indian ceremonial," similar to the annual event that had been staged in Gallup, New Mexico, for two years (and has continued through today). Burke replied that "the Indian is not to be deprived of his occasional feast days, his periods of play and recreation and his religious ceremonials," but he also needed to be taught that "these things do not relieve him from hard work, thrift, self-help, and the necessity for individual energy." If the Indians' cultures could not be suppressed, the "old-time habits and pagan ways" could at least be limited in the interest of instilling the Indians with a proper work ethic.[5]

The tide was clearly against the Office of Indian Affairs' efforts to prevent Indians from performing. By 1925 Jermark estimated that between five hundred and fifteen hundred Lakotas were participating in fairs, circuses, and shows in the United States and Europe. He further stated that 150 to 200 professional performers among the Lakotas were "willing to travel around the country for little or no salary, so long as traveling expenses and beef are provided." There was plenty of opportunity for a performer, including the chance to travel to Europe. Though the Miller Brothers did not return to Europe, Joe Miller continued assisting European shows in acquiring Indians to perform. In 1925 he contracted with eighteen Indians from Pine Ridge to travel to London and perform on behalf of the Bertram Mills Circus. D. L. "Shorty" Mack accompanied the group as a representative of the Miller Brothers. The group included Black Horn and his wife, Bessie. Black Horn was a cousin of Luther Standing Bear and had previously appeared in Europe with Buffalo Bill's Wild West during its 1902–1906 tour. Sam Little Bull and his wife also had appeared in Europe previously. Jennie LaPoint returned to Europe for her fifth time and first visit since World War I. Others also had show experience, like William Ghost Bear, who had appeared with Buffalo Bill's Wild West in 1906, 1907, and 1910. After the appearance in London with Bertram Mills, the group proceeded to Dresden, where they joined the Sarrasani Circus.[6]

The tour did not go smoothly. Black Horn and four other members of the troupe wrote to Jermark from Dresden in February 1926 that Joe Miller had overcharged them for their passports. On September 14 James Grass, who had been one of the signers of the earlier letter, wrote Jermark that Miller and Sarrasani had broken the contract and noted that they were also pocketing a fee for exchanging the Indians' money. He asked Jermark to look into these matters as well as noting that some of the Indians were sick because of the climate. One of the sick was Mrs. William Ghost Bear. She was part of an extended family on the tour, including her husband, their son, William Ghost Dog, plus the son's wife and two children. On September 23 her son wrote that she had been ill for three days but the family's requests for health care had been ignored. He reiterated what Black Horn had written earlier, that the contract was being ignored. His biggest concern was that there had been a fire in the circus tent that morning, and his mother had been badly burned. He asked that she be returned to the United States if she recovered. A few days later he wrote Jermark that she had died in a hospital in Essen, Germany. He was upset that the Sarrasani Circus had ignored his request to bury her near Dresden where Edward Two Two had been buried in 1914. Instead they buried her in Essen. He specifically asked that he and his family be sent home, but Shorty Mack would not let them leave. The letter ends with an appeal for assistance from Jermark.[7]

William Ghost Dog's letter of September 23, 1926, advised Jermark, " Mr. Sarrasani the director is not suitable to have Indians from Pine Ridge. Don't you send no more Indians from Pine Ridge to Germany." Despite that advice, Jermark continued to allow Indians to go to Germany. In fact some of those who had taken part in the 1926 tour with the Circus Sarrasani returned later to work for the circus, despite their complaints. As performers they may have had little choice, since by the 1920s, Sarrasani was the largest employer of show Indians in Europe—perhaps in the world.[8]

Large was a matter of perspective, however. Whereas fifty Indians had participated in Buffalo Bill's Wild West during its European tour at the beginning of the century, the Millers provided only eighteen to Sarrasani in 1925. Joe Miller wrote Jermark, "It is not little trouble to assemble these Indian troupes to send abroad." He continued, "The expense of sending a group of eighteen to twenty people to Europe and returning them is enormous." It was expensive to put shows together, and the old days, when scores of Indians participated in reenactments and villages, had clearly ended. The reenactments, when there were reenactments at all, were small. Instead, Indian villages, with dances and demonstrations of Indian life, were becoming the order of the day. People in Europe, as in America, were still fascinated with the exotic aspects of Indian cultures, but re-creations of battle scenes, hurt in part by the rising popularity of western movies, with their own re-creations, were becoming a thing of the past. For Lakota performers, the options were narrowing.[9]

The Lakotas' return to the Circus Sarrasani may have also been motivated by a new player on the scene, one who ensured that the problems of 1926 wouldn't be repeated. Shorty Mack, whose mismanagement had caused many of the earlier problems, was no longer working for Miller and Sarrasani in 1927. Miller's new representative was Clarence Shultz. Shultz

Here, flanked by Clarence Shultz and his wife, the Lakotas with the Sarrasani Circus pose at one of their German locations in 1928. This photograph was sent by Shultz to Pine Ridge superintendent Jermark as a souvenir, perhaps also to demonstrate that all were well and accounted for. *PR2800, Record Group 75, National Archives and Records Administration, Kansas City, Missouri*

A group photo on the ship *Westphalia* of eighteen adults and three children en route to Europe, where they would perform with the Sarrasani Circus in 1928. *PR2801, Record Group 75, National Archives and Records Administration, Kansas City, Missouri*

Above left: Sam Lone Bear and Mark Spider, the only single men among the group of Lakotas who performed for Sarrasani Circus during the 1928 tour of Europe, are pictured on this souvenir postcard. *PR2802, Record Group 75, National Archives and Records Administration, Kansas City, Missouri*

Above right: White Buffalo Man (Thomas Stabber) and his wife Sallie. Clarence Shultz, who was in charge of the Lakota contingent for the Sarrasani Circus in 1928, had these souvenir postcards made for the performers to sell. *Steve Friesen Collection*

began his career in show business as a cowboy with the Miller Brothers 101 Ranch Real Wild West and had worked with the show for more than a decade. Like the Millers, he was based out of Marland, Oklahoma. With Shultz handling things, Joe Miller was able to report to Jermark about the 1927 season, "The troupe that I sent from the ranch over to Germany, in place of Black Horn and his band, are getting along very nicely." That year Black Horn traveled around the United States with the Miller Brothers 101 Ranch Real Wild West instead of traveling to Europe.[10]

The 1927 season would be the last one coordinated by Joe Miller on behalf of the Circus Sarrasani. He died unexpectedly that October. That ended the Miller Brothers' coordination of Indian performers for the circus. Clarence Shultz stepped into the gap in 1928. That year he became the Circus Sarrasani's exclusive representative to Pine Ridge. In that capacity he hired several Buffalo Bill's Wild West veterans: Sam Lone Bear, Yellow Thunder, John Milk, and Thomas Stabber (known also as White Buffalo Man). Stabber acted as chief of the group. There were eight families plus two single men, Lone Bear and Mark Spider. That made a total of eighteen men and women, plus three children. Shultz had several group photographs taken on the boat, the *Westphalia*, while they were on their way to Europe. Once they reached Europe, he had each family pose for photographs. The photos were made into postcards to be sold as souvenirs to circus visitors. The backs of the cards explained in German and English, "Real Sioux Indians from Pine Ridge South Dakota. They are in Europa with Clarence Shultz, the well known cowboy from Marland Oklahoma U.S.A."[11]

Throughout his first season coordinating the Indians with the circus, Shultz sent monthly reports from Germany, certifying that they were being paid. The reports often included little margin notes like "Everyone getting along fine." The July and September notes included the comments that nobody had gotten sick, since there had been reports of illness during those months during the 1926 tour. The reports continued through December. Shultz's missives assured Superintendent Jermark that any previous concerns about the well-being of the Indians, as well as concerns about wages, were unnecessary on Shultz's watch.[12]

Taking some time away from the circus in 1928, Shultz and the Indians visited the Karl May Museum. Karl May probably saw his first Indians during his visit to Buffalo Bill's Wild West in Dresden in 1890. He didn't particularly care for Buffalo Bill, whom he may have seen as a real-life rival to Old Shatterhand, the fictional German hero of his books. He also felt that the Indians in the show had betrayed their people because they did not fit his Indian ideal. May visited the United States only once, in 1908, getting no farther west than Buffalo, New York. He died in 1912, and the Karl May Museum was opened at his home in Radebeul, near Dresden, in 1928. The Karl May Museum was a log building, filled with Indian artifacts collected by May's widow, Klara, and her curator, Patty Frank. While near Dresden the Lakota also paid a visit to the grave of Two Two, something that other Indians with the Circus Sarrasani had done in the years after his burial there in 1914.[13]

The only complaint that season came not from those new to the wild west business but from veteran performer John Milk. Milk wrote to Jermark complaining that Shultz was not being fair to them with their wages and was taking half of the money they made by selling the postcard souvenirs. He also said that Chief White Buffalo Man, as leader of the group of Lakotas, was in collusion with Shultz to take the Indians' money. The handling of that complaint demonstrated Shultz's effectiveness as a manager on behalf of Sarrasani. Shultz wrote Jermark refuting the accusations, stating that he had gotten all the Indians together to discuss the letter, and that Milk had claimed it had been translated to English incorrectly and that was why it sounded so critical. Shultz then went through each accusation, stating why it was wrong. He confided in Jermark that "John Milk is a man who likes to drink" and didn't like Shultz preventing the Indians from leaving the show at night when the bars were open. A typed copy of Milk's original letter was attached with the handwritten phrase "This letter is untrue." It was signed by the other nine males with the Indian group. Shultz's response apparently calmed any concerns that Jermark might have had. Without further incident, the group later departed from Hamburg on the S.S. *Cleveland*, arriving in New York City on January 20, 1929.[14]

The following year, Clarence Shultz once again arranged for a group from Pine Ridge to travel to Germany and take part in the Circus Sarrasani. The process began on February 26, 1929, with an initial contract between Shultz and Jermark. The agreement was similar to those that had been in use for more than thirty years. Shultz would provide a bond of $3,000. The bond would be returned at the end of the season, in whole or in part, if he carried out all the conditions in the agreements he made with the performers. Each agreement included a specific salary and a commitment to provide transportation to and from Germany. There was still a moral clause in the agreements stating that Shultz and Sarrasani would make "reasonable effort" to keep the Lakotas from "intoxicating liquors and other immoral influences." The responsibilities of the performers included furnishing "all headdress and other Indian regalia" for use in "portraying Indian life and entertainments." The agreements' duration was from March 1929 through March 1930.[15]

Shultz typically hired a combination of persons who had already toured in Europe, persons who had performed in the United States but not been to Europe, and persons who were completely new to performing. Those performers who were returning to Europe were critical to the shows because they were used to performing in a foreign context and knew what the audiences expected. Thus it was in the best interest of show coordinators like Shultz to have several veteran performers in their troupes.

Veteran performers Sam Lone Bear and Thomas Stabber once again traveled to Dresden to perform with the Circus Sarrasani. Lone Bear further signed each letter of agreement as an interpreter. William Ghost Bear, whose wife had died during the tour with Sarrasani in 1926, was back with a second wife. The group totaled fifteen adults and two children. The oldest performer was David Flies Above, at age seventy-three, and the youngest was Steven Swallow's one-year-old. Most members of the group, like forty-five-year-old Joe Elk Boy, were in their forties and fifties. After a year of traveling, the group returned to the United States from Hamburg on March 29, 1930, on board the S.S. *Albert Ballin*.[16]

Later, in 1930, Shultz sent another group to Dresden, numbering eighteen adults and three children. The group included Lone Bear, Stabber and his wife Sallie, and Elk Boy and his son, all from the previous year. Joining them after a break of several years was Mark Spider. By this time, perhaps motivated by the treatment of Mrs. William Ghost Bear by Shorty Mack in 1926, the contract between Shultz as a representative of the Sarrasani Circus and the performers included some new conditions. It stated that appropriate medical care would be given to the performer as needed and that, in the event of death, the performer would be properly embalmed and sent back to Rushville, Nebraska, the nearest train station to Pine Ridge. All costs associated with proper care of the ill or deceased were to be absorbed by the Sarrasani Circus. In his letters back to Pine Ridge, Shultz continued to assure Jermark that he was watching out for the health of the performers, noting that he sent Sam Lone Bear to the hospital for several days but that Lone Bear was now out and "getting along allright." The group returned from Hamburg on the S.S. *Deutschland*, arriving in New York City on January 30, 1931. When they reached the Rushville station on February 2, 1931, Shultz requested that new superintendent James McGregor provide two large trucks to transport them to Pine Ridge. Shultz clearly valued the performers and was thorough in his efforts to ensure their well-being.[17]

After several successful years, it seems that Clarence Shultz's role as a coordinator for Circus Sarrasani was solidified. Yet in 1931 he had a falling out with Hans Stosch-Sarrasani. Early that year Shultz wrote Superintendent McGregor that he had not recontracted with Circus Sarrasani because Sarrasani had refused to reimburse him $852.75 that he had spent "gathering, paying passports & returning the Indians home" in 1930. He emphasized his experience coordinating six troupes of Indians for appearances in both Europe and South America, stating that the new Sarrasani representative had no such experience and that there could be trouble. At the same time McGregor received a letter from Sarrasani introducing a Captain C. A. Henning as his representative and asking for eleven men, seven women, and four children to perform with his circus.[18]

Sarrasani had not been advancing funds to Shultz, who had ordinarily paid for expenses out of pocket to be later reimbursed by Sarrasani. Sarrasani may have felt Shultz was taking advantage of him and thus did not reimburse Shultz for some of the 1930 costs. At any rate, Sarrasani decided he could do it more inexpensively by sending his own representative. Henning, that representative, soon found that the process was more expensive than expected, and a flurry of correspondence began between him and Sarrasani. Henning requested more money, stating that "Shultz and Miller advanced Indians money for clothes, shoes, trunks, stores also spent large sums for dances feasts" and that he was "only asking for necessary actual expenses." Sarrasani wrote one of the field agents in Pine Ridge that he was "appalled at the expense and requirements necessary to take such a troupe to Europe." In his frustration, he blamed Henning.[19]

One of the largest expenses was for clothing in which the Indians could perform. Henning wrote, "It would be impossible to bring the Indians over in the clothes they have at present." Few of the Lakotas still had the traditional clothing they were expected to use in the performances. By this time, their everyday attire was just like that of everyone in the West. Before joining a show, they often had to acquire their costumes from other Lakotas or from traders, many of whom had acquired the clothing specifically for the purpose of selling it to performers. Even if they had costumes during a previous season, Henning wrote, "practically all Indians, returning from shows sell everything they have acquired such as their costumes, trunks, etc., and there are few exceptions." Clarence Shultz, and Joe Miller before him, had not advanced the Indians money for their clothing; typically, their agreements with the performers required them to furnish their own costumes. Henning clearly was confused on this issue. His confusion was not helped by a telegram he received en route to the States from Sarrasani, stating that the Lakotas "must have first class costumes and arms." As Henning saw it, Sarrasani wanted the best but was unwilling to supply the funds to acquire it.[20]

There were other complications. Since Stabber and some of the other Indians had worked with Sarrasani in the past, he had assumed they would jump at the opportunity to come work for him again. But that was not the case. Stabber wrote McGregor that they were suspicious of Henning. "No Americans work for that man yet, so Indians are afraid to work for him." He said he was not interested in returning to Germany that year and would stay on Pine Ridge to raise his crops. He further stated that he might work for Shultz the following year if Shultz was interested in hiring him. He did note that Sam Lone Bear would probably take Henning's offer and work for Sarrasani that season.[21]

As the correspondence between Henning and Sarrasani got more strained, relations also deteriorated between Henning and the Indians. He wrote Sarrasani in May, "Most Indians refuse to go with Tom [Stabber] and Sam [Lone Bear] and I hear Shultz said he would not take them out again. Shultz has done his best to turn the Indians against me and your show. I have also seen letters where Tom has also maligned your circus and the treatment they received in Germany."[22]

By mid-June there was still no resolution. The Indians continued to be reluctant to work with Henning, Sarrasani refused to send Henning any more money, and the situation was worsening. Finally, on June 23, Sarrasani wrote the superintendent at Pine Ridge that Henning was no longer authorized to represent him. A few weeks later Henning wrote Bertram Mills in London, stating he was no longer with Sarrasani and offering to coordinate a group of Indians for his circus. It does not appear that Mills hired him.[23]

With the departure of Henning, Sarrasani was forced to return to Clarence Shultz. On August 31, James McGregor wrote the commissioner of Indian affairs that he had authorized Clarence O. Shultz of Marland, Oklahoma, to take a party of Indians to Germany to join the circus. They left on August 29, 1931, on the S.S. *Albert Ballin* of the Hamburg-American line. Twenty-one Indians in all were with the group. While they were late for most of the 1931

Lakotas with the Sarrasani Circus in 1932 paid a special visit to the statue of Father De Smet in Dendermonde, Belgium. Young Stanley Adams, who did a special dance at the statue, is pictured on the far left. *François Chladiuk Collection*

season, their agreements with Shultz and Sarrasani stated that they would perform through September 1933 if needed. The performers included Thomas and Sallie Stabber. They had apparently decided that, with the return of Shultz, they would rather perform than farm. Black Horn and Bessie returned to the circus for the first time after their unfortunate experience with Shorty Mack. Mark Spider, who had been in the 1928 group but had not returned to Europe since, also rejoined the circus, as did William White Belly and his family from the 1929 season. Among the newcomers were Charles High Hawk and his wife. High Hawk had performed with Buffalo Bill's Wild West eighteen years earlier during its 1912 and 1913 tours in the United States. Sam Lone Bear, who had considered joining the group earlier that summer, chose to remain at Pine Ridge.[24]

In the earlier years wild west shows, particularly those with reenactments, focused on "celebrities" from the Indian Wars. When Buffalo Bill's Wild West traveled through Europe in 1891, the show featured leaders from the Ghost Dance, which had recently been put down by the army. Crowds turned out

Above: In March 1932, the group of Lakotas with the Sarrasani Circus appeared in downtown Brussels, where they clothed the famous Manneken Pis (pissing boy) fountain (*upper left corner*) in a ceremonial Plains Indian outfit, attracting a large crowd. *François Chladiuk Collection*

Right: This souvenir postcard from 1932 shows Manneken Pis in Brussels, wearing his Plains Indian attire. *François Chladiuk Collection*

Far right: The 1932 Manneken Pis outfit as preserved today in the City Museum of Brussels. *Musée de la ville de Bruxelles-Maison du Roi*

to see the participants in the history-making events of the American West. But by the 1920s most of the earlier celebrities, who had participated in the Indian Wars, had retired or died. In order to draw crowds, it was still necessary to create an atmosphere of celebrity around the performers.

John Burke, publicist for Buffalo Bill's Wild West, originated publicity stunts such as inserting show participants in important places and events. Thus, in 1887, Red Shirt and Buffalo Bill both appeared at British Parliament, a visit covered extensively by London papers. Burke also created human interest stories around the celebrities that were judiciously released to the newspapers. When the Indians visited Genoa and saw Christopher Columbus' statue, the show released a story about one of the Indians seeing the statue and saying, "It was a damned bad day for us when he discovered America."[25]

Twentieth-century shows like the Circus Sarrasani no longer had performers who had participated in actual events like the Ghost Dance, so they followed Burke's example and built up the notoriety of their performers however they could. Those among the Lakotas who were assigned leadership roles in the show were given the title of "chief," whether or not they were. When the Indians traveled through Europe, they were promoted and treated like diplomats, meeting important local governmental leaders and posing for pictures, as well as being escorted to special places and being filmed in them. While touring with Circus Sarrasani, groups in 1926 and in 1931 were hosted by city officials in the Dutch town of s-Hertogenbosch and photographed visiting its ornate gothic cathedral. Even though they hadn't been participants in the Battle of Little Bighorn, they were promoted as "direct descendants of the tribe" that had defeated Custer.[26]

The 1931 visit, with Black Horn as chief, continued into 1932 with a visit to Belgium by the Circus Sarrasani. There the group made two "diplomatic" visits. The first was January 31, to the town of Dendermonde, the hometown of Father De Smet, a missionary to the Indians and an acquaintance of Sitting Bull. There they performed a ceremony, and Stabber, as White Buffalo Man, gave a speech to a large crowd of onlookers. The event ended with a dance by Stanley Adams, a young boy with the group. He had caused some trouble during the tour but redeemed himself with the performance. In March the group appeared in downtown Brussels, where they clothed the famous Manneken Pis (pissing boy) fountain in a ceremonial Plains Indian outfit with headdress. Completed in 1619, the fountain was and still is one of Brussels' most famous landmarks, attracting visitors from all over the world. Over the years a tradition evolved of dressing the boy in ethnic and other costumes. The Plains Indian outfit put on him in 1932 can still be seen today in a museum near the fountain. As with the stop in Dendermonde, this visit became a ceremonial occasion, attended by hundreds of onlookers. The group completed its tour with the Circus Sarrasani and returned to Pine Ridge in July.[27]

In 1933, because of his disdain for the Nazi party, Hans Stosch-Sarrasani chose not to tour Europe and instead took his circus to South America. Two Lakotas are portrayed enjoying the sights in this souvenir program for that tour.
François Chladiuk Collection

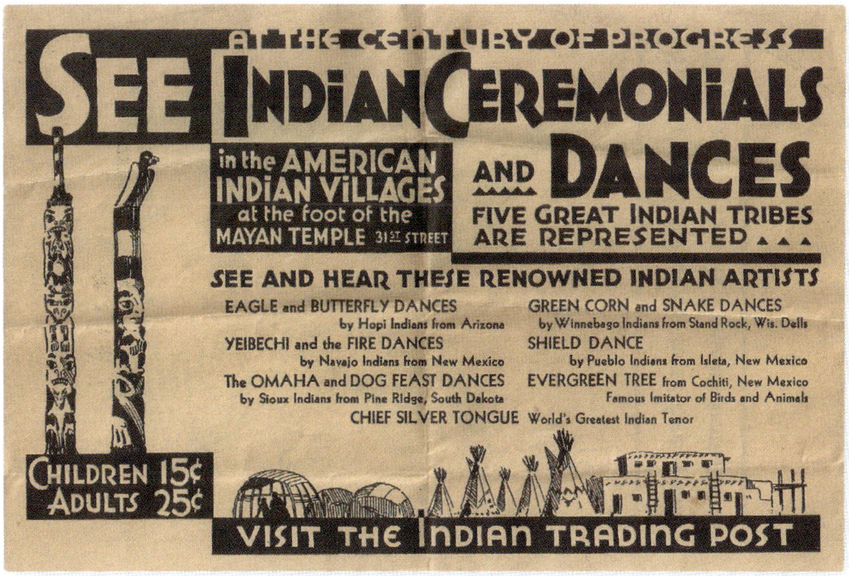

Clarence Shultz did not join the Sarrasani Circus tour in 1933 but instead took a group of Lakota performers from Pine Ridge to the Century of Progress in Chicago to participate in the Indian village.
Steve Friesen Collection

During 1932 the Nazi Party became the largest political party in the German Reichstag. Then, in January 1933, Hitler became chancellor of Germany, and Nazi control of the country was established. Hans Stosch-Sarrasani, who did not like the Nazis, took the circus on tour through South America, where he died in 1934. Circus Sarrasani continued, but without its founder. No longer needed by Sarrasani to coordinate Indian performances, Shultz sought out another employment opportunity. He found it with the 1933 Century of Progress in Chicago, held from June 1 to November 1.[28]

Shultz was engaged by the American Indian Villages and Ceremonials Company to provide and coordinate Lakotas from Pine Ridge in an exhibition of their dances and culture at the Chicago World's Fair. They would be part of Indian villages that included the Winnebagos from Wisconsin, Hopis from Arizona, and Navajos from New Mexico. The World's Fair was spread along the shore of Lake Michigan, occupying Burnham Park. Unlike the Seminole Indian Village, which offered alligator wrestling on the Midway as an amusement, the Lakotas were in the Indian villages located in an area intended to offer anthropological information. The area included the Mayan Temple, which contained an exhibit from the Office of Indian Affairs touting the work being done to better the lives of the Indians. The temple also included exhibits of Indian arts and crafts. Each afternoon, and for a minimal fee, it was possible to see performances of "Indian Ceremonials" in the villages.[29]

The anthropological area was, perhaps ironically, surrounded by a U.S. Army camp. Despite that presence, the emphasis of the area was not on the conflicts of the past but on the value of American Indian culture. In this respect it reflected a newer Office of Indian Affairs policy that encouraged the maintenance of Indian culture rather than its suppression. In 1932, President

Franklin Roosevelt had appointed John Collier the new commissioner of Indian affairs. In a visit to Pine Ridge a year later, Collier stated that the Indians' heritage was as valuable as any other heritage in America and condemned the practice of suppressing their customs. His efforts, supported by Roosevelt, amounted to a New Deal for all American Indians, in which they would be viewed and treated not as a vanishing and vanquished people but as a valued part of American life and culture. This approach toward the diverse tribal cultures across the country, as well as efforts to get more autonomy for the reservations, was a marked change from previous policy. The government not only ceased its labors to discourage Indians from performing, but actually encouraged their cultural expressions. Following that lead and borrowing from the title of the Chicago exhibition, the letterhead for the American Indian Villages and Ceremonials Company stated, "The ceremonies of the Hopi, Navajo, Sioux and Winnebago survive a century of progress." It would take time for the old policies of suppression and paternalism to disappear, but it was a start. After spending nearly a century trying to destroy the cultures of American Indians, the government was finally acknowledging the value of those cultures; the old discussions about assimilation and extinction had largely disappeared.[30]

The Lakotas performing at the Indian village numbered thirty-six, including seven children. Recently returned from performing in Europe with the Circus Sarrasani were Black Horn, Dave Charging, and William White Belly. The group performed for the full five months of the fair but, when informed it had been extended for two more weeks, chose to leave "on account of the weather getting too cool to live in the tepees." Shultz wrote Superintendent McGregor that "[t]hey all want to come home anyhow" and asked him to send several trucks, at Shultz's expense, to meet them at Rushville and drive them back to Pine Ridge. He noted that the Indian village had been one of the outstanding shows at the Century of Progress.[31]

After spending six years soliciting and coordinating performers for the Circus Sarrasani, Clarence Shultz had ventured out on his own with successful results. And those results had been achieved in an exposition setting rather than a circus venue. This experience would serve him well when he returned to Europe just over a year later for the Exposition Universelle et Internationale de Bruxelles.

That exposition marked a critical intersection between Lakota performers and three Belgians: an artist, an anthropologist, and a butcher. The Belgians would each experience Lakota culture at the exposition and then, in their own ways, play a role in its transition from the twentieth century into the twenty-first.

CHAPTER 6

EXPOSITION UNIVERSELLE ET INTERNATIONALE DE BRUXELLES

THE PERFORMERS

Joe and Rosa Little Moon gathered the children together in front of the tepee. Joe held one-year-old Wilson in his arms, while Gilbert and Pauline stood proudly next to their mother. Francis wasn't very happy to be part of the photograph; he had other things he would rather have been doing. Mr. Shultz, director of the group, had told Joe the photograph would be used to make postcards. The extra income they made selling the cards would be useful to the family when they returned to Pine Ridge.

Like the 1910 exposition in Brussels and Chicago's Century of Progress in 1933, the 1935 Brussels International Exposition was intended to showcase modern advancements. Countries from throughout the world created pavilions promoting their products, history, and achievements. The event's theme was colonization, celebrating the fiftieth anniversary of the establishment of the Congo Free State by King Leopold II of Belgium. There was little to celebrate in that founding, though, since the Free State had been anything but free. Under Leopold's rule, which began in 1885 and was supposedly undertaken for humanitarian purposes, the country had been mercilessly exploited, and many atrocities had been committed against its people. Finally, the Belgian parliament intervened, taking the land away from Leopold and annexing the Congo as a colony in 1908. The Brussels exposition ignored the earlier history and emphasized the progress that had been made since 1908. Twenty-five countries were official participants in the exposition. The United States was not among them. U.S. representatives had chosen not to have a pavilion, perhaps because the California Pacific International Exposition was being held in San Diego in 1935. Moreover, the extremely successful Century of Progress had closed only months before, and preparations were already

As he had done in the past, Clarence Shultz had the Lakota performers pose for photographs that would be made into postcards. This postcard of the Little Moon family was sold as a souvenir to fair visitors. It shows (*left to right*) three-year-old Francis, one-year-old Wilson, Joe, six-year-old Pauline, Rosa, and seven-year-old Gilbert. *François Chladiuk Collection*

beginning for the 1939 World's Fair in New York. The United States was not without representation, however. There were several corporate exhibits, and more importantly, there were the Lakotas.

The Belgians wanted to include an American Indian village at their exposition, as had been the practice at other world's fairs, including the exposition that had been held in Brussels twenty-five years earlier. The organizers set about making arrangements in 1934. They knew that the Circus Sarrasani, which had visited Brussels just three years earlier, had a wild west component. In fact the Indians with the circus had dressed Manneken Pis in Plains Indian attire to much fanfare during that visit. It would be ideal to get those performers again for the exposition. But the Circus Sarrasani was in South America, and Hans Stosch-Sarrasani had just died while on tour there. Clarence Shultz, always wearing a cowboy outfit and doing some performing himself, had been a conspicuous figure during the circus' tour of Belgium. Presumably on behalf of the exposition's organizers, the Belgian embassy in Washington, D.C., made an informal inquiry with the U.S. State Department about Shultz's relationship with the Indians. The response was that the 1931 visit "appears to have been satisfactory to the Indians involved." That response, plus any other information the exposition organizers had gathered on Shultz, must have been satisfactory as well. By the end of 1934, Shultz was the general director of Indians for the Associated American Indian Group. The goal of the group, and his task, was to create an American Indian village at the International Exposition in Brussels in 1935.[1]

The letterhead of the Associated American Indian Group stated, in French, that "the 1,000 year civilization of the red-skins" would live again at the exposition. Six tribes from reservations in the United States would be represented, including, as listed on the letterhead, Navaho (Navajos), Hames (probably Apaches), Pueblo Indians, Hopis, Lagona (Lagunas), and Sioux (Lakotas). The Sioux received top billing among the six tribes and their chiefs.

So the United States would be represented after all, even if not by an official pavilion, and foremost among the representatives would be the Lakotas. For more than fifty years, despite the best efforts of the U.S. government and reformers to repress American Indian cultures, Lakota performers, each an oskate wicasa, had kept their culture alive, demonstrating it in wild west shows, circuses, and expositions. By 1935 the U.S. government had finally recognized that and other Indian cultures, allowing them free expression on reservations and elsewhere. The performances of the Lakota people had made an indelible imprint on the

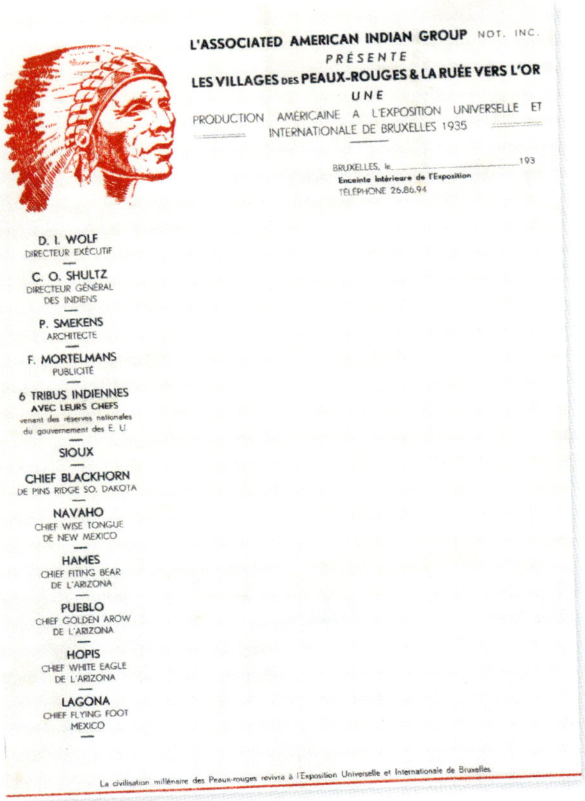

L'ASSOCIATED AMERICAN INDIAN GROUP NOT. INC.
PRÉSENTE
LES VILLAGES DES PEAUX-ROUGES & LA RUÉE VERS L'OR
UNE
PRODUCTION AMÉRICAINE A L'EXPOSITION UNIVERSELLE ET INTERNATIONALE DE BRUXELLES 1935

BRUXELLES, le ________ 193
Enceinte Intérieure de l'Exposition
TÉLÉPHONE 26.86.94

D. I. WOLF
DIRECTEUR EXÉCUTIF

C. O. SHULTZ
DIRECTEUR GÉNÉRAL DES INDIENS

P. SMEKENS
ARCHITECTE

F. MORTELMANS
PUBLICITÉ

6 TRIBUS INDIENNES
AVEC LEURS CHEFS
venant des réserves nationales du gouvernement des E. U.

SIOUX

CHIEF BLACKHORN
DE PINS RIDGE SO. DAKOTA

NAVAHO
CHIEF WISE TONGUE
DE NEW MEXICO

HAMES
CHIEF FITING BEAR
DE L'ARIZONA

PUEBLO
CHIEF GOLDEN AROW
DE L'ARIZONA

HOPIS
CHIEF WHITE EAGLE
DE L'ARIZONA

LAGONA
CHIEF FLYING FOOT
MEXICO

La civilisation millénaire des Peaux-rouges revivra à l'Exposition Universelle et Internationale de Bruxelles

Letterhead used by the Associated American Indian Group while coordinating the Indian village for the 1935 exposition in Brussels. Clarence Shultz is listed as coordinator of the Indian groups, while Black Horn is designated as chief. *François Chladiuk Collection*

people of Europe during the preceding fifty years, gaining sympathy among some, imitators among others, and fascination among all. Together with the other performers in the wild west shows, Lakotas had helped create impressions, and stereotypes, about the American West that would last well into the next century. The exposition's organizers, and the Associated American Indian Group, were confident that the Lakotas would be a successful addition to the exposition.

The Lakotas arrived in Europe to some fanfare on April 25, 1935. The United Press distributed a posting from Paris with the headline "Redskins Block Paris Traffic." The performers arrived at Gare Saint-Lazare on the boat train, after a trip to Europe on the S.S. *Bremen*. Fourteen adults and children, plus one infant, were met on the train platform by astounded passersby and the press. The United Press reporter described them as garbed in "war paint and all of the trimmings" and stated that they had come "all the way from Pine Ridge, South Dakota, to set up a typical Sioux village at the Brussels exposition" and to demonstrate their customs. A *New York Times* reporter, also present at the Lakotas' arrival in Paris, described the event somewhat flippantly: "They are en route to the Brussels exposition where they will set up a typical Sioux village to show the world how the Red Man solves the high cost of living."[2]

According to the *New York Times* reporter, he drew upon his own "Indian vocabulary" and asked "Heap-big Injun likum Paris?" This stereotype-laden query was met with a reply from Chief Black Horn: "I think it might facilitate matters for you if I refer you to our interpreter, Sam Lone Bear." At that point the reporter asked Lone Bear in English if he spoke French. "Oh yes, and I also speak German," he replied. Lone Bear then pointed out to the gathered

Lakotas arrived at the train station in Paris en route to Brussels on April 25, 1935, and created quite a commotion. Among the most striking in appearance, and certainly the tallest, was White Buffalo Man (*in the center*). *François Chladiuk Collection*

reporters that he had made a point to learn these three languages and that he had visited Europe off and on for years since his first time there with Buffalo Bill's Wild West. It was in fact his eighth trip to the continent.[3]

The three most prominent and most experienced performers among the Lakotas were Sam Lone Bear, Daniel Black Horn, and Thomas Stabber (White Buffalo Man). Their predecessors, such as Red Shirt, Rocky Bear, and American Horse, had either retired or passed away. Even Iron Tail, who had the highest profile of all wild west performers (his visage had even been used for the Indian head/buffalo nickel), had died. Black Horn's cousin Luther Standing Bear had moved from performing in shows to acting in movies and advocating for Indian rights. These men and more had all performed with Buffalo Bill's Wild West, but Lone Bear, Black Horn, and Stabber, who had been young men when they had begun with Cody, were the remaining links to that earlier time. Now middle aged, they were on the verge of retiring as well. It was to the three of them that Clarence Shultz had gone to form his troupe. He had worked with all three at various times, and he trusted them. Because of their prominence, they were also trusted by the other Lakotas. For the International Exposition, Black Horn acted as head chief of the entire village, including the other tribes represented. Stabber would be chief of the Lakotas, and Lone Bear would be their interpreter.[4]

At fifty-six years of age, Sam Lone Bear had performed with wild west shows for longer than anyone else in the group and was the best known in the troupe. Lone Bear has also been the most misunderstood of all wild west performers. Historians and anthropologists alike have labeled him not only a performer, but also a Peyotist and a felon. On April 13, 1935, when Sam Lone Bear signed a contract with Clarence Shultz to appear in Brussels, another Sam Lone Bear was finishing off a two-year prison sentence at McNeil Island Federal Penitentiary in Washington State. Lone Bear was not a person with different aspects of his personality, who could also be in two places at once. There were two different men named Sam Lone Bear. One was a performer and the other a Peyotist.[5]

The performer Sam Lone Bear (also Samuel, Sammie, and Sammy) was born in Beaver Creek, South Dakota, in 1878. On the Indian census records, his father was simply known as Lone Bear, although Sam once referred to himself as Sam Lone Bear Junior, suggesting his father had the same name. Both of them did bear the Lakota name Mato Wanjila. Sam's mother was Lizzie Walks at Night, and his sister was Alice Lone Bear. Sam attended Indian school until third grade and later reminisced that school had aroused his curiosity about the rest of the world. There, the teachers had told him about the cities and marvels of civilization, and he had decided that he wanted to see them firsthand. When Buffalo Bill visited the reservation, Sam listened to the stories of his travels and concluded that Buffalo Bill's Wild West would be his ticket to the world. He started

Because Sam Lone Bear could speak English, French, and German, in addition to Lakota, he acted as interpreter for the group at the Brussels 1935 exposition. Photographer unknown. *François Chladiuk Collection*

with Buffalo Bill's Wild West at age sixteen in 1894.[6]

Sam Lone Bear's command of the English language, which he had learned in school and had continued to polish, enabled him to rise quickly in the ranks of Buffalo Bill's Wild West. At age twenty-two, six years after joining the show, he was listed as one of two interpreters for the forty-one-person Indian troupe in the *Wild West Route Book* for the 1900 season. Sam Lone Bear was one of the celebrities of Buffalo Bill's Wild West. A featured performer in the Wild West, he was present in many photographs of the show. He posed for portraits by Gertrude Kasebier in 1898 and by William Rau in 1900. Both were noted photographers of the era. Sam Lone Bear's father also posed for photographs by Kasebier, but whether his father performed with the Wild West is unclear. During this time Sam had business cards printed with his name and the years he had served with Buffalo Bill's Wild West. In addition to acting as interpreter, Lone Bear was chief of the show's Indian police for several seasons. He also served intermittently as a policeman on the reservation.[7]

Sam Lone Bear was a critical contact person on the reservation for recruiters from wild west shows, circuses, and fairs. He had worked with Buffalo Bill's agent William McCune recruiting performers for the Wild West early in his career. Being able to drop McCune's name and, more importantly, Buffalo Bill's name gave him special cachet with outsiders. It

was to Lone Bear and his friend Stabber that C. A. Henning first went in his ill-fated effort to recruit performers for the Sarrasani Circus in 1931. Because of their experience with show, they had a credibility with other members of the community, and their lack of confidence in Henning was one reason he was unsuccessful in his endeavor. Lone Bear's signature as translator is often found on contracts with shows, whether or not he joined them as a performer.

Opposite: Sam Lone Bear was one of ten Lakota performers with Buffalo Bill's Wild West who posed for Philadelphia photographer William Rau in 1900. At the time he was around twenty-two years old. *Buffalo Bill Museum and Grave*

In 1913 Sam Lone Bear joined William F. Cody; Cody's foster son, Johnny Baker; Ghost Dance leader Short Bull; and a cast of thousands in a movie re-creating the Indian Wars. Critical to the film was the Wounded Knee sequence, illustrating the massacre of Chief Big Foot and several hundred of his people by the U.S. Army. Sam Lone Bear played the role of Big Foot. When Lone Bear left Buffalo Bill's Wild West after its demise in 1913, he was presented with a letter of appreciation by Cody. Lone Bear prized the letter, which assisted him in gaining employment with other shows. He performed in wild west shows for at least fifteen seasons between 1894 and 1930. During that period he traveled to Europe seven times. One of those trips was in 1923 to help promote a movie, *The Covered Wagon*, in which he may have had a role. His performance at the Brussels exposition in 1935 would mark his eighth and last trip to Europe.[8]

Unlike other performers, who often brought their wives on tour, Sam traveled by himself when performing. His first and only marriage occurred sometime after 1900. In 1907 Buffalo Bill wrote to Superintendent John Brennan that he was sending Sam Lone Bear home to be with his wife, who was quite ill. After she passed away, Lone Bear never remarried, nor does it appear that he had any children.[9]

In 1923 Sam Lone Bear traveled to Paris to promote the opening of the movie *The Covered Wagon*. There he was sketched by French artist Marthe Antoine Gerardin. *François Chladiuk Collection*

That was Sam Lone Bear the performer. Sam Lone Bear the Peyotist was, according to anthropologist Omer C. Stewart, "lawless, immoral, exploitative, overbearing, acquisitive and dishonest—a real scalawag." Stewart and those who have based their writings on his findings have postulated that Sam Lone Bear led almost a double life, acting in wild west shows on the one hand while spreading Peyotism and engaging in various nefarious activities on the other. But Sam Lone Bear did not live a double life. There were, in fact, two different Sam Lone Bears. Both were born around the same time in Pine Ridge, and they were probably related, but they were different individuals.[10]

Sam Lone Bear the Peyotist is credited with spreading the Peyotism movement through much of the West, particularly among the Utes. According to Stewart's research, while Lone Bear made a positive contribution to Peyotism and helped lay the groundwork for the Native American Church, he also engaged in various scurrilous activities that eventually led to a federal charge against him for engaging in "white slavery." Lone Bear had engaged in sexual liaisons with several women over the years, even transporting an underaged girl across state lines, which had led to the federal charge.[11]

Sam Lone Bear the Peyotist was born in 1879. His father was Oliver Lone Bear, and his mother was Plenty Brothers. His siblings were Julia, Abraham, Benjamin, Henry, and Susie. Unlike the other Sam Lone Bear, who was rarely around at Indian census time after he joined Buffalo Bill's Wild West, this Sam Lone Bear is present and accounted for with his family on nearly every census from 1894 until 1902. He was still in Pine Ridge in spring 1910, when the other Lone Bear was rehearsing with the rest of Buffalo Bill's Wild West in New Jersey, in preparation for the season to follow. He brought peyote to Pine Ridge in 1915, according to his sister Susie. By 1922 he had a three-year-old son, Oliver, living with him at Pine Ridge but no wife. He also had a one-year-old son, Sam, who was living with the boy's mother, Sue Sirawap, among the Uncompaghre Utes in Utah. By 1924 he had another son, a one-year-old named Peter, living with him in Pine Ridge as well as a wife, Ella Sirawap, in Utah. Ella had a one-year-old son named Fred Lone Bear. According to Stewart, Lone Bear traveled between Pine Ridge and Utah for most of the 1920s, then did not return to the reservation after 1929. By 1930 there was a warrant for his arrest, and Lone Bear was hiding from the law; his home might have been in Pine Ridge, but his whereabouts were unknown. The law finally caught up with Sam Lone Bear, and he went to prison at McNeil Island on February 3, 1933. There he remained until May 26, 1935, when he was released. He married May Charles and returned to Pine Ridge, where he died two years later on February 4, 1937.[12]

This is a tale of two Sams, each from Pine Ridge and nearly the same age, yet with divergent paths. Sam Lone Bear the performer was clearly of different parents and an upstanding enough member of the community to serve in both Buffalo Bill's police and the Pine Ridge police. From March 1, 1929, through March 1930, Sam Lone Bear was in Europe, in keeping with his letter of agreement to work for Shultz, not in Utah nor in Nevada promoting Peyotism to the Utes. In fact he was recorded in the 1930 U.S. census as working for the "cirqus [*sic*]." And in keeping with years of policy, the agreement made between Lone Bear and Shultz was very clear about immoral behavior. Federal authorities at Pine Ridge would have been aware if Sam Lone Bear the performer had had a reputation for immoral behavior, as well as a warrant for his arrest. He would not have been allowed to travel to Europe. Sam Lone Bear the Peyotist may have traveled around the West proselytizing, but he never traveled to Europe and never traveled with the Wild West shows. His relationship with the law had landed him in prison during the time when the other Lone Bear was preparing to go to Belgium. Sam the Peyotist had relationships with women that were definitely more complicated than those of Sam the performer, who wrote to friends on December 1, 1936, "I am single man[;] my wife died along [*sic*] time ago." Finally, Sam Lone Bear the Peyotist died in 1937. Sam Lone Bear the performer had at least five more years of living ahead of him when he traveled to Brussels in 1935.[13]

Sam Lone Bear poses in front of an Indian village tepee with Pauline and Gilbert Little Moon for a visitor's photo. *François Chladiuk Collection*

Sixty-year-old Thomas Stabber was almost as experienced at performing as his friend Sam Lone Bear. Stabber could not read or write but was well spoken enough to make a speech at the De Smet statue during his visit to Belgium in 1932. Born in 1874, he was given the name Wacapa, or Stabber. Not long after his birth, he received the first name Thomas. He also went by the nickname Sam. Stabber began his career in Buffalo Bill's Wild West during the 1895 season and appeared with the show again in 1899 and in 1900.[14]

In early 1903 Stabber traveled to Great Britain on the S.S. *Etruria* with his first wife, Julia, as part of Buffalo Bill's Wild West. They performed for three weeks in Manchester then left the show when it got to Liverpool, traveling by themselves back to the States, again on the S.S. *Etruria*. On May 16, 1903, they arrived in New York City, a place Stabber had already visited several times, then returned to Pine Ridge. Stabber returned to Europe in 1905, where he posed for a photograph at the Champ de Mars in Paris, where the Wild West was performing.[15]

Sometime after 1910 Julia passed away or she and Stabber parted company. By 1913 Stabber had remarried, to Sallie Three Stars. Sallie and he traveled together performing with wild west shows and circuses for the next twenty-plus years. This travel included appearances with the Sarrasani Circus in Europe from 1928 to 1932 as well as appearing at the 1933 Century of Progress. The Brussels exposition would be his seventh and last trip to Europe.

Over time Stabber adopted the stage name White Buffalo Man, following the lead of men like William F. "Buffalo Bill" Cody. White Buffalo Man was more inspirational as a stage name and perhaps less violent than Stabber for audience appetites. By the late 1920s, the re-creations of battles had

White Buffalo Man, aka Thomas Stabber, and his wife Sallie in front of their tepee at the Indian village. Stabber acted as chief of just the Lakota contingent. *François Chladiuk Collection*

almost disappeared from wild west shows and circus programs, reflecting changing audience tastes as well as the much-changed reality of Indian life in the West. A name like Stabber may have simply been less desirable to a show business career.

White Buffalo Man was striking. He was described in 1932 as a broad-shouldered, attractive man of six feet four inches with a very strong handshake. He was soft spoken and courteous, with a gentle humor. White Buffalo Man spoke very good English and wore regular clothing when not performing. When asked if he was enjoying his work, he replied, "Very well. I like very much the life with the circus. We are traveling and we see many countries. And on top of this we are making good money selling postcards." His take on Belgium: "It's a nice country and I like very much Brussels. But it rains too much."[16]

Despite the weather in 1932, White Buffalo Man returned to Belgium in 1935. So did Daniel Black Horn, who had been in Belgium with White Buffalo Man on that earlier trip. In 1935 Black Horn acted as chief of the Lakotas and of the entire Indian village. He had begun his career with Buffalo Bill's Wild West in 1902, when he and his cousin Luther Standing Bear had been recruited by William McCune. Black Horn spoke no English at the time. Standing Bear, on the other hand, had attended the Carlisle Indian School and spoke English, so he was recruited to act as chief interpreter for the show. Both took their families with them and had a good experience. Standing Bear later wrote that, though he had packed conservatively, Black Horn had taken a large bag, like an oversized duffel, filled with rawhide, tanned skins, awls, and sinew, as well as clothing. Buffalo Bill not only allowed but encouraged the Indians to make and sell goods to visitors, which was probably Black Horn's intention. Wild West performers often supplemented their income by making beadwork moccasins, purses, and watch fobs, which they sold to show visitors. When the group returned from Europe in 1902, the supplies and goods in Black Horn's duffel had been replaced with clothing and souvenirs from their travels. Some in the group had purchased so many items that they had needed to cut up the show's canvas tepees, worn out from travel, to create bundles.[17]

The following year both Daniel and Luther signed up with the Wild West, intending to return to Europe. En route to the coast, however, the train in which the performers were riding crashed, and Luther Standing

Bear was badly injured. Standing Bear, after he recovered, appeared with other shows in the United States and eventually began acting in films. Uninjured, Black Horn continued with the show to Europe for the 1903 season. When Buffalo Bill's Wild West returned to the United States, Black Horn worked with the show until it closed in 1913.[18]

In 1925, Black Horn returned to Europe with Bessie, who had accompanied him to Europe twenty-two years earlier. Just as before, she went prepared to make souvenirs for show visitors. According to Newton Turvey, who had gotten to know the Black Horns during their first engagement in London, she showed him how to make Sioux clothing and beadwork. When the Black Horns left London, Turvey was presented with the gift of a pipe and pipe bag.[19]

The London engagement, with the Bertram Mills Circus, was followed by a tour of the continent with the Sarrasani Circus. That was a rather ill-fated tour, with several Lakotas falling sick and Mrs. William Ghost Bear dying. The Black Horns did not return to Europe for the next season, although they did perform in the United States with the Miller Brothers 101 Ranch Real Wild West and Great Far East. By 1931, Clarence Shultz was coordinating the Lakota performers for Sarrasani, and the Black Horns returned to Europe with him.[20]

Bessie Black Horn died in 1933. Daniel continued in show business, appearing at Shultz's Indian village at Chicago's Century of Progress. In 1935, Daniel Black Horn returned to Europe for the fifth time. It would be his first time without Bessie and his final visit. At seventy-three, he was the oldest member of the group.[21]

Although Lone Bear, White Buffalo Man (aka Stabber), Sallie Stabber, and Black Horn were the most experienced of the group in Brussels, others had show experience as well. Joshua Spotted Owl had been with Buffalo Bill's Wild West and had just performed at the Century of Progress in 1933 with Black Horn. He could speak, read, and write English and was also a member of the Lakota Tribal Council under the Indian Reorganization Act, representing the Wounded Knee District. The Indian Reorganization Act was an effort by Collier and others in the Roosevelt administration to give the Indian tribes more opportunity for self-government.[22]

Daniel Black Horn, because of his experience, acted as the chief of the entire Indian village at the Exposition Universelle et Internationale. This placed him above the Apaches, Pueblo Indians, Navajos, and other American Indians, as well as the Lakotas. *François Chladiuk Collection*

This was Spotted Owl's first trip to Europe. Like the others, he had gotten his start with Buffalo Bill's Wild West. He first performed during the 1907 season, after the show returned from several years in Europe. The 1907 season began with two months in New York City's Madison Square

Above left: The appearance in Brussels was the first trip to Europe for both Joshua Spotted Owl (*left*) and Charles Little Boy, although Spotted Owl had performed with Buffalo Bill's Wild West in the United States. *François Chladiuk Collection*

Above right: John and Lucy Little Elk, pictured here at the 1935 Brussels exposition, brought their three-year-old granddaughter, Virginia, with them to Brussels. *François Chladiuk Collection*

Gardens, then toured the States, advertising "Here We Are; Home Again from Foreign Lands." Spotted Owl undoubtedly heard stories of Europe from other performers who had been there, perhaps influencing his decision to go to Brussels twenty-eight years later. In 1907 he had a wife and four children, and within a decade, his family had added two more children. To support his family, his primary employment was as a laborer doing road work. During this time, he performed occasionally, for example, taking his wife and a daughter with him to the Belle Fouche Roundup in 1925. By 1928 his wife had died, and most of his children had left home. That year he returned to the Belle Fouche Roundup by himself, leaving his two remaining daughters, both teenagers, at home. When he went to Brussels in 1935, they were on their own, and he was alone. At sixty-three he was the second oldest member of the group.[23]

John Little Elk (Heraka Ciqala) and his wife, Lucy, had been married for thirty-six years, longer than the other couples in the 1935 Brussels group. Early in their marriage, John had performed with the John Robinson Combined Ten Big Shows during the 1905 season, providing "public exhibitions of American frontier life." He joined Buffalo Bill's Wild West in 1906 and performed through the season of 1911. Little Elk traveled to Europe for the first time in

1929 with the Circus Sarrasani, where he performed with Sam Lone Bear. When not performing, he was a farmer at Pine Ridge. Fifty-three-year-old John and fifty-one-year-old Lucy brought their three-year-old granddaughter, Virginia, with them to Brussels in 1935.[24]

Like Lone Bear, Black Horn, and Spotted Owl, Charles Little Boy was not accompanied by family members when he went to Brussels in 1935. At age forty-three, this was probably his first time with a wild west show, and it certainly was his first trip to Europe. He did have some exposure to performing; his older brother, Thomas, had performed with Buffalo Bill's Wild West in 1911.[25]

Sam Lone Bear was a seasoned performer with seven past trips to Europe when he took part in the 1935 exposition. Charlie Little Boy, behind Lone Bear, was performing in Europe for the first time. *François Chladiuk Collection*

The Little Moon family was the largest group among the 1935 Brussels performers. James, better known as Joe to his family and friends, and his wife, Rosa, brought four children, Gilbert, Pauline, Francis, and Wilson. By bringing his family, Joe Little Moon was following a tradition that had begun with Buffalo Bill's Wild West. The Indian village approach, with family units demonstrating life and culture, had been very successful in the sixty years of wild west performances. In fact, by 1935 the battle re-creations that had been a mainstay for the earliest wild west shows had diminished in importance, while the opportunity to wander through an Indian village, meeting "real" Indian families, had continued to be popular. From the perspective of the performers, keeping the family unit together reinforced the village traditions that they were trying to interpret for visitors as well as helping maintain cohesion as the performers traveled through strange lands.[26]

Joe Little Moon was making his first trip to Europe in 1935, although it may not have been his first time performing. In 1914 a Little Moon had signed on with the Young Buffalo Wild West. This was probably Joe, who would have been nineteen at the time. Working with Lakota chiefs Red Shirt and Flat Iron, both of whom were experienced performers, would have been exciting. The experience was short lived, however, with the Young Buffalo Wild West going out of business during that season. No records indicate that Little Moon performed again until 1935. That year, as a married father of four and with a bit of show experience himself, he took his family to the exposition in Brussels.[27]

The pay received by each head of household in attendance at the exposition was based primarily on the number of persons in the household, not on performing experience. The single men, Sam Lone Bear, Joshua Spotted Owl, and Charlie Little Boy each received thirty dollars per month. Black Horn, the other single man, served as chief of all Indians in the village, so he received a bit more pay per month, thirty-five dollars.

Those who had wives along, Thomas Stabber, John Little Elk, and Joe Little Moon received fifty-five dollars per month. According to the letters of agreement drawn up between Clarence Shultz and the performers, they could receive additional pay of five dollars per month for each minor child. Little Elk's agreement mentioned his wife and a baby, his three-year-old granddaughter, Virginia. Since Virginia was listed as a baby, he probably did not receive the five dollars each month for her presence. Joe Little Moon's agreement listed himself, his wife, and two children (Gilbert Aloysius, or Al, and Pauline). There were two other children along, three-year-old Francis and one-year-old Wilson, but like Virginia, they were considered babies rather than minors, and Joe did not receive any extra money for them.[28]

The Indian village setting offered the Lakotas a chance to interact with many visitors. The experience was enlightening for the Europeans in particular. Some, like the *New York Times* reporter who had met the Lakota performers earlier in Paris, were surprised at the Indians' facility with language. A dispatch to American papers on May 20 was entitled "Surprise for Belgians" and went on to state that "fourteen Sioux Indians from Pine Ridge, S.D. have disillusioned the little boys of this city. Some of the Indians who are participating in the 1935 Brussels Fair speak fluent French, English and several other languages." Europeans, expecting to find the half-naked savages of the American dime novels, discovered that Lakotas were well spoken and were neither savage nor ignorant. During the late nineteenth century, U.S. reformers and their government allies had claimed that the wild west shows would encourage the Indians to "remain" savage and ignorant. The situation, however, was quite the opposite for performers like Sam Lone Bear and Thomas Stabber, each of whom had traveled to Europe more often than most Americans. Both men's experiences and travels with the shows had enabled them to develop a sophistication that surprised the Europeans while still allowing them to remain in touch with their heritage.[29]

Three-year-old Virginia Little Elk in front of the tepee she shared with her grandparents in the Brussels exposition Indian village. *François Chladiuk Collection*

CHAPTER 7

EXPOSITION UNIVERSELLE ET INTERNATIONALE DE BRUXELLES

THE COSTUMES

Clarence Shultz browsed through Pawnee Bill's Trading Post. Now that Ray Lyon had moved down from Nebraska to join forces with Pawnee Bill, Shultz only needed to drive thirty miles from Marland to shop. With Lyon's inventory of feathered items from Lakotas and Pawnee Bill's inventory of beaded Pawnee materials, it was so much easier for Shultz to find what he wanted for the performers he would send to the Brussels exposition.

The costumes of the Indians were critical to the success of the shows, circuses, and exhibitions that featured them, particularly as the emphasis on battle re-creations receded and emphasis on culture increased. A Miller Brothers 101 Ranch Real Wild West program in 1926 had no mimic battles like those that could be seen in Buffalo Bill's Wild West, but it did emphasize an Indian pageant, where visitors could see "the greatest aggregation of the native Americans ever made, all gorgeously costumed with bead adornments and exquisite garments of their race."[1]

In the nineteenth century, when Buffalo Bill's Wild West had hired Lakotas from Pine Ridge and the other reservations to perform, they came wearing their traditional clothing. Thus photographs taken of Lone Bear over the years he performed with the Wild West depict him wearing the clothing he had traditionally worn. The same could be said of the Pawnee and Lakota chiefs who posed for photos during Wild West's performances at Erastina in Staten Island in 1886. In 1898 a booklet advertising Buffalo Bill's Wild West described Indians in the show as "painted from head to foot—yellow, red, green and blue, legs, arms, bodies and faces, plain and in designs. They wear enormous head-dresses, and great fans of eagle feathers stick out from their backs."[2]

Before long, however, Buffalo Bill, Pawnee Bill, and the other wild west show operators felt it necessary to remind their audiences that the Indians, or at least the image of Indians they depicted in the shows, were disappearing. In 1900 Pawnee Bill could point out that in his show, everything was real and that "the Indians, dressed and accoutred as they always have been"

An 1898 advertisement for Buffalo Bill's Wild West described Indians in the show as "painted from head to foot—yellow, red, green and blue, legs, arms, bodies and faces, plain and in designs." These colors and designs can be seen in this colorized photograph of performers around 1900. *Buffalo Bill Museum and Grave*

could be observed. But by 1909, after Pawnee Bill combined his show with Buffalo Bill's Wild West, a program emphasized that "touched by the tragic hand of civilization their slow and relentless elimination will soon leave nothing but a legacy to posterity in art and history."[3]

That "elimination" was seen as the inevitable result of continued government efforts to suppress Lakota cultural expressions and of the Indians' adaptations to the dominant culture. The constant pressure from the government, from the Indian schools, and from the reformers did result in a certain degree of assimilation. In 1908 the program for Pawnee Bill's Great West pointed out that it featured "the best known braves still left as survivors of the Indians wars of recent years. They are not 'exhibition' Indians whom contact with civilization has brought into such close resemblance to the white man that the color of the skin and the form of the features are the only distinguishing marks between the two races." Those "exhibition" Indians were what most of the Lakota performers were resembling, at least in dress, by 1908, as more and more of them dressed in the clothing of the times while on the reservations. This was foreshadowed in 1901 when John Burke, publicist with Buffalo Bill's Wild West, commented to a reporter that, while the Indians wore their own traditional garments in the show, ordinarily they often wear "clothing woven by the pale face." Over time the clothing and

Lakota women and children with Buffalo Bill's Wild West pose for a colorized photograph, some in eagle feather headdresses. Neither women nor children would have traditionally worn headdresses, but performers wore them because audiences expected to see headdresses. *Buffalo Bill Museum and Grave*

accessories of the past were stored away or sold, replaced by the clothing of the surrounding and dominant culture.[4]

Despite this, show managers expected performers to bring their own costumes, as was spelled out in the contract used by Earl Gandy with the Lakotas who performed for the Red Man's Syndicate at Earl's Court in 1909. "The Performer shall provide free of charge proper native costume suitable to a Wild West show, blankets, tepees, bow and arrows, and proper full equipment suited to the character which may be allotted to the said Performer and the Performer further agrees to bring any and every thing he can that is native to help the looks of village." Gandy did allow each performer to "take 100 lbs of personal baggage to dispose of as he likes for his own benefit." Performers were thus able to bring items to sell, as Black Horn had done when he had appeared with Buffalo Bill's Wild West in 1902.[5]

Show managers' expectations that performers bring the proper equipment became more and more unrealistic. Even in 1910, Adrian Jacobsen, while recruiting performers for Hagenbeck's Volkerschau in Hamburg, remarked that it was necessary to purchase headdresses and other items that the Germans expected to see since the performers did not have them.[6]

The costumes themselves did vary from tradition, in part because of the influence of the wild west shows. Show business being what it was, it emphasized some aspects of Indian culture and deemphasized other aspects. This was particularly the case with the costumes. Indian women, who would not have worn headdresses traditionally, would pose in them for photos at the shows.

Some aspects of dress that were originally reserved for certain groups within Lakota culture were worn by all performers to present a look that the audience, or the show organizers, desired. As early as 1894, a visitor to Buffalo Bill's Wild West observed that never, "even in Indian camps out West, have I seen a more gaudy, brilliant, and bewildering spectacle than they presented." He noted that paint, feathers, elk teeth, buckskins, bear claws, and beadwork appealed to "a sense of the romantic and the picturesque as no other costume in the world [can] begin to do." Performers also adopted and adapted as they created their costumes, adding American flag designs, brass buttons, and wool shirts or pants to them. This led to a hybridization of dress, combining traditional forms with modern introduced elements.[7]

By 1932 the performers were often seen in regular street clothes behind the scenes. That year, a reporter from Le Petit Vingtième, a youth supplement to the Belgian newspaper Le Vingtième Siècle, went behind the scenes of the Sarrasani Circus, where he found White Buffalo Man wearing a European suit. The reporter also met two children, one of them in European-style clothing and wearing a "Jackie Coogan" hat. The reporter noted that they wore their Indian costumes only during the shows.[8]

At the same time, much of the traditional clothing and other decorative items from

By 1935 Lakotas involved in shows dressed specifically for performance. When the Little Elks posed for this souvenir postcard, they wore clothing influenced by tradition but much more extravagant. John and Lucy's granddaughter, Virginia, is even wearing an eagle feather headdress and carrying a small medicine stick. The reverse side of the souvenir postcard has the family members' names handwritten on it and a postmark showing that it was sent from a postal station at the Brussels exposition. *François Chladiuk Collection*

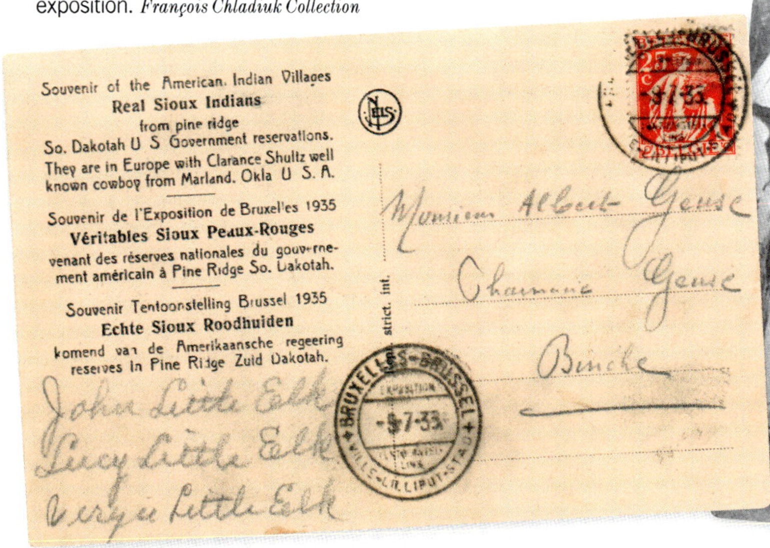

the nineteenth century had disappeared from the reservations, entering private and museum collections by 1935. Drawn by the uniqueness of the costumes and well aware that the culture of the Lakotas was changing, collectors were already traveling to the reservations to purchase artifacts in the 1890s. Men like David Charles Bristol, operator of the Kickapoo Medicine Company, acquired materials from Lakotas and other tribes for private museums. His collection went to the Nebraska State Historical Society in 1906. Artist Emil Lenders, who made several paintings for Buffalo Bill, amassed a study collection on his trips to the reservations. Those materials ended up in the American Museum of Natural History and the Gilcrease Museum in the early part of the twentieth century.[9]

With traditional clothing and accessories disappearing from active use, performers needed a source for the clothing. If they did not have traditional clothing in storage at home, they had to purchase it, either from their neighbors or from trading posts. As Luther Standing Bear noted in 1902, a store in Rushville "provided costumes for those of the Indians who had none themselves." Ironically, some of the performers were probably purchasing clothing that, only scant years before, they or family members might have sold to the trading posts.[10]

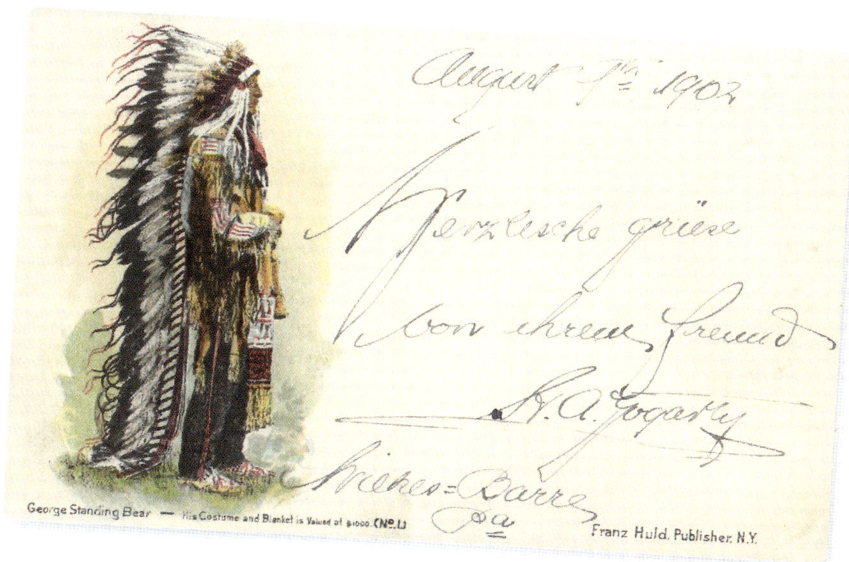

This postcard shows Luther Standing Bear's father, George, in clothing valued at one thousand dollars in 1898. Made from an image created at some earlier time (George died in 1898), the postcard was sent from Pennsylvania to Germany in 1902.
Steve Friesen Collection

Stores also had new clothing and accessories made that they then sold to performers. In addition to "recycled" clothing, performers could also purchase newly made beaded goods, sometimes produced as far away as Oklahoma, where the Pawnee had a strong beadwork tradition.

The store in Rushville mentioned by Standing Bear was probably operated by James F. Asay, who also assisted shows in getting performers from the reservations. After 1902 his business was replaced by another store in Gordon, Nebraska, operated by W. H. Barten. Barten offered a one-stop business to show operators, providing performers as well as traditional clothing should the performers have none. The performers ended up paying Barten so much for both clothing and processing expenses that they made little for themselves, existing in a situation similar to indentured servitude. This cycle was not desirable, but for one who wished to be a performer, it was a necessary evil. The demand from show operators for performing Indians and from Indians for costumes in order to perform made Barten a tidy profit until the 1920s.[11]

As the efforts of the government to suppress Indian cultures subsided in the 1920s and 1930s, the demand for costumes by growing numbers of performers increased. Despite Indian performers having few or any articles suitable for exhibition, contracts with performers often continued to state that they must provide their own costumes. After Captain Henning's ill-fated attempt to recruit Lakotas for the Sarrasani Circus in 1931, he wrote to Bertram Mills, offering to recruit Indians for a show in London. Regarding arrangements, he stated, "Very few have complete or even part costumes, as even when they are fitted out for a show, on their return, they invariably re-sell their costumes and everything else which will bring in money." He noted that costumes cost anywhere from seventy-five to one hundred dollars per adult. Customarily, that amount was deducted weekly from performers' salaries, thus enabling performers to meet the contractual requirement to provide their own costumes.[12]

A primary source of clothing during the 1920s and 1930s was the Lyon Curio Store in Clinton, Nebraska. It provided the "largest line of sinew sewn Sioux Indian bead work in the world," with a catalog of more than fifty offerings, ranging from skin dresses to warbonnets. Ray Lyon, the proprietor, bragged, "If it was made by a Sioux Indian—We Have It!" He provided costumes to Indian performers at fairs, in movies, and even for plays in Indian schools, noting, "I take great pride in furnishing the Indians with outfits[,] for every time that I have done this, it has sure been a good advertisement for me." Lyon also assisted representatives of shows seeking to hire performers, positioning himself to provide costuming for those performers as well. Pawnee Bill's prediction concerning "exhibition Indians" had surely come true.[13]

Clarence Shultz went to Ray Lyon when he needed materials for Lakota performers. In 1933 Lyon assisted Shultz in obtaining costumes for the Indians who would appear at the Century of Progress in Chicago. At the end of the fair, Shultz, who had paid Lyon for the costumes and reimbursed himself with money from performers' wages, then assisted the performers with selling their costumes. It was not unusual for performers to sell part or all of their costumes at the end of a season in order to have cash for the coming year. The costume might be sold back to a trading post like Lyon's or to other performers preparing for a new season. In this manner, the materials circulated around Pine Ridge.[14]

Around 1930 Ray Lyon became Pawnee Bill's business partner. Pawnee Bill had gotten out of the wild west show business after his combined show with Buffalo Bill had gone bankrupt in 1913. He maintained a large ranch in Pawnee, Oklahoma, which featured a wild west town and trading post. Ray Lyon moved from Nebraska to Oklahoma to operate the trading post, citing a desire to "be among more tribes" and "be more centrally located." Pawnee Bill's Trading Post offered goods from American cowboys and from

Ray Lyon moved from Nebraska to Oklahoma in the early 1930s, combining his business with Pawnee Bill's Trading Post. This became an ideal location for Clarence Shultz, who lived in nearby Marland. *Steve Friesen Collection*

Old Mexico but, like Lyon's curio shop, specialized in Indian goods. The primary market was "collectors of museum specimens" who were seeking Indian items that were "becoming very scarce and will be past procuring in a very short time." In addition to providing historical artifacts, the trading post offered handicrafts, both retail and wholesale, created by local craftspeople, including beadwork by Pawnees. The trading post, incidentally, could also "furnish Indians for celebrations and show purposes."[15]

Clarence Shultz purchased a vest from this catalog for Gilbert Little Moon to wear while performing at the Exposition Universelle et Internationale. *François Chladiuk Collection*

As in the past, performers at the 1935 International Exposition in Brussels were expected to provide their own costumes, as spelled out in the contract: "The party of the second part agrees to furnish all head-dress and other Indian regalia required for such performances." If the performers could not provide their own regalia, they had to buy them from other Lakotas or from the trading post. The prices for costumes and costume materials were clearly established. Breastplates ranged in price from fifteen to twenty-five dollars, leggings eight to twenty-two dollars, moccasins four to five dollars, pants twenty-five to thirty-five dollars, war shirts fifty to seventy dollars, and warbonnets fifty to sixty dollars.[16]

Some of the performers did have their own costumes. One of the shirts Black Horn wore at the 1935 exposition had been made for him by Bessie sometime prior to 1923. During his previous trips to Europe, he had shaken hands with many visitors, so she had commemorated this with the shirt, decorating it with beaded hands to represent what he called "many handshakes." Handshaking was very important in many American Indian cultures as not only a greeting but a gesture of friendship. Lakotas in Buffalo Bill's Wild West were frequently photographed shaking hands with visitors, as well as with other performers. Despite his "Many Handshakes" shirt

Right: Chief Black Horn pictured at the Brussels exposition in his "Many Handshakes" shirt, made by his wife, Bessie. It commemorated his many handshakes with royalty and others during previous trips to Europe. *François Chladiuk Collection*

Opposite: Today Daniel Black Horn's "Many Handshakes" shirt is in the collection of the Denver Museum of Nature and Science. *Denver Museum of Nature and Science*

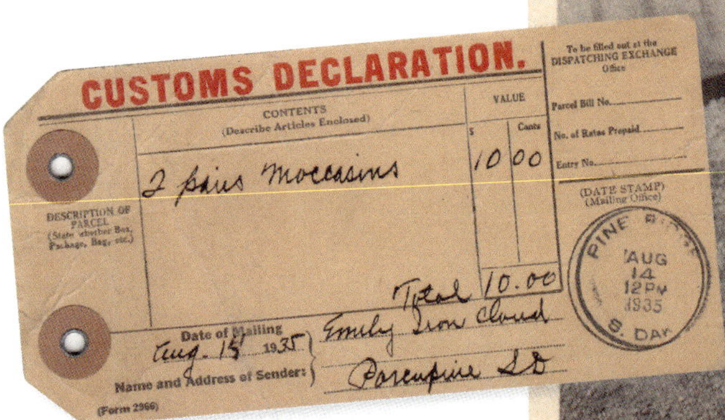

CUSTOMS DECLARATION.

CONTENTS (Describe Articles Enclosed)

VALUE $ Cents

2 pairs moccasins 10 00

DESCRIPTION OF PARCEL (State whether Box, Package, Bag, etc.)

Total 10.00

Date of Mailing Aug. 15 1935

Name and Address of Sender: Emily Iron Cloud, Porcupine SD

(Form 2966)

To be filled out at the DISPATCHING EXCHANGE Office

Parcel Bill No.

No. of Rates Prepaid

Entry No.

(DATE STAMP) (Mailing Office)

PINE ... AUG 14 12PM 1935 S. DAK

On August 14, 1935, Emily Iron Cloud sent two pairs of moccasins from Pine Ridge to Chief Black Horn at the Indian village in Brussels. He probably intended to sell them as souvenirs to exposition visitors. *François Chladiuk Collection*

and his years of experience performing, however, even Black Horn found it necessary to acquire additional costume materials. Halfway through the exposition, he had two pairs of moccasins, valued at ten dollars, sent to him from Pine Ridge. He may have worn out his other pairs or he may have acquired the new moccasins to sell to visitors.[17]

Shultz, who lived in Marland, Oklahoma, not far from Pawnee, was able to work once again with Lyon to supply needed costume materials to the 1935 performers. As usual, he purchased the costumes and took the

cost out of their wages. Although it was possible to find some adult clothing items in Pine Ridge, it was more of a challenge to outfit the children of the performers. In 1932 he wrote that the young boy Stanley, a performer Shultz had found for the Sarrasani Circus, "had hardly no clothes at all." Shultz had needed to acquire the boy's entire costume. When that season ended, Shultz kept Stanley's vest. He later gave it to three-year-old Francis Little Moon to wear during the 1935 exposition. Shultz also purchased a newly made vest from the Pawnee Bill Trading Post for Joe Little Moon's seven-year-old son, Gilbert. Neither vest went back to Pine Ridge when the exposition closed; both were acquired by August Hermans, a frequent visitor to the Indian village.[18]

Handshaking as a sign of friendship was very important to the Lakota performers. Near the conclusion of the Brussels exposition, Black Horn received a postcard from a visitor that said, "I shake hands from Antwerp."
François Chladiuk Collection

CHAPTER 8

EXPOSITION UNIVERSELLE ET INTERNATIONALE DE BRUXELLES

THE VISITORS

The day was gray and gloomy, but August Hermans barely noticed as he hurried through the fairgrounds. Up ahead he saw a tepee, then another. It was the Indians. He hoped he would be able to see White Buffalo Man again. August's excitement increased as he entered the small amphitheater and took his seat on a bench. The dancing would begin soon.

The arrival of the Lakotas in Brussels caused as much of a stir as it had in Paris. Black Horn and the others descended from the train in their full regalia, with eagle feather headdresses, breastplates, and beaded clothing. One newspaper photographer posed a Belgian boy with the group to contrast his clothing with theirs. Then, like the many visitors who would be arriving for the exposition, they traveled from the station to the exhibition grounds. The area where the Indians would be demonstrating their cultures was described as Le Village des Peaux-Rouges, the Redskin Village, or Indian Village. It was considered one of the exposition's entertainments, which included a hall of science, planetarium, and zoo, as well as the customary midway rides and attractions. The village was not, however, located near the Plaine des Attractions, as the midway was called. Instead it was located at a convenient spot near the tram station and near a number of restaurants within the exposition complex. An estimated twenty million people visited the exposition in 1935. Because of the Indian village's location, many of them likely spent some time there.[1]

Photograph of Lakotas dancing taken by a Brussels exposition visitor seated in the amphitheater.
François Chladiuk Collection

The Indian village had its own enclosed space. It was bordered by a large building replicating Pueblo Indian architecture, by wooden walls separating

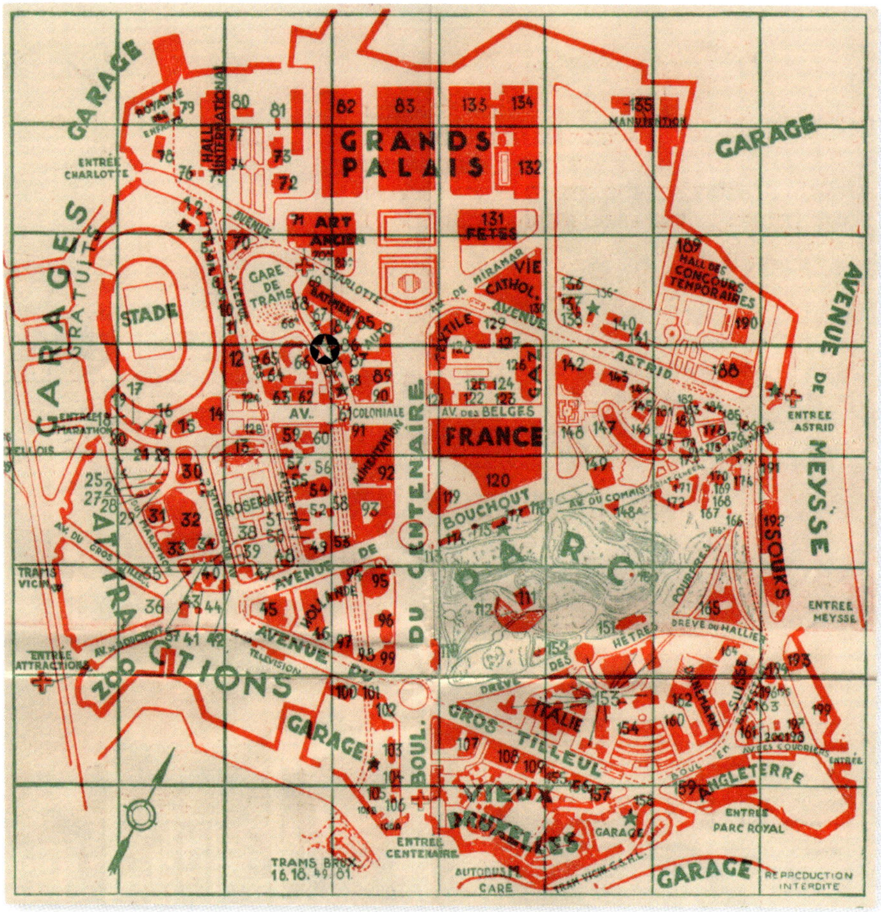

The Indian village, with its semicircular amphitheater, was located beside a major tram station for the 1935 Brussels exposition. The star on this map of the exposition marks the location of the village. *François Chladiuk Collection*

domestiques, auxquels une tortue géante des Iles Galapagos tenait compagnie ; une superbe allée de perroquets conduisait à des rochers sur lesquels vivaient dans une entente parfaite des ours, des lions, des tigres.

∴

LE VILLAGE INDIEN.

Cet ensemble de constructions, d'une authenticité rigoureuse et colorée, avait été réalisé par l'« Associated American Indian Group », avec la participation de plusieurs organismes, tels que les Musées d'Histoire Naturelle, de Folklore, etc.

Dans un décor de roches rouges, s'élevaient des bâtiments représentatifs des diverses régions américaines : il y avait des maisons basses, comme il s'en trouve dans tous les villages du Nord. Encore, un blockhaus, semblable à ceux où les premiers colons se défendaient des incursions des Peaux-Rouges, une taverne, pareille à celles où les chercheurs d'or jouaient leurs gains, à celles que tant de films, dont « la Ruée vers l'Or », nous ont montrées avec leurs clients étranges et pourtant attachants. Un peu plus loin, un restaurant évoquait les bâtiments du Nouveau-Mexique; et des tentes de cuir brun, rehaussée de motifs aux vives couleurs, abritaient des Peaux Rouges authentiques, venus à Bruxelles au prix d'un long et pénible voyage.

Il y avait là toute une tribu, du grand chef qui, au cours de son séjour aux Etats Unis, avait décoré le général Balbo, commandant en chef de l'Aviation italienne; des vénérables « Squaws », préposées à la préparation des mets familiaux, des vaillants guerriers, des gosses ravissants hauts comme trois pommes et qui déjà portaient avec crânerie le costume national, les mocassins, les pantalons de cuir, la veste brodée, la coiffure de plumes.

Dans un cirque voisin, les Peaux Rouges donnaient des échantillons de leurs talents divers. L'un lançait le lasso avec une étourdissante virtuosité; l'autre, tireur émérite, faisait mouche à tous les coups. Le « médecin » de la tribu montrait comment, en Amérique, on guérit les malades en les berçant de chansons nostalgiques, en exécutant autour d'eux des danses magiques. Des cavaliers initiaient le public aux mystères du dressage des chevaux sauvages; et l'on vit, un beau jour, Son Excellence l'Ambassadeur des Etats-Unis recevoir, des mains du Grand Chef, une investiture solennelle, symbolisée par un tomahawk enrubanné aux couleurs de la République étoilée.

Le Village Indien. Photo L'Ex.

∴

LES SOUKHS.

A l'ombre du Parc Forestier et du Palais de la France d'Outre-Mer, toute une cité bariolée avait surgi; sous les arbres, on trouvait le kiosque où se dégustaient les vins d'Algérie; et le coquet pavillon où, plus modestes, moins connus, les crus marocains ne laissaient pas de plaire à des dégustateurs nombreux. Avec sa terrasse aux parasols multicolores, sa vaste salle à huit pans, éclairée de larges verrières, le Restaurant des Colonies françaises ajoutait aux charmes de la cuisine métropolitaine, les savoureux prestiges du « couscous » et des plats orientaux.

A quelques pas, le « Café des Oudaïas » dressait sa façade blanche percée de fenêtre ogiva-

602

A souvenir guidebook to the 1935 Exposition Universelle et Internationale with a page devoted to describing the Indian village. *François Chladiuk Collection*

it from a road used by the trams, by an artificial "setting of red rocks," and by a stadium of bleachers, which curved around to form a large outdoor amphitheater. The stadium, which could seat several hundred persons, was twelve rows high, with a large central covered area and uncovered seating on either side. The complex also included several smaller structures representing the gold rush, a western tavern, a "blockhouse" of logs, and a tile-covered restaurant with outdoor seating that "evoked buildings of New Mexico." There were two main approaches to the village: a ground-level entrance at one end of the amphitheater and a walking bridge that crossed over the tram roadway. The open space in the center of this enclosure was devoted to four tepees clustered near the bridge and a performance area in front of the bleachers.

Below: Photograph of the Indian village showing the relationship of the adobe building, the tepees, and the walking bridge over the tram roadway. Gilbert Little Moon appears to be the only member of the group who notices the photographer. *François Chladiuk Collection*

Lakota performances in the amphitheater included demonstrations of skills, like marksmanship, lasso throwing, and horse taming. There were also dances. The Indian village complex, with the buildings surrounding it, was the sole representation of American culture at the exposition. Yet the absence of a United States pavilion did not keep the American ambassador from attending. Not long after the exposition's opening, he paid a special visit to the Indian village, where Chief Black Horn presented him with a tomahawk decorated with the colors and stars of the American flag.[2]

In 1935, the transition from earlier wild west shows, with their re-creations of battles, to circuses with Wild West components to expositions that emphasized cultural life was completed. The battle re-creations had played

Right: Some of the Lakota dancers, with Sam Lone Bear in the center, stand under a shelter erected in the amphitheater. Behind them is the adobe building illustrating pueblo architecture. *François Chladiuk Collection*

an increasingly less prominent role in the wild west shows and then in the circuses until there were no more re-creations of old battles. Instead Indian village areas, offering visitors an opportunity to see and meet real people demonstrating their cultures, had become more popular than sham battles. And in the 1930s, the battle that the U.S. government had waged against Lakota culture was ending. In Buffalo Bill's day, he had insisted that his Wild West was not a show but an educational exhibition. But the mock battles had to end, and cultural understanding begin, before that vision could be fully realized. At the 1935 exposition, visitors from all over Europe would learn that American Indians were not half-naked ignorant savages. They met men like Sam Lone Bear, who spoke several languages and was well traveled, and were surprised to see that the Lakota, when not performing, dressed similarly to them.

During the months of the exposition in Brussels, literally millions of people visited the Indian village. Among them were three people for whom the village had a particular impact. One was an anthropologist, another was an artist, and the third was a butcher.

Georgette Van Zwieten was a twenty-year-old anthropologist when she met and photographed the Lakotas at the fair. She took a number of photographs of the village and its inhabitants. The interest she developed there ultimately led her to become director of the American collections at Belgium's Royal Museums of Art and History in 1968. The photographs she took at the exposition would also become an important record of the village, the performers, and their costumes.[3]

Eric Wansart was related to Father De Smet, the Belgian missionary to the American Indians. Wansart's mother, Lucie, was De Smet's niece. She was an artist, as was Eric's father, Adolphe, a well-known Belgian sculptor. Eric first met an Indian when, at age eleven, he visited the 1910 exposition in Brussels. That visit, combined with stories told him of his grand-uncle's life among the Indians, led Eric to an interest in the Lakota people that would continue throughout his life. Following in the family's artistic tradition, he took a sketchbook to the exposition and drew the re-created Indian attack

This letter opener, sold in Brussels in 1935, capitalized on the popularity of the Indian village at the exposition. *François Chladiuk Collection*

These three photographs by Georgette Van Zwieten show the amphitheater, the Lakota performers in front of the bleachers, and the "setting of red rocks" as backdrop to the Indian village and the walking bridge that led to the rest of the exposition.
François Chladiuk Collection

Above left: One of Eric Wansart's 1910 illustrations showed Sitting Bull in a battle. Later, as a commercial artist, he would also depict Sitting Bull's adventures. *François Chladiuk Collection*

Above right: At age eleven, Eric Wansart visited the 1910 Exposition Universelle in Brussels, where he had his first encounter with American Indians. He was so fascinated that he entitled his newly acquired sketchbook "The Adventures of Sitting Bull and the Moonlight." *François Chladiuk Collection*

Right: Eric Wansart (in a headdress), his artist father, his grandmother, and his artist mother posed for a family photograph in 1910. *François Chladiuk Collection*

on a settler's cabin, a part of the program in the wild west area. Another sketch he made that year showed Sitting Bull fighting an enemy with the caption "The tomahawk of Sitting Bull crushed the skull of the Blackfoot." A photograph taken of the Wansart family that same year shows young Eric wearing a feather headdress. He posed for photos in Indian outfits several times over the next years. He also continued to add more images of Indian and frontier life to his sketchbook.

Above left: Three years after his first encounter with Lakotas at the 1910 World's Fair, Eric Wansart posed for a portrait wearing a headdress and a bear claw necklace while holding a toy gun. *François Chladiuk Collection*

Above right: Young Wansart's artistic abilities were already evident by 1910, when he sketched this attack on a settler's cabin as reenacted at the World's Fair. This is one of several sketches of the American Wild West Show done by him during his visit to the fair. *François Chladiuk Collection*

Left: Eric Wansart's artistic abilities were considerably more sophisticated by the time of his visit to the exposition in 1935, as can be seen in this pen-and-ink drawing of White Buffalo Man using a microphone to address the crowd in the Indian village. *François Chladiuk Collection*

Like Georgette Van Zwieten, Wansart visited the Indian village at the 1935 exposition. Now thirty-six years old, he sat in the bleachers of the amphitheater, executing an ink drawing of a performance, showing one of the Indians, probably White Buffalo Man, addressing the audience with a microphone.[4]

August Hermans was a local butcher and a man who, like Georgette and Eric, was enthralled with the American West. His profession became a way to forge a deeper bond with the Lakotas than the other two could. Hermans grew up with Lakota artifacts in the house, items his father had acquired from performers at the 1910 exposition in Brussels. These included a breastplate from Chief Red Shirt, two pairs of moccasins, and several other beaded items. His father, who had been fascinated by the Indians, passed that fascination on to August. As a young man, August joined the Boy Scouts of Belgium, which sought to emulate the scouting techniques and other skills used by the Indians and frontiersmen in the American West. Hermans first met White Buffalo Man in 1932 during the Lakota's visit to Brussels with the Sarrasani Circus. At that time he also purchased a headdress, a hair decoration, and a bone necklace choker from Charles High Hawk, presumably to add to his father's collection from 1910. When he later visited the Indian village at the 1935 exposition, Hermans was twenty-six years old.[5]

August Hermans first made the acquaintance of White Buffalo Man during the Sarrasani Circus tour of Belgium in 1932, when Hermans painted this portrait of him. *François Chladiuk Collection*

Like Eric Wansart, Hermans had an interest in art as well as in the Indians. But, unlike Wansart, his work was somewhat crude, suggesting minimal, if any, art training. His paintings depicted scenes in the American West, ranging from Indian life to mountain scenery and images of hunting. One of the paintings was a portrait of White Buffalo Man, made during the Sarrasani Circus visit to Brussels in 1932.

Hermans' previous meeting with White Buffalo Man may have provided an entrée to the group performing in the Indian village. He forged friendships with the Lakota performers and, as a butcher, provided meat to them. In return he received gifts from the visitors from Pine Ridge and, when the exposition ended, was given an opportunity to purchase some of the artifacts they had used. That was how August had acquired the artifacts from Charles High Hawk in 1932 and how his father had acquired the moccasins and breastplate back in 1910. With the season over, the sales to Hermans provided the Lakotas with extra income to take back to Pine Ridge.

August Hermans' purchase involved more materials than usual. Perhaps there was a sense that change was in the wind and that the selling and buying that had been happening back in Pine Ridge was coming to a close. Or perhaps they were just sales of opportunity, with the Indians receiving a better price from Hermans than they would have at home. Certainly August's friendship with the performers had something to do with it as well. Whatever the reason, it was the first and last time that such a large collection of Indian materials would be left in Europe. Hermans acquired them and then put them in steel boxes in a safe place in his home.

Visitors to the Indian Village were invited to take photographs with the performers. It was possible to pose, possibly for an extra fee, with a pony and a sign that read "Souvenir de l'Exposition Bruxelles 1935 (Village Peaux Rouges)." In these images (*above left*) Gilbert Little Moon and the pony pose with two visitors; (*above right*) Gilbert Little Moon and three young visitors pose in front of a tepee; and (*left*) a female visitor poses with Gilbert and Chief Black Horn.
François Chladiuk Collection

Three visitors pose with Joe, Rosa, Pauline, and Francis Little Moon in the New Mexican restaurant.
François Chladiuk Collection

Eight visitors pose with John Little Elk, Sam Lone Bear, Joshua Spotted Owl, Francis Little Moon, Charlie Little Boy, and Gilbert Little Moon (whose face is blurred).
François Chladiuk Collection

CHAPTER 9

BACK TO THE RESERVATION

Sam Lone Bear walked around the farm. After returning from Europe in late 1935, he had joined his friends Thomas and Sallie Stabber in their home. Tom, who was nearly his age, continued to farm, but Lone Bear just didn't have the interest or stamina. With a roof over his head, his government subsidy, and the money he had made from performing, he could live comfortably enough. He didn't have the energy to sit a horse and engage in mock battles any more either, but he sure missed performing.

The Exposition Universelle et Internationale de Bruxelles closed on November 3, 1935. With the exposition ended and war on the horizon, the Lakotas returned to Pine Ridge. They arrived in New York City from Cherbourg, France, on the ship S.S. *Deutschland* on December 8. None, not even Lone Bear, would return to Europe. With all the modern advancements the exposition had showcased, it had also given visitors one last chance to see Lakotas perform before Europe was thrown into the chaos of war.[1]

The Little Moon family poses with a visitor to the Indian village in Brussels, 1935. More children, including Joe and Rosa's youngest, Walter, would be born to the couple after they returned to Pine Ridge. Joe was killed by lightning eight years after their return, and Rosa had to raise their seven children on her own. *François Chladiuk Collection*

Visitors to the 1935 exposition did not realize it, but they had also been witnesses to the end of the wild west, at least the wild west that Buffalo Bill had experienced and then promoted. Buffalo Bill himself had predicted this back in 1901 when he wrote, "the life of the Wild West Show proper is limited to the present generation. For only men who have lived the life it reproduces can preserve its quality and reality." Men like Stabber, Lone Bear, and Black Horn, at one time the youngest to have lived that life, were now old. Their departure from Europe at the end of 1935 marked the end of the wild west as a living reality for the people of Europe. The old advertisements for Buffalo Bill's Wild West, which drew parallels between the vanished dinosaurs and the vanishing West, had come true. Lone Bear, with his understanding of European ways and facility with languages like French and German, was a part of that change. The wild American West was now a historical event, and the wild west as live presentation was over. The 1935 Indian village with its dances and feats of skill heralded the rise of rodeo and powwows as new presentations of culture rather than of conflict. This shift would be finalized by the advent of World War II, which brought sweeping changes to both the United States and Europe.[2]

Wild west shows at one time had been the only venues where Lakota culture could be practiced with minimal government interference, even if it was transformed somewhat for show business. Over time the restrictions had eased, with wild west performances and Indian villages being allowed in circus, fair, and exposition settings. Pioneers like Standing Bear had asserted their right to extend their performance to the movies as well, with grudging concessions from the U.S. government. The Roosevelt administration's reforms of 1934 spelled the end of decades of restriction and outright suppression of the Lakotas' culture. While it took a while for those reforms to take effect and be accepted, they were nevertheless a change and a positive one.

One of the greatest changes allowed Lakotas and other American Indian groups to organize and perform in their own shows. The result of this was the powwow. The term powwow was originally used to describe a gathering. The modern powwow, still a tribal gathering, evolved over the twentieth century and was built on fifty years of resistance, adaptation, and accommodation.

The Lakotas and other tribal groups had found ways during the years of government suppression to continue their traditional dances, performing them as part of holiday celebrations, particularly the Fourth of July. The

By 1958, when this postcard was printed, powwows had become common throughout the United States. Though the powwow had its roots within American Indian traditions, its resurgence encouraged new cultural expressions. Powwow clothing was, and still is, frequently quite different from that worn by performers in the earlier Wild West shows. *Steve Friesen Collection*

government grudgingly allowed the dancing since it was done within the context of accepted holidays. For the same reason dances were also allowed at occasional tribal fairs, staged by the government to demonstrate progress in agriculture on the reservations. In the latter 1920s, a visit to Rapid City, South Dakota, by President Calvin Coolidge was observed with a great celebration, including a re-creation of the Battle of Little Bighorn as well as Indian dancing. A chief attraction was the Sun Dance, with government restrictions to "tone down the extreme tortures of the dance." That event, however, was the exception, not the rule. The predominant opportunity for public dancing was in the wild west shows and circuses, reluctantly allowed by the government. Except for private and usually illegal dancing, all observance of these primarily religious traditions was relegated to performance. The shows also demonstrated that money was to be made in performance, influencing the commercial aspects of the powwow.[3]

The transformation of traditional dancing from spiritual observance to performance occurred at the same time as other changes were shaping what would become the powwow. There were early pan-Indian movements like the Ghost Dance and Peyotism, which eventually led to the formation of the Native American Church. There were dances that had great similarities across different tribal groups, like the Grass Dance and Sun Dance. But, for the most part, specific traditional dances had been unique to each tribe. The wild west shows and other performance venues promoted greater intertribal cooperation as different tribes found themselves thrown together in places where their differences were minimal compared with the foreign cultures in which they found themselves. The shows themselves, like Colonel Cummins' Indian Congress, encouraged intertribal contact by promoting pan-Indian exhibition.

The changes in official policy during the 1930s also brought change to the Indian schools. Teachers and students formed "Indian clubs" to value and encourage tribal traditions. Traditional music, songs, and dances were now allowed. Where the Indian schools had once been a primary tool for suppressing and eliminating tribal cultures, many now attempted to foster those cultures.[4]

In 1941 the official program for the annual Oglala Sioux Fair and Festival in Pine Ridge gave a history of the relationship between the government and the Lakota people. The program authors noted that the previous policy had been "immediate Americanization," with restriction on native customs, but emphasized that recent changes had reversed those practices. The event included traditional dancing and dance contests as well as an opening grand entry onto the grounds by participants, all things that are part of modern powwows. [5]

With the easing of regulations, Lakotas returned from Belgium to the United States with more opportunities for performance than ever before.

Circuses like Hagenbeck-Wallace continued to offer a wild west component, and there were occasional opportunities to act in the growing western movie market. The Indian Actors Association advocated for the hiring of more American Indians, rather than white stand-ins, for movie roles.

Even though the old wild west shows had diminished in popularity, some shows were still on tour. Western movie stars Tom Mix, Tim McCoy, and Ken Maynard all tried their hands at the wild west show business. The cowboy skill demonstrations in Buffalo Bill's Wild West had laid the groundwork for competitive rodeos that were held throughout the West. Not only did many of the rodeos offer Indian villages as an added attraction, the competitions offered Indians a chance to demonstrate their horsemanship. State, county, and reservation fairs also continued to offer exhibitions of Indian cultures and ways of life.[6]

After his brief time with Buffalo Bill's Wild West, Chief Luther Standing Bear became a strong voice for American Indian rights. He would become the oldest member of the Indian Actors Association, which advocated hiring Indians for film roles. *Buffalo Bill Museum and Grave*

As experienced performers with résumés that included a recent appearance at a European world exposition, members of the Brussels group were in demand. Daniel Black Horn did some performing near Pine Ridge, then joined Colonel Tim McCoy's Real Wild West and Rough Riders of the World in 1938. McCoy was a cowboy who had made it big in movie westerns. An admirer of Buffalo Bill, his show emulated Cody's. McCoy's was short lived, however, and closed midseason, leaving Black Horn and twenty-three other Lakotas out of work.

After the failure of McCoy's show, a last-ditch effort to revive the large traveling wild west shows of the past, Black Horn returned to the reservation. Unlike his cousin Standing Bear, he chose not to go into the movies and stayed on the reservation until his death in 1953, when he was accidentally struck by an automobile. In 1951, at sixty-nine years of age, John Little Elk danced with nine other Lakotas at the Sheridan County Fair in Gordon, Nebraska. He coordinated the performance, which suggests that he had been doing that during the sixteen years following the exposition in Brussels. Joe Little Moon and his family returned to their farm on the reservation after 1935. In addition to farming, Joe Little Moon continued to perform at powwows on the reservation. He also conducted sacred ceremonies and drummed.[7]

Thomas Stabber (White Buffalo Man) did not get back to Europe again, but he did maintain contact with Elk Eber in Germany. The two had gotten to know each other when Stabber had visited Munich in 1929, while touring with the Circus Sarrasani. Eber was an artist very interested in depicting the Indians, who later painted *Custer's Last Battle* for the Karl May Museum. During their Munich meeting, which took place at the Munich Cowboy Club, Eber made several paintings of Stabber. During the following decade, the two of them corresponded and exchanged goods. Stabber traded old Lakota artifacts to Eber in return for European eagle feathers, beads, and medicine. Eber also purchased some artifacts from Stabber. The correspondence and trading continued throughout the 1930s. The year after the group returned from Brussels, Stabber expressed an interest in returning to Europe to perform in Germany. But by the end of the decade, the Nazis were fully in control of Germany. Eber was a member of the SA, the Nazi paramilitary wing, and remained so until his death in 1941. Stabber could not return to Europe and, with the Depression in full swing, found few opportunities for performance in the United States. He returned to farming.[8]

In 1938 Daniel Black Horn joined Colonel Tim McCoy's Real Wild West, appearing in the show's Indian village. Unfortunately the show was not successful and closed midseason. *Buffalo Bill Museum and Grave*

The most experienced performer of the group, Sam Lone Bear, returned to farming but had little heart for it. After meeting Mrs. Alfred Angell, a Swiss immigrant who lived in Columbus, Nebraska, he began corresponding with her in 1936. In a letter written in October of that year, he complained about conditions in Pine Ridge and longed for a return to Europe. Farming was hard because the country was too dry, and the grasshoppers ate all his crops. About his time in Europe he wrote, "I have good time every day." He also wrote that he got a letter from the Circus Sarrasani inviting him back to Europe. In early December he wrote that the return had been postponed to January 1937. By the end of December, he no longer mentioned the circus, and it appears that he never did make a return visit. Around that time Lone Bear retired from performing and moved in with his friends Sallie and Thomas Stabber on their farm. By 1940 the sixty-five-year-old Lone Bear was no longer able to do any work around the farm because of illness.[9]

Thomas Stabber continued to farm into his sixties and, like Lone Bear, did not return to show business. He did appear with at least one more delegation. When Cardinal Francis Joseph Spellman visited South Dakota to install a new bishop in 1947, Stabber traveled to Rapid City with a group of other Lakotas to present the cardinal with a warbonnet. Charlie Little Boy also returned to farming. Joshua Spotted Owl did some performing in 1936

When the Brussels exposition closed, the performers sold some of their outfits to collectors like August Hermans, put on their regular clothing, and returned to Pine Ridge. The following year Sam Lone Bear wrote nostalgically to his friends the Angells about his experiences in Europe and enclosed this photograph, taken during the exposition. *Courtesy of Kristi Angell*

but primarily returned to his involvement with tribal politics, traveling to Washington in 1937 to protest those provisions in the Wheeler-Howard Act (aka the Indian Reorganization Act) that he felt undermined assistance to Indians. As originally introduced in 1934 by the Roosevelt administration, the act had been intended to give the Indians more autonomy, more control over their lands, and more freedom to observe traditional practices. By the time it passed Congress, much of that had disappeared, a concern for men like Spotted Owl.[10]

John Collier, the Roosevelt administration's commissioner of Indian affairs, ordered government schools on reservations to emphasize traditional Indian practices and culture. The gutting of the Wheeler-Howard Act by Congress, however, allowed some of the assimilation efforts to continue. These efforts were felt by the Little Moons. Four more children were born to the family after their return from Brussels in 1935, including a daughter who died at age one. Joe Little Moon was struck by lightning and died on July 27, 1943. Living in poverty and confronted with raising their seven children alone, Rosa Little Moon eventually allowed those of school age to be taken to the government boarding school at Pine Ridge. It was not one of the schools that was emphasizing or even accepting of Indian culture. The richness of culture that had so fascinated visitors to the Brussels exposition was actively suppressed. In the school, children were treated harshly and frequently punished for speaking Lakota or observing other traditional practices. Abuse was so common in the school that the Little Moon children, and many other Lakotas who attended, grew up with a stress-induced numbness toward life. They lived in something that Joe and Rosa's youngest son, Walter, described as "a dark fog." Like the Lakota artifacts in Hermans' house in Belgium, the heritage of Walter and the other Little Moon children was hidden away in a figurative steel box as they tried to survive in a repressive, abusive environment. The culture that had been so admired in Europe was still taking a beating in the United States.[11]

CHAPTER 10

LIKE A TIME CAPSULE

August sat looking at the Lakota artifacts he had bought in 1935. He wore a few pieces now and then but knew that he had to stop if they were to be preserved. When he showed the artifacts to his friends, they wanted to put them on and handle them. To keep the collection safe, he had to stop sharing it. He had kept the collection hidden from the Nazis; now he would keep it hidden from his friends.

As suppression slowly, too slowly for the Little Moon family, ended in the United States, suppression of a different kind was increasing in Europe. By 1935 Nazism had already enveloped Germany, and the Nazis had fixed their focus on the rest of Europe. Perhaps because of their growing war effort, the Nazis chose not to participate in the International Exposition. But though the Nazis were not present in Brussels in 1935, they came in force in 1940, with the invasion and occupation of Belgium.

Before that invasion, the Nazis had already set their sights on occupying the story of the American West. Adolph Hitler and other Nazi leaders had been avid readers of Karl May in their youth. May's most popular novels were about the American West and featured a German immigrant named Old Shatterhand, a role in which May fancied himself. During Shatterhand's adventures in the West, he became allied with the Apache chief Winnetou. Together the two encountered many men, good and bad, in the West. Shatterhand rose above them all, demonstrating what May depicted as an innate Germanic strength of character and even a certain amount of superiority. In Shatterhand the Nazis saw reinforcement of their own beliefs in the Germanic master race. Hitler quoted May and even had copies of May's novels distributed to his troops. Nazi propaganda further promoted an affinity between the Indians and Germans, manipulating stories about Sitting Bull and Tecumseh to promote their National Socialist ideals. Although this propaganda was grounded largely in May's writings, May, a professed pacifist who died in 1912, would probably have been appalled to see how the Nazis used his writings.[1]

Hans Stosch-Sarrasani, who in 1933 had taken his circus to South America to avoid the Nazis, would also have been appalled by the direction in which his son took the circus after his death in 1934. Hans Sarrasani Jr.,

Western artist Robert Lindneux (*on the far left*) visited the Munich Cowboy Club in 1938 as an honored guest for its twenty-fifth anniversary. After World War II the club moved away from dressing like Indians, and today most members wear cowboy clothing.
Buffalo Bill Museum and Grave

perhaps seeing few other alternatives, became a Nazi supporter. In 1940 he staged a Wild West show "like Karl May" at the Rathen outdoor theater in Saxony. While the image of an Indian was featured in advertising for the show, no Indians were involved; all the roles were played by Germans. By that time, all such events were part of the Nazi propaganda machine. The first Karl May Festival at Rathen, held eleven years earlier in 1929, had been arranged by the Hitlerjugend, or Hitler Youth.[2]

Not only was the American West where, according to readers of Karl May, Teutonic superiority had been demonstrated, but the battles in the wild west shows had proved to the Nazis that the Indians were enemies of the American government. There was, after all, the old adage that "the enemy of my enemy is my friend." As the Nazis were coming to power, Hans Rudolf Rieder stated, "The Indian is closer to the German than to any other European." Thus it is not altogether surprising that the Nazis hoped American Indians would become their allies. Nazi propagandists broadcast messages through long-distance radios and pro-Nazi organizations to tribal peoples in the States claiming common ancestry and denouncing earlier American suppression of the Indians. The propaganda, with its emphasis on race and the effort to revive issues long dead, missed its targets. Some of the information provided was so inaccurate and outrageous that many of the Indians saw no sense in it. For those who didn't see through the propaganda, there was John Collier, the man who a few years earlier had led the efforts to reform government policy toward the Indians. He pointed out that Hitler's ultimate goal was not freedom for them, but slavery. The propaganda did appeal to one group, the Nazis themselves. Completely convinced of their affinity with the American Indians and of the Indians' disaffection with the United States, they were quite surprised when the Indians did not rise up to support them.[3]

The response should not have been completely unexpected; during World War I more than seventeen thousand Indians registered to serve with the U.S. forces. At the time one newspaper explained, "Indians see Germany trying to do to all the world what the white man did to the Indian." Below that somewhat simplistic explanation may have been the real truth, that participation in the war appealed to the warrior ethic of tribes like the Lakota. The mock battles of the wild west shows were replaced with real battles with new opportunities to demonstrate bravery and sacrifice. The earlier war songs created by the Lakotas after fighting other tribes or the American military were modified to include references to World War I and the Germans. Participation in World War II led to repeating these songs, with modifications to include such German allies as the Japanese.[4]

When the United States entered World War II, around twenty-five thousand Indians enlisted to serve. Some tribal governments, exhibiting the autonomy allowed after the Indian Reorganization Act of 1934, issued their own declarations of war against the Axis in 1941. In the Southwest, Navajos took part in a multitribe resolution to outlaw the use of the swastika as a symbol in native designs. Lakotas danced the Sun Dance as they prepared to make war on the Nazis and Hitler, whom they derisively referred to as "Mustache-Smeller." Although Collier was surprised by the response, he reasoned that the Indians "have identified the struggle of democracies the world over with their own struggle of the last century." A U.S. congressman at the time stated that the Indians were "fighting for America because America has made a conscientious effort to right old wrongs and improve the life of our Indians." Finally, what the Nazis didn't understand was that Lakotas had always fought to defend their families and their lands. The very ferocity with which they had defended their homes in the nineteenth century, the ferocity they had demonstrated on the arenas of the wild west shows, was now directed at a new threat.

That ferocity did manifest itself on the battlefield in Europe. After World War I, a German general observed that the Indian "is the one American soldier Germany must fear." That fear continued into World War II and was not unfounded. Even though wearing a very different uniform from that of their ancestors, Lakotas and other American Indians revived warrior traditions, like counting coup on fallen enemies and occasionally scalping them. Both the literal and psychological impact on their German enemies was effective.[5]

So Lakotas, who had once visited Europe as curiosities in feathers and paint, now returned as defenders and liberators, wearing the clothing of the modern warrior. But the traditional clothing that Sam Lone Bear, Joe Little Moon, and the others had worn remained in August Hermans' house, safe

While Europe was in the throes of World War II, with Belgium occupied by Germany, Hermans' interest in the American Indians abided. This painting of a Lakota ceremony was done by Hermans in 1942. His collection may have provided inspiration for some of the designs on the clothing in the painting. *François Chladiuk Collection*

and undisturbed by the arrival and then final departure of the Nazis from Brussels.[6]

The conclusion of World War II left much of Western Europe in ruins, with little to attract traveling shows; but there weren't that many left to attract. In the decade prior to World War II, around seventeen wild west shows or circuses featuring wild west shows were traveling the United States and Europe. After the war, fewer than five such shows were traveling the United States. It is not surprising that few wild west shows visited Europe, which was still reeling in the aftermath of World War II.[7]

Europeans' interest in the Indians of America's Old West, however, had not abated. Late nineteenth- and early twentieth-century visits by wild west shows had made their mark. This interest fueled the resurgence of wild west hobbyist groups, many begun prior to the war. Wild west shows and circuses, plus the writings of Karl May, led to the rise of wild west hobbyist groups throughout Europe prior to World War II. This was particularly the case in Germany, where the oldest was the Cowboy-Club München Süd (Munich Cowboy Club), founded in Munich in 1913. Participants in the club learned about and dressed like cowboys and Indians in the American West. Two other clubs, the Cowboy Club Buffalo and the Wild-West, were formed in Freiburg in 1919. A performance by Black Horn and his Lakota warriors with the Sarrasani Circus in Dresden in 1926 helped stimulate the creation of the Indian-und Cowboyclub Manitou in Dresden in 1930. Though these early clubs included enthusiasts for both cowboys and Indians, eventually more clubs were formed around an interest in Indians. In 1934 the Indianer Club Frankfurt West was begun in Frankfurt to meet and discuss Indian life as well as to make traditional Indian costumes.[8]

World War II brought Indian-related activities in Europe to a near standstill, but after the war, some clubs were revived. Even more were created. The Indianer Club Frankfurt was restarted in 1954. Other clubs were founded in the 1950s. In addition to holding meetings, these clubs published newsletters like *Der Indianerfruend* (*The Indian Friend*) and *Rauchzeichen* (*Smoke Signals*). The newsletters included studies about American Indian life as well as promoting the clubs' activities. Over time those activities grew to include members assuming Indian identities and lifestyles. Some of the clubs functioned behind the Iron Curtain with grudging tolerance, based on framing the Indians as victims of American imperialism, from the East German government. During this time, hobbyists near Dresden began caring for Edward Two Two's grave, a practice they have continued to the present day.

In 1940 the Sarrasani Circus sponsored a Wild West festival. Inspired by Karl May's writings, the festival was promoted using an image of a Lakota warrior and was clearly a part of Nazi propaganda efforts. The festival ran from May through August, during which time Germany invaded France, the Netherlands, and Belgium. *Steve Friesen Collection*

Today, with the reunification of Germany, hundreds of Germans travel around the country to spend weekends in tepees. They re-create Plains Indian tribal lore as they believe it was practiced more than a hundred years ago. Accurately or inaccurately, they seek to capture a bit of the past. While critics might say that the practice of dressing up as Plains Indians by non-Natives perpetuates stereotypes and racism, most Germans who participate indicate that they do it out of admiration, not derision. When members of the Lakota tribe and other tribal groups journey to Europe, they are met with respect by these white re-creators of past Indian life.[9]

In 1929 Hans Rieder had stated that the Germans had more affinity to the Indians than any other group in Europe. But the Germans were not alone in this feeling. "We are the Indians of Europe" was a phrase used by members of other nationalities as a statement of their own unique and sometimes disaffected identities. Or, in other cases, individuals were simply fascinated by the American Indians and joined with other like-minded individuals to create organizations. As a result, Germany was not the

Lakota performer Edward Two Two became ill while traveling with the Sarrasani Circus in Germany and asked to be buried near Dresden. After World War II, Indian hobbyists began to care for the grave and continue to do so today. *Steve Friesen Collection*

A group of Indian hobbyists and friends in Belgium after World War II. *François Chladiuk Collection*

only country with Indian hobbyists. In the decades after World War II, clubs were formed across Europe in France, Italy, Russia, England, Sweden, the Netherlands, and Belgium.[10]

Georgette Van Zwieten, Eric Wansart, and August Hermans, the three Belgians whose enthusiasm for Lakota people and culture had been excited by their visits to the Indian village at the Brussels exposition, continued their interest in the Indians after the war. That interest took them on slightly different paths, but paths that were, nevertheless, influenced by their experiences at the exposition. The photos Georgette Van Zwieten had taken of the Indian village went into a souvenir album from the exposition, which she kept for the rest of her life. She continued her interest in anthropology, taking a job doing educational programs at the Royal Museums of Art and History in Brussels in 1939. She worked there throughout the war and for twenty-five years after, becoming director of the American Section of the Royal Museums in 1968, dealing primarily with materials from American

A photo from Georgette Van Zwieten's album, showing a friend posing in the amphitheater in front of the Indian village. *François Chladiuk Collection*

Indians. She served in that capacity until retiring in 1979. Her family inherited her photo album after her death.[11]

Eric Wansart resumed his art and graphic design activities after the war. In 1943 a friend had written him requesting some drawings of the American West that could be shown to the Martougin Chocolate Company in Antwerp at the war's conclusion. The result was a series of collector cards that were enclosed in chocolate bar wrappers. The cards and the collector books associated with them dealt with the lives of Sitting Bull and Buffalo Bill. Wansart's interest in the American Indians led him to join an Indian hobbyist group near Brussels called Wigwam.[12]

This book was one of two issued by the Martougin Chocolate Company to hold Sitting Bull and Buffalo Bill collector cards that were enclosed with the chocolate bars. The scenes on the various cards as well as on the covers of the books were designed by Eric Wansart. *François Chladiuk Collection*

Eric Wansart and August Hermans probably met for the first time at one of the meetings of Wigwam. Hermans and several other members of the group had gotten to know each other as youngsters in the Boy Scouts of Belgium. The members of Wigwam took Indian names and dressed like Indians. Wansart was Tatanka and Hermans was Wambli-Sapa. One reporter who visited the group in 1955 said they "lived like Indians in a forest during the weekend." He stated that the group was not to be taken lightly because in addition to "playing like Indians" they were experts who had done research on the Indians. That research included talking with Indians who had visited Brussels with a circus. Since no Lakotas had visited Belgium with circuses after World War II, the reporter was probably referring to the tour of the Sarrasani Circus in 1932. That tour, like the Indian village at the 1935 exposition, included both Black Horn and White Buffalo Man. The reporter referred to both Lakotas as good friends of Wambli-Sapa, or August Hermans. He noted that Hermans had artifacts good enough to be in

A French magazine named *Western Gazette* carried an article about August Hermans' ranch, Colorado, in 1966. The article included an illustration of him dressed as a Lakota and wearing one of the shirts he had purchased in 1935. *François Chladiuk Collection*

a museum, including a stone war club he had purchased from Black Horn and a peace pipe. Like some of the items Hermans wore when he dressed as an Indian, he had acquired the club and pipe from Lakotas at the 1935 exposition.[13]

Hermans told the United States Information Service that his collection completed the work his father had begun at the Brussels exposition of 1910. That collection, comprising primarily the materials he had purchased at the close of the 1935 exposition, was used to organize an "Indian folkloric group." The war interrupted that effort, but following its conclusion, he reorganized the group, which provided presentations in various venues, including on Belgian national television, as a cooperative effort with the Belgian-American Association and the United States Information Service.[14]

When the American Wild West Show and Rodeo appeared at the 1958 Brussels World's Fair, August Hermans attended. By 1958 the world had entered the nuclear era. The theme of the fair was demonstrated with a giant atom, an Atomium, through which visitors could travel as they visualized the progress that awaited them in the atomic era. The days of the Indian Wars were long

August Hermans had several photographs taken of himself with Lakota performers at the 1958 fair. The costume materials he is wearing in this photo were not in his collection and may have been loaned to him by the performers. *François Chladiuk Collection*

August Hermans wearing a vest he acquired from John Little Elk at the 1935 exposition, posing here with a friend. *François Chladiuk Collection*

past. One of the oldest Lakotas from that time, Dewey Beard, a survivor of both the Battle of Little Bighorn and the massacre at Wounded Knee, had passed away three years earlier. He had performed with Buffalo Bill's Wild West in the 1890s. The other Lakotas who had participated in the wild west shows' heyday had also passed on. But there was an Indian village at the fair, with sixty Lakota performers, most of them new to the business. Hermans posed with them, wearing a headdress, armbands, and vest that they may have loaned to him.[15]

Two years after the World's Fair, Hermans explored purchasing a ranch in Colorado, with the idea of turning it into a dude ranch. He made a number of inquiries regarding land in the Walsenburg area. He never did acquire a Colorado ranch, perhaps discouraged by the difficulty of the endeavor. Instead he purchased land outside of Liège, Belgium, and opened a small ranch that he named Colorado. The ranch consisted of a corral with a barn and a small building that served as a saloon. There it was possible for visitors to hire horses equipped with western saddles and ride through the neighboring woods. It became a destination for other Old West enthusiasts, like Eric Wansart, French movie actor Joe Hamman, and French anthropologist and writer Paul Coze. Hermans presided, wearing cowboy clothes or Indian outfits. In his Indian persona he wore items from his collection, including a war shirt and vest he had acquired in 1935. But he was becoming increasingly uncomfortable about wearing or showing off his collection.[16]

At some point in the 1960s, Hermans and his friend Eric Wansart stopped "playing like Indians." The few items he had occasionally worn were returned to his house, no longer to be removed or even shown for that matter. Hermans kept the collection in several metal trunks, left over from World War II. One trunk came from a fellow Belgian who had served with the British Army of the Rhine, a group that occupied the western portion of Germany bordering Belgium following the war. The trunks, and the artifacts in them, were jealously guarded by Hermans. Most of his friends knew he had a collection of artifacts but had never seen them. Wansart died in 1976, and Hermans died four years later, on January 31, 1980. The artifacts, sequestered away from the curious, remained in August Hermans' house for the next twenty-four years.[17]

CHAPTER 11

THE TIME CAPSULE OPENED

Young François ran around the yard playing "cowboys and Indians." Extending his first finger and cocking his thumb like a pistol, he imagined himself in the American West. His parents worked hard to provide for the family, but post-war Belgium was a difficult place to grow up. Some kids had cap guns and costumes; François settled for his imagination and dreamed of the Old West.

Just a five-minute walk from Brussels' Grand Place, with its fifteenth-century town hall, is an unexpected sight: a store with the sign "Western Shop." Part of a row of late nineteenth-century buildings, the five-story shop has paintings of American Indians in its upper story windows. The storefront window display features western shirts, boots, and cowboy hats. The shop doors have handles that reproduce an American nickel, with an Indian head on one side and a buffalo on the other. Behind those doors is a "western superstore," with an inventory of Stetson hats, western snap shirts, silver Navajo buckles, and more than two thousand boots. The smell of leather is pervasive. Here in the center of Brussels, capital of the European Union, is the American West.

Like August Hermans, François Chladiuk thought about the Old West a lot while he was growing up. He often

Western Shop's door handles reproduce, in large size, an Indian head nickel. One of the models for the nickel was Iron Tail, who traveled to Brussels with Buffalo Bill's Wild West in 1906. *Steve Friesen Collection*

François Chladiuk stands in front of his store, Western Shop, in downtown Brussels. *Steve Friesen Collection*

played "cowboys and Indians" with his friends. He later remembered, "Even when I was young my spirit felt more free when I was thinking about the West. I always knew I would make my life around the West, and the things and people I imagined all of my life."[1] As he grew older, he read about the American frontier, watched western movies avidly, and polished his English in anticipation of eventually visiting the West. Buying and selling several businesses, he eventually had the money he needed to begin collecting western artifacts. Chladiuk traveled around Europe finding what he could and made the first of many trips to the United States. One thing led to another, and eventually he opened his own shop in the heart of Brussels in 1990, specializing in contemporary western clothing. Over the years Western Shop has become the premier location for all things western in Europe, patronized by everyone from rock star Bruce Springsteen to members of the Belgian royal family. As Chladiuk's business thrived, so did his hobby, with his collection of saddles, artwork, and Indian artifacts occupying a gallery in the second floor of the shop. The artwork included a set of drawings by Eric Wansart, including images of Indians performing at the 1935 exposition in Brussels.

On a warm August day in 2004, Chladiuk was contacted by a friend regarding a local antiques dealer. The dealer had a collection of American Indian materials that Chladiuk's friend thought might be of interest. They had belonged to a local man, a butcher named August Hermans, who had died with no will and no immediate heirs. It had taken several years to track down his nearest family members and clear up the inheritance, but when it was done, the dealer had purchased the antiques in his estate. The estate included a collection packed with mothballs in several metal trunks. The trunks had resided in storage at the butcher's house since his death and had apparently not been opened for years. Though the dealer had not seen everything, they were clearly Indian items, and she thought Chladiuk would be interested.

François Chladiuk and his friend went to see the dealer, who had the trunks in her garage. She had not unpacked the artifacts, so he could only see the top layer of them. François immediately recognized that the collection had some value. They appeared to be Indian materials from the 1920s and 1930s. Since the dealer handled mainly nineteenth-century items, she was not interested in them and didn't really know what she had. He was impressed by the pristine condition of the artifacts, which hadn't been used in many years. Based on what he could see, he immediately purchased the collection and hoped he had not made a mistake. While he knew that the collection had belonged to August Hermans and could see that the materials were Lakota, he did not realize they had been in the 1935 International Exposition. Nor did he know who had originally owned them.

As Chladiuk went through the collection, he found other materials from

August Hermans' trunks, which had held Lakota materials for sixty years following World War II. The artifacts were discovered in these trunks in 2004. *François Chladiuk Collection*

Hermans. There were several color photographs and some letters. Then he had a breakthrough. He found a little notebook with several names and addresses in it. He was able to track down one of the names, Guy Huygens, and met with him. From Guy he learned that Hermans had collected the items from performers at the exposition.

Chladiuk also found a small box tucked in among the moccasins and headdresses. In it were tags, handwritten in French. They appeared to refer to different items in the collection. He started matching the tags to the artifacts as best he could. Some had fairly comprehensive descriptions like, "Sioux beaded deer skin vest. Different geometric forms. Very beautiful work. Comes from Alosius Little Moon who wore it." The other side of that tag continued "until November 3rd 1935 date when I purchased it. Son of Joe Little Moon." He was able to match it with one of the vests. As he looked through the tags, he found more names of the original users. Examining the color photographs, he saw they showed tags attached to some of the items. But at some point the tags had been removed from all the artifacts and placed in the small box. That proved fortuitous for Chladiuk because had the tags still been on the items, the dealer might have chosen to sell them individually rather than as a collection. Many of the artifacts were wrapped in newspapers. As he dug through the trunk, Chladiuk also found small typewritten notes wrapped within the newspapers, sometimes in association with the artifacts they described. With the tags, the color photographs,

August Hermans had carefully recorded information about the artifacts on small tags, sometimes with small illustrations. These were found in this tin box, buried in the clothing. *François Chladiuk Collection*

and the notes, he was on his way to identifying the original owners of the artifacts.

Two months after purchasing the collection, Chladiuk had another breakthrough. He found a souvenir postcard from the 1935 exposition in an antiques shop. It was of an Indian family posing in front of a tepee. One of the boys was wearing a vest; it was a vest in Chladiuk's collection. The boy was Gilbert Aloysius "Al" Little Moon, whom Hermans had noted as "Alosius" on the tag for the vest. On the back was the imprint "Exposition Universelle et Internationale de Bruxelles." For François Chladiuk, it was the Rosetta stone for the collection. With the realization that the Little Moon family had been in Brussels for the exposition, the names and dates on the artifact tags now fell into place. With this information he began advertising in collectors' magazines for other postcards and photos associated with the 1935 exposition.

Chladiuk was well aware that the Royal Museums of Art and History had a collection of American Indian materials. Armed with the information he had gathered, he visited Sergio Purini, a curator in the American Section at the Royal Museums. Purini immediately realized the collection's importance, stating that he had seen other American Indian collections, and the documentation and quality of this collection made it unequaled. Purini showed him photos taken by Georgette Van Zwieten of the Indian village at the exposition. Having been director of the American Section of the Royal Museums, she had left copies of the photos in her album with the museum before her death. There in her photographs, Chladiuk recognized more artifacts from the collection.

Despite the artifacts' age, most were in pristine condition, having been carefully stored for nearly seventy years. Though there were some nineteenth-century items, most were early twentieth century, reflecting the changes that had occurred in life on the reservations as well as changes in Lakota performances. For example, there was the newly made vest that had come from the Pawnee Bill Trading Post just before the 1935 exhibition. François later found it listed in a catalog from the trading post. Clearly some of the items were relatively new in 1935. Because of this, and because Hermans had kept them so secure, most of the items were in nearly new condition.

The 157 items, packed carefully together in the trunks, clearly composed a single and related collection. Although 12 of the items had belonged to Hermans before 1935, 145 artifacts appeared to date to the 1935 exposition in Brussels. Chladiuk was concerned that a number of artifacts were still without tags. He reexamined the color photographs, which appeared to have

One of eight color photographs showing tags still affixed to the artifacts. Some of the photos had notes about the artifacts' original owners, such as the reference in this photo to Spotted Owl. *François Chladiuk Collection*

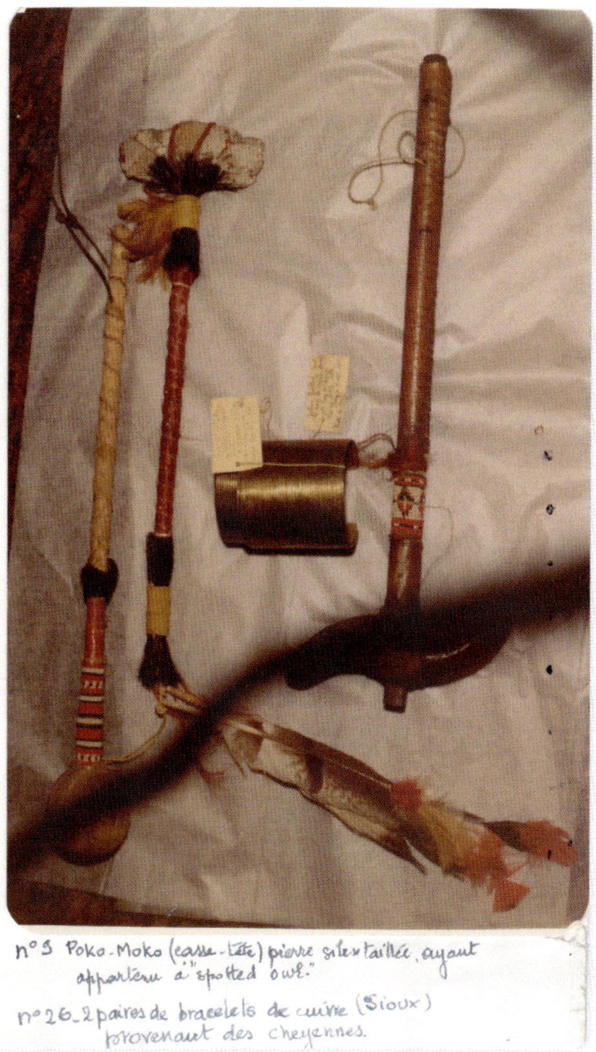

been taken by Hermans in the 1960s. Some of the artifacts in the collection had clearly had tags at one time, tags that were missing. Despite this, plenty of artifacts in the trunks could be tied to performers at the exposition.

August Hermans had worn some of the artifacts in his collection. Even though he had played "cowboys and Indians" as a child, François Chladiuk had no interest in "playing Indian" like Hermans and Wansart had done in their day. Nor was he content with simply possessing the collection. Instead, his purchase in 2004 began a journey of discovery as he sought to uncover more about the artifacts. He acquired more postcards and photographs, compiling visual documentation of thirty-five items in the collection, all worn by the 1935 performers. He also found newspaper articles about the Lakotas at the 1935 exposition and about Hermans himself. One article suggested that Hermans' collection included items that his father had acquired at the 1910 exposition. Through careful examination of the tags, Chladiuk determined that out of the 157 artifacts in the collection, 9 had been collected by Hermans' father. Three items, including one of the headdresses, were acquired by Hermans when he met the group traveling through Brussels with the Sarrasani Circus in 1932. The remaining 145 artifacts were from the 1935 Exposition Universelle et Internationale de Bruxelles. The provenance and the condition of the materials made them an incredible find.

The following pages include a comprehensive sampling of Hermans' collection, along with photographs, when they are available, showing the performers wearing the artifacts. Where tags or notes were associated with the artifacts the information from those tags is included. Those items without identifying tags, notes, or photos were packed in similar wrapping and in the same trunks as identified materials and are thus presumed to have also been acquired in 1935 unless otherwise noted. All the artifact images were provided by François Chladiuk.

1910

In 1910 August Hermans' father visited the American Wild West Show put together by Earl Gandy and his partners. It was located in the Plaine des Attractions portion of the Exposition Universelle et International de Bruxelles. The highest-profile performer at the show was Red Shirt, who had first traveled to Europe with Buffalo Bill in 1887 and had returned several times in the intervening years. The trunks contained several items collected in 1910, identified by small typewritten labels, similar to those created by Hermans for the items he collected in 1935.

A typewritten label identifies this breastplate as belonging to Red Shirt, who was the chief of the performers at the Brussels exposition of 1910. In 1914 Red Shirt appeared at the Anglo-American Exposition in London, performing with the 101 Ranch Real Wild West. That was his last trip to Europe. The cover of the program for the 1910 performances shows Red Shirt wearing this breastplate, which is made of bone hairpipes. It also includes glass beads, shell discs, and wool tassels in spent cartridges. *Length 63 cm, width 33 cm.*

A typewritten label identifies this fan as coming from Little Bull. Like Red Shirt, Little Bull was one of the thirty-six Lakotas who performed at the 1910 Brussels exposition. The fan is made of eagle feathers secured to a wooden paddle that was held by the user. *Length 66.5 cm, width 19 cm.*

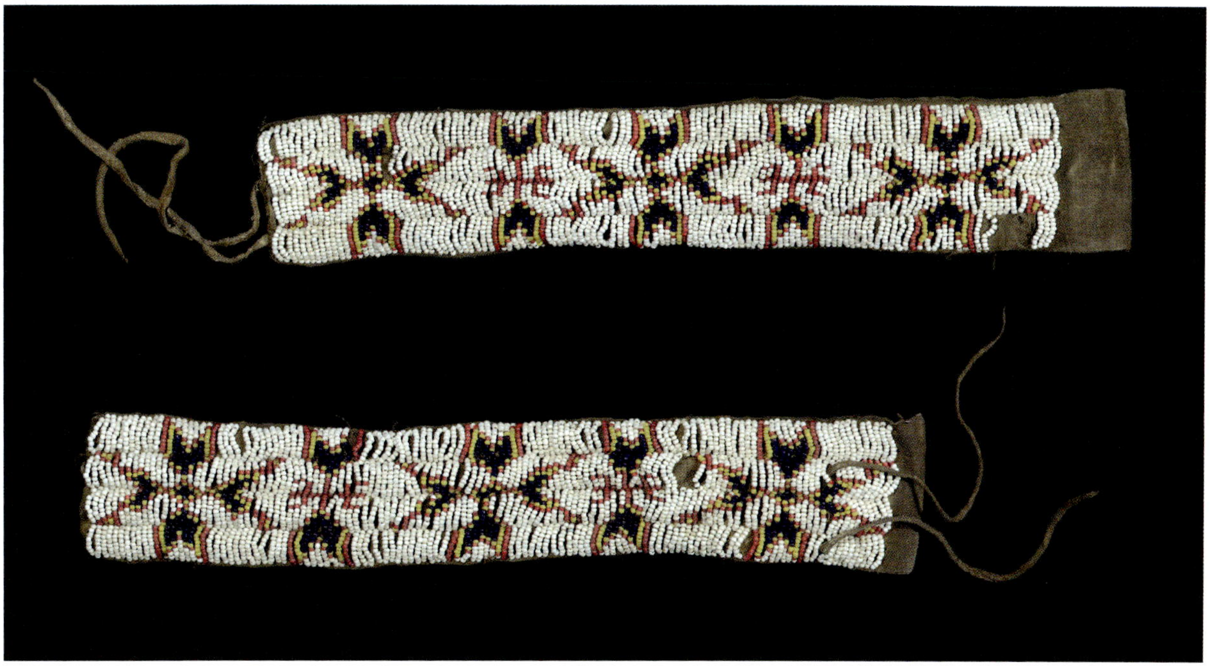

Pair of armbands from 1910, made of hide and glass beads. Top: *length 29.5 cm, width 5.5 cm.* Bottom: *length 30.5 cm, width 5.5 cm.*

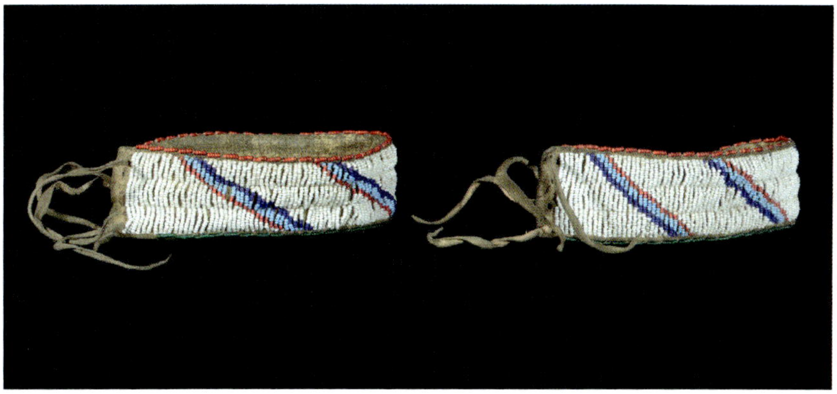

Pair of armbands from 1910, made of hide and glass beads. Left: *length 31.5 cm, width 4.5 cm.* Right: *length 32 cm, width 4.5 cm.*

Pair of armbands from 1910, made of hide and glass beads. Left: *length 33.5 cm, width 5.5 cm.* Right: *length 35 cm, width 5.5 cm.*

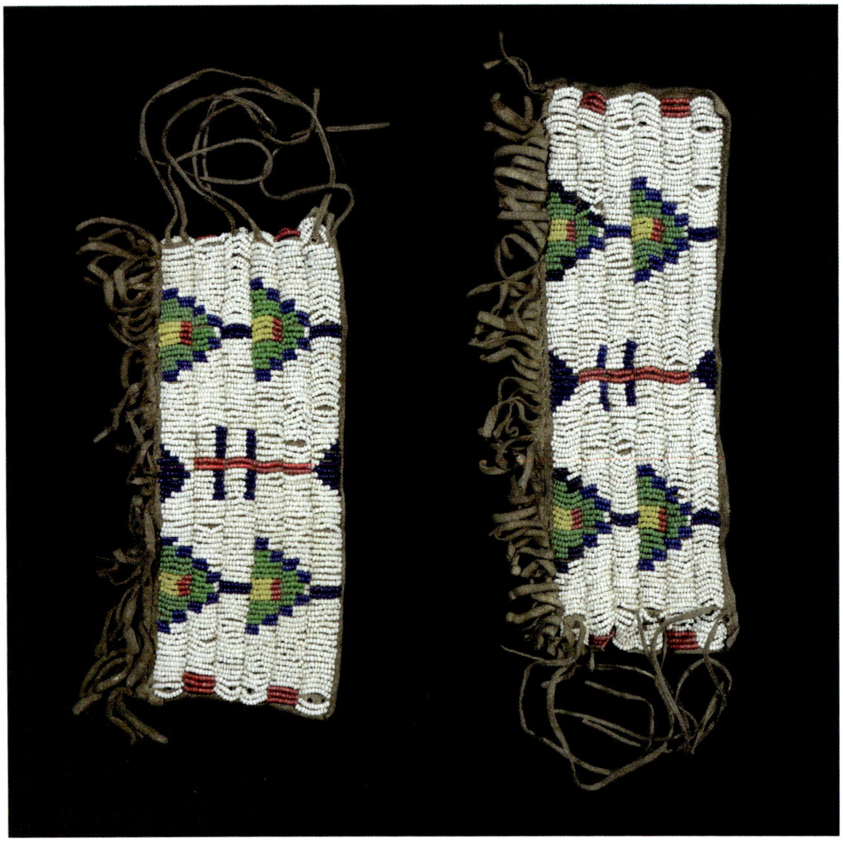

Pair of cuffs from 1910, made of hide and glass beads. Left: *length 20 cm, width 11 cm.* Right: *length 22 cm, width 11 cm.*

Pair of cuffs from 1910, made of hide and glass beads, lined with cloth. *Length 18.5 cm, diameter 7.5 cm at one end and 10.5 cm on the other end.*

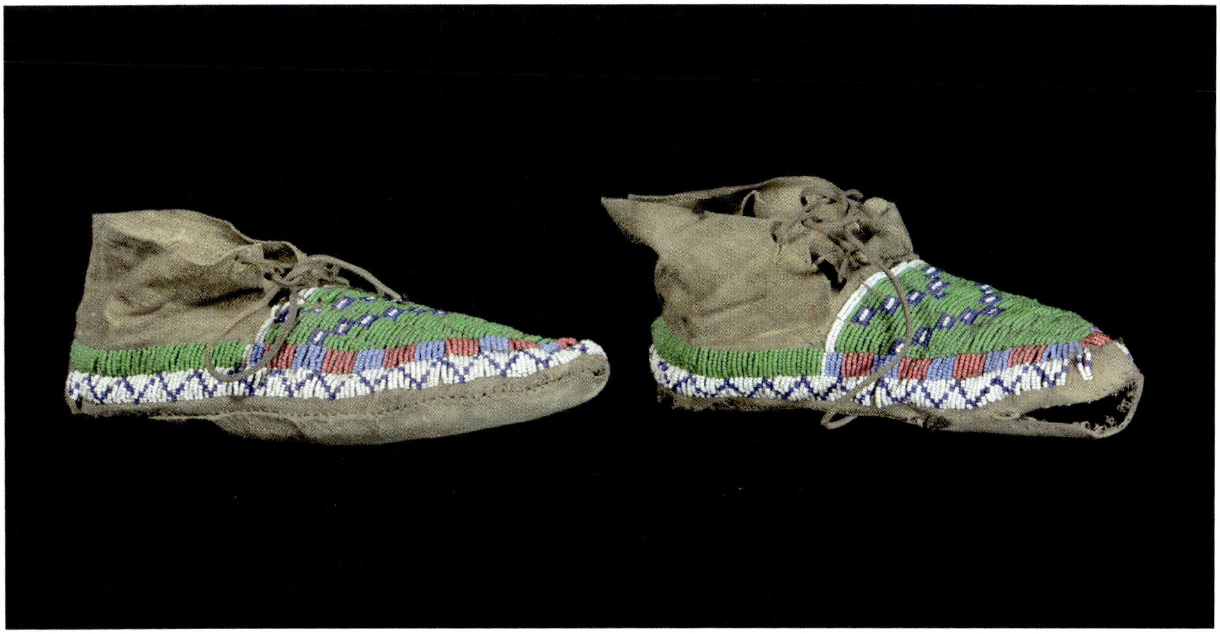

Pair of moccasins from 1910, made of hide and glass beads. *Length 25 cm, width 9 cm, height 10 cm.*

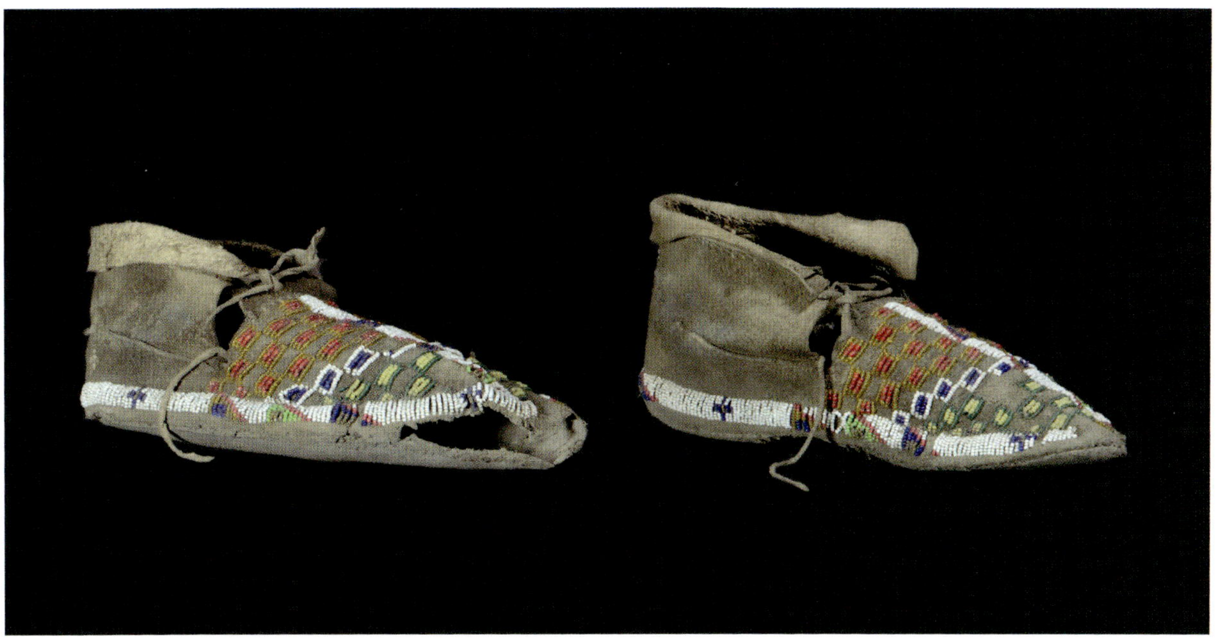

Pair of moccasins from 1910, made of hide and glass beads. *Length 25 cm, width 9 cm, height 10 cm.*

1932

In March 1932 the Circus Sarrasani visited Brussels with a group of Lakota performers organized by Clarence Shultz and led by Daniel Black Horn as chief. During this visit August Hermans first met White Buffalo Man (aka Thomas Stabber). Another performer with the group was Charles High Hawk, who was traveling to Europe for the first time. Twenty-three-year-old Hermans followed in the footsteps of his father, who had purchased items from the Lakotas during the 1910 exposition in Brussels, and purchased three artifacts from High Hawk.

This pendant was probably made by Charles High Hawk to sell as a souvenir. Note the initials CHH in beadwork above the Indian figure. *Length 25 cm, width 8 cm.*

This eagle feather headdress with a beaded headband was worn by Charles High Hawk and purchased by August Hermans in 1932. *Length 96 cm, width 50 cm, depth 80 cm.*

A choker made from bone and glass beads. Purchased from Charles High Hawk by August Hermans in 1932. *Length 65 cm, width 4 cm.*

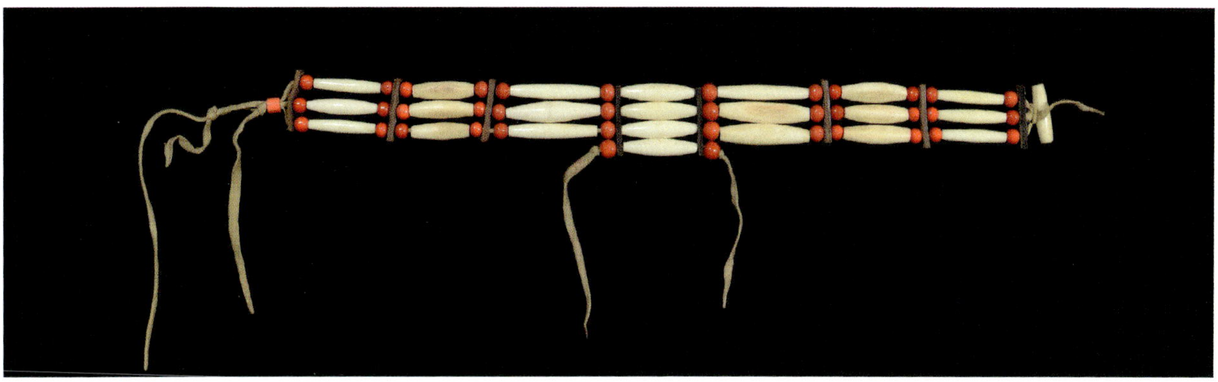

1935

In 1935, August Hermans frequently visited the Exposition Universelle et Internationale de Bruxelles to see White Buffalo Man and the other Lakota performers. During this time he received gifts and made purchases from the Lakotas. The artifacts ranged from headdresses and shirts to moccasins and breastplates. Some of the artifacts were of no great value but were curiosities, like the rattlesnake rattle he received from Joe Little Moon and a piece of the American flag given to him by Joshua Spotted Owl.

War shirt worn by Charles Little Boy and pictured on a 1935 exposition postcard. Hermans' tag for the shirt reads, "A War shirt from Sioux Indian, Elk skin with fringes and beads and Cheyenne hair, Souvenir of war between Sioux and Cheyenne and Sioux and Crow; Interesting and very rare piece. Only brave Indians could wear that kind of shirt. Come from a[n] old Sioux Indian from Iowa. This shirt was made more than 60 years ago. Was worn by Charly Little Boy until October 1935. Purchased October 20th 1935." *Length 110 cm, width 172 cm.*

Shirt worn by Wilson Little Moon. Hermans' tag for the shirt reads, "War shirt from Wilson Little Moon. Purchased October 6th 1935 (Deer skin and beads)." *Length 47 cm, width 74 cm.*

Leggings worn by Wilson Little Moon. Hermans' tag for the leggings reads, "Leggings from Wilson Little Moon. Deer skin and beads. Purchased October 6th 1935." *Length 26.5 cm, width 19.5 cm.*

This shirt's broken cross symbol, adopted by the Nazis as the swastika, was common to many cultures worldwide, including some American Indian tribes. They had various names for it, such as "whirling log." While one of the Lakotas was performing in this shirt in Brussels, the swastika was gaining a more malevolent prominence in Germany, on the shirts and flags of the Nazis. *Length 100 cm, width 165 cm.*

Decorative elements on this shirt include rifle cartridges and porcupine quills encasing the locks of hair. *Length 93 cm, width 159 cm.*

This dress was worn by Lucy Little Elk. Hermans' tag for the item reads, "A Indian woman dress. Special blue fabric. The shells go from generation to generation. The top is a B yoke made of shells (Indian name: WASU HULA see my notes) Belonged to Lucy Little Elk. Purchased October 16th 1935." *Wasúhula* is the Lakota word for dentalium shells. No further notes from Hermans regarding this piece were discovered in the boxes. Dress: *length 140 cm, width 90 cm.* Yoke: *height 40 cm, width 79 cm.*

The yoke of this dress is decorated with dentalium shells and teeth, possibly from a horse. It is colorfully decorated with silk strips on both the yoke and the bottom hem area. Dress: *length 138 cm, width 80 cm.* Yoke: *height 60 cm, width 53 cm.*

Leggings worn by Joe Little Moon. He can be seen wearing these in several postcards and photographs from the exposition, including this one taken by Georgette Van Zwieten of him seated with his children, fellow performer Charlie Little Boy, and a visitor. *Length 87 cm, width 36 cm.*

Leggings worn by John Little Elk. He is pictured wearing them and a vest with beaded buffalo, which Hermans also purchased, on this souvenir postcard from the exposition. Left leg: *length 86 cm, width 34 cm.* Right leg: *length 83 cm, width 35 cm.*

These appear to be leggings that were worn on the calf and extended down to moccasin-covered feet, acting like gaiters. Their size suggests they were worn by a woman or a child. *Length 34 cm, width 20 cm.*

Loincloth worn by Spotted Owl. It can be seen just below his cloth shirt in his photograph with Charlie Little Boy. *Length 119 cm, width 39 cm.*

Vest purchased by Clarence Shultz from Pawnee Bill's Trading Post, ca. 1929, as evident in the Trading Post catalog page shown. Worn by Gilbert Aloysius "Al" Little Moon. Hermans' tag reads, "Sioux beaded deer skin vest. Different geometric forms. Very beautiful work. Comes from Alosius Little Moon who wore it until November 3rd 1935 date when I purchased it." *Length 42 cm, width 42 cm.*

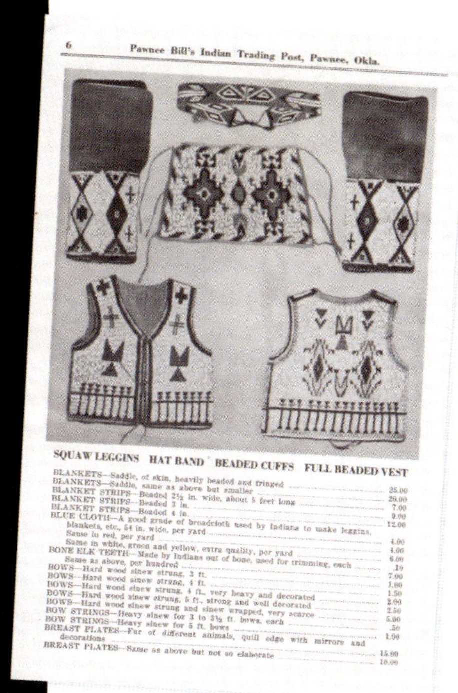

6 Pawnee Bill's Indian Trading Post, Pawnee, Okla.

SQUAW LEGGINS HAT BAND BEADED CUFFS FULL BEADED VEST

BLANKETS—Saddle, of skin, heavily beaded and fringed 25.00
BLANKETS—Saddle, same as above but smaller 20.00
BLANKET STRIPS—Beaded 2½ in. wide, about 5 feet long 7.00
BLANKET STRIPS—Beaded 3 in. 9.00
BLANKET STRIPS—Beaded 4 in. 12.00
BLUE CLOTH—A good grade of broadcloth used by Indians to make leggins, blankets, etc., 54 in. wide, per yard 4.00
Same in red, per yard 4.00
Same in white, green and yellow, extra quality, per yard 6.00
BONE ELK TEETH—Made by Indians out of bone, used for trimming, each .... .10
Same as above, per hundred 7.00
BOWS—Hard wood sinew strung, 3 ft. 1.00
BOWS—Hard wood sinew strung, 4 ft. 1.50
BOWS—Hard wood sinew strung, 4 ft., very heavy and decorated 2.00
BOWS—Hard wood sinew strung, 5 ft., strong and well decorated 2.50
BOWS—Hard wood sinew strung and sinew wrapped, very scarce 5.00
BOW STRINGS—Heavy sinew for 3 to 3½ ft. bows, each .... .50
BOW STRINGS—Heavy sinew for 5 ft. bows 1.00
BREAST PLATES—Fur of different animals, quill edge with mirrors and decorations 15.00
BREAST PLATES—Same as above but not so elaborate 10.00

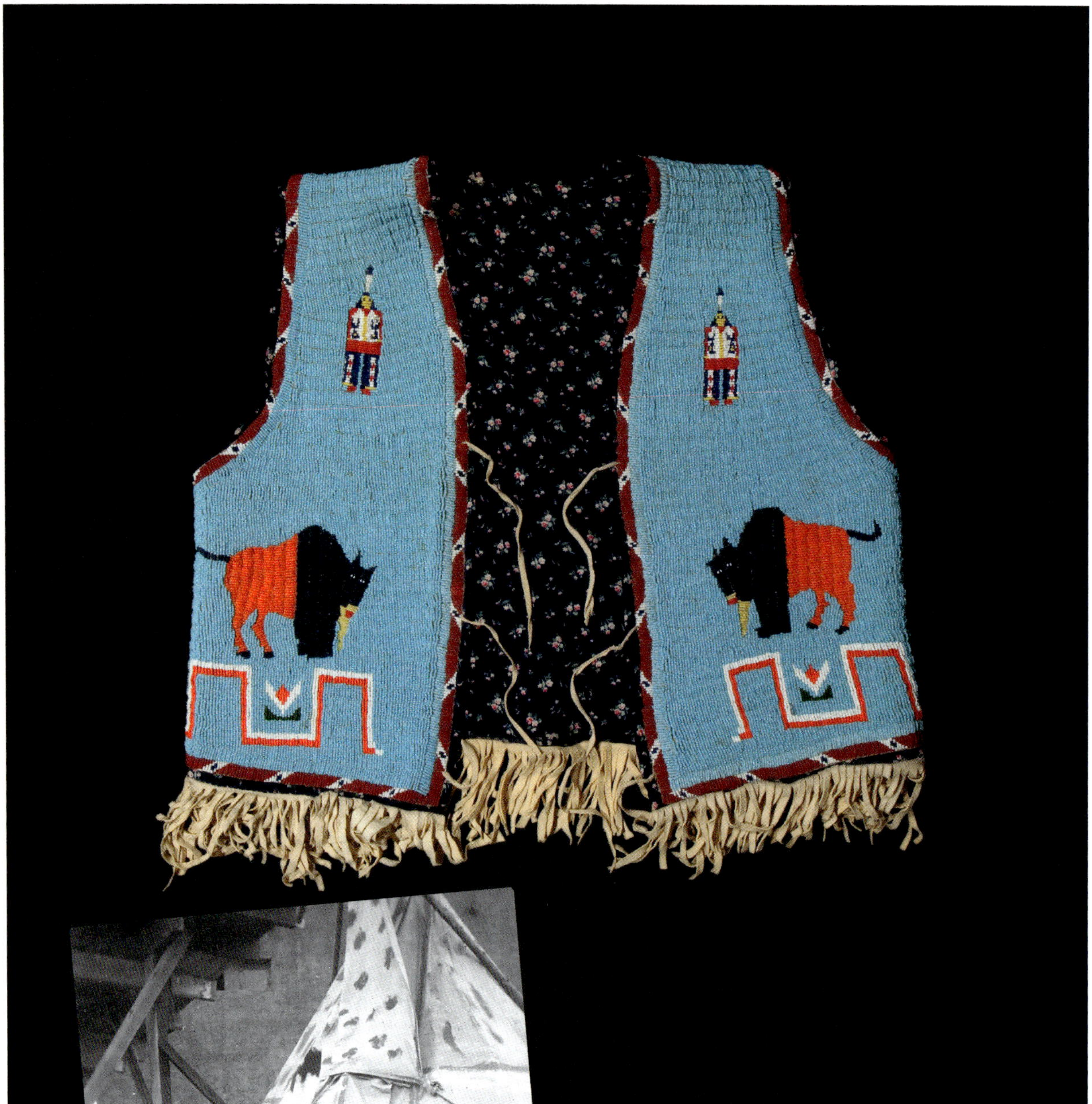

Vest worn by John Little Elk. This vest had no tag from Hermans but can be seen on Little Elk in several different photographs and postcards, including in the photo at far left. Hermans later wore the vest during reenactments, also shown. *Length 62 cm, width 62 cm.*

This vest was worn by Francis Little Moon. Hermans' tag for the item reads, "A Sioux vest, beaded deer skin, Eagles and Sioux on horses. Very beautiful work. Come from the little Indian B. Herbert Little Moon (2nd son of Joe Little Moon). Purchased November 3rd, 1935." Francis' complete name was Hobert Francis Little Moon, according to his younger brother Walter. Hermans must have miswritten the name on the tag. Francis is clearly wearing this vest in photographs taken at the 1935 fair, including in the photograph at right taken by Georgette Van Zwieten in the arena where the group danced. *Length 41 cm, width 43 cm.*

This vest bears a combination of beadwork and cowrie shells on its front. The decoration on the back consists of animal teeth, a few cowrie shells, and a small medallion of beadwork. These decorative variations are unusual. *Length 67 cm, width 59 cm.*

Several men in the 1935 Brussels exposition group can be seen in photographs wearing relatively simple vests decorated with cowrie shells and beads. It is not clear from photos which of them wore this vest. *Length 56 cm, width 53 cm.*

This vest is decorated with cowrie shells and two teeth (on the left and right sides). Each pocket also has three coins, one animal tooth, and teardrop-shaped glass beads dangling from it. *Length 59 cm, width 51 cm.*

This eagle feather headdress was worn by Joshua Spotted Owl. He is shown wearing it in several photos and postcards, including this image with a group of visitors. Spotted Owl is in the center. *Length 72 cm, width 54 cm, depth 49 cm.*

Opposite: August Hermans did not identify the owner of this eagle feather headdress nor can it be seen in any photographs or postcards collected thus far by François Chladiuk. *Length 96 cm, width 78 cm, depth 89 cm.*

This headdress features a combination of red, white, and blue colors that was very popular among Lakotas. By 1935 the headdress could have served as a patriotic representation of the United States at the exposition. *Length 86 cm, width 69 cm, depth 69 cm.*

Eagle feather headdress with a beaded headband and silk ribbons hanging from the sides. *Length 101 cm, width 55 cm, depth 43 cm.*

This eagle feather headdress includes decorative strips on its sides of both cloth and ermine fur. *Length 83 cm, width 66 cm, depth 45 cm.*

In addition to the eagle feathers and beaded headband, with small medallions on each side, this headdress has decorative cloth ribbons and feathers hanging from each side. *Length 93 cm, width 63 cm, depth 63 cm.*

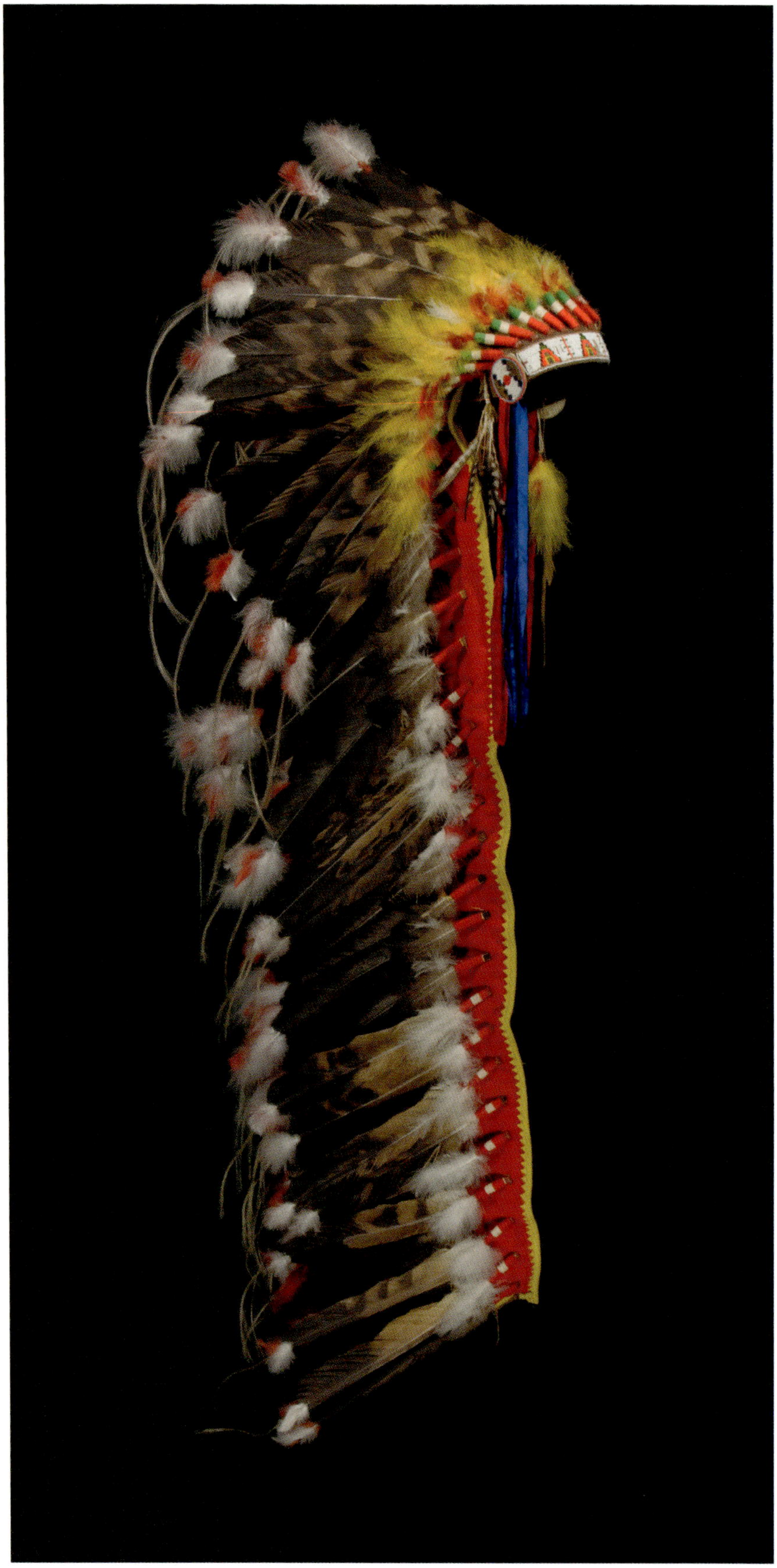

This colorful headdress has beaded medallions on its headband and a double train with eagle feathers on each side. *Length 195 cm, width 65 cm, depth 80 cm.*

This headdress has decorative silk ribbons and ermine fur on the sides in addition to the beaded headband and medallions. It has a single train with one row of eagle feathers. *Length 238 cm, width 62 cm, depth 82 cm.*

Opposite: Roach worn by Joshua Spotted Owl. A typewritten note from Hermans in the trunk with the roach identifies this item's user. *Height 47 cm, length 53 cm, width 20 cm.*

Roach worn by John Little Elk. There is no identifying tag from August Hermans, but the roach can be seen in a postcard of John Little Elk, in which he is also wearing a vest from the collection with beaded decorations of buffalo. *Height 100 cm, length 45 cm, width 25 cm.*

Beaded headband from headdress worn by John Little Elk in 1935, which he is pictured wearing in this photograph. Hermans' tag reads, "Head band from John Little Elk's bonnet made with eagle feathers. Was made in 1915. Purchased November 3rd 1935." *Length 29.5 cm, width 4.5 cm.*

Beaded headband from headdress worn by Daniel Black Horn in 1935, which he is pictured wearing in the photo. Hermans' tag reads, "Head band from the warbonnet (wapaka) made of eagle feathers from Sioux Chief Black Horn. Very interesting piece made in 1915. Gift from the big chief on November 3rd 1935 in memory of his friendship for me." *Length 36.5 cm, width 4 cm, rosette diameter 5 cm.*

A loose piece of typewritten paper left with the collection by Hermans identifies this as a headband made by Lucy Little Elk for a headdress. The beaded headband has decorative strands of beads on either side. Headband: *length 33.5 cm, width 4 cm.* Bead strands: *length 18 cm.*

Four beaded headbands from headdresses. As pictured from top to bottom: *length 30.5 cm, width 4 cm; length 32.5 cm, width 3.5 cm; length 29 cm, width 3 cm; length 28 cm, width 4.5 cm.*

Beaded headbands that were made to be tied or otherwise secured at the back of the head. As pictured from top to bottom: *length 30 cm, width 2 cm; length 30 cm, width 2 cm; length 30 cm, width 2.5 cm; length 28.5 cm, width 5 cm.*

Headband with cloth ties. Some headbands may have been made to sell as souvenirs. *Length 54 cm, width 4.5 cm.*

Headband with leather ties. *Length 59 cm, width 3 cm.*

Headband with leather ties. *Length 55 cm, width 4 cm.*

This hair ornament belonged to Joshua Spotted Owl. Hermans' tag for the artifact reads, "Scalp Lock, Beads and pony tail, Belonged to J Spotted Owl." Scalp locks, or portions of human scalps taken in combat, were worn by Lakotas until the latter nineteenth century. Twentieth-century performers maintained that tradition by creating scalp locks with horse hair. *Length 80 cm, width 6 cm.*

This hair ornament came from John Little Elk. Hermans' tag for this piece reads, "Sioux hair ornament, placed in the back (above) little mirror, wooden beads, color beads—porcupine quills, red feathers—cow tail. Made in 1930. Was worn by John Little Elk until October 1935. Purchased October 11th 1935." The ornament, also made of beads, spent cartridges, metal cones, and quills, has a now-corroded metal mirror on one end and the portion of cow tail on the other. *Length 77 cm, width 6.5 cm.*

This hair ornament belonged to Sallie White Buffalo (aka Sallie Stabber, formerly Sallie Three Stars). Hermans' tag for it reads, "Hair ornament for Sioux squaws. Red beads and brass beads ended with American Dimes. They are fixed on the plaits in the back left and right. Comes from Sallie White Buffalo Man, wife of Thomas White Buffalo Man. She has worn these until October 27th 1935. Purchased October 28th 1935." *Length 26 cm, diameter of coins 1.5 cm.*

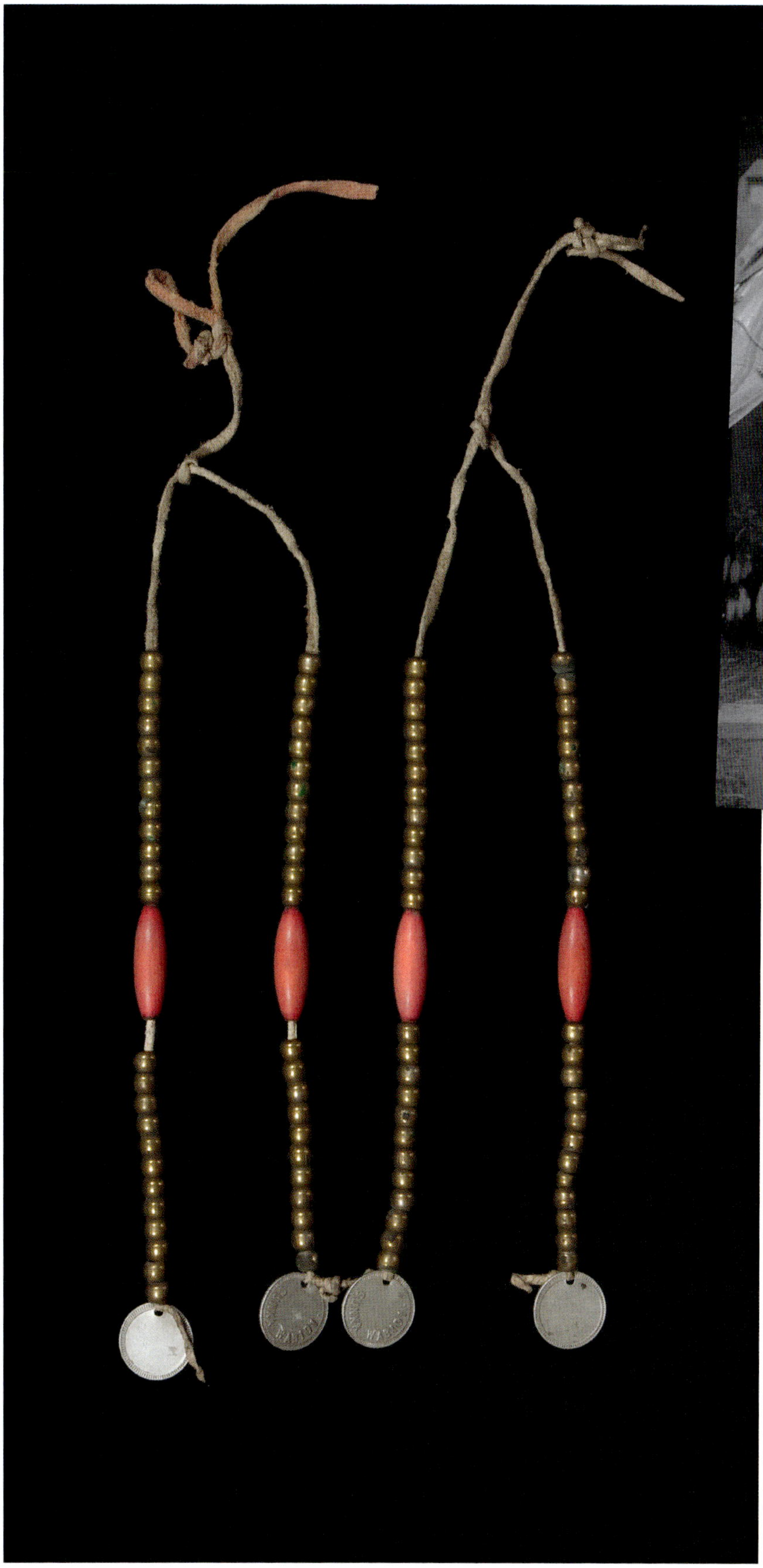

Lucy Little Elk braided these two hair ornaments into her hair while performing at the exposition. They can be seen attached to her hair in this photograph of her with her granddaughter Virginia. Hermans' tag for the ornaments reads, "Sioux hair ornament with brass beads and tubular wooden beads[.] The ends are round metallic pieces (aluminum) with the inscription 'sunka wabidi.' (Indian language). Only Sioux women and girls are wearing this ornament. It is attached to their plaits in the back. It belonged to Lucy Little Elk who wore it for more than 30 years. Purchased October 31st 1935." The words on the metal pieces are a mystery. The first word, *sunka*, can mean dog or horse, but *wabidi* does not appear to be a Lakota word. *Length 98 cm.*

Hair decoration from John Little Elk. Hermans' tag for the artifact reads, "Wooden pin with quill colored with red feathers. Is worn by men in their hair on the right side. Made in 1930. Comes from John Little Elk. Purchased October 15th 1935." *Length 42 cm, pin length 18 cm.*

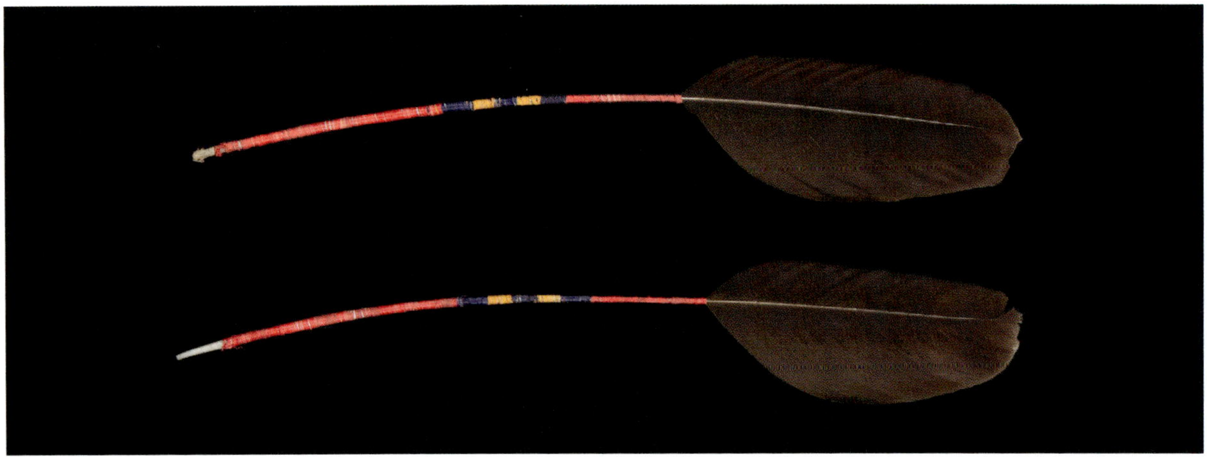

Hermans did not identify who wore these hair ornaments, but his tag for the artifacts does identify them as feathers from the head of an eagle. Each feather is partially wrapped with dyed porcupine quills. *Length 37 cm, width 6 cm.*

This hair ornament is made of quill-wrapped hide and decorated with cone-encased feathers. *Length 36 cm.*

Opposite: These hair ornaments were probably woven into a woman's or girl's braids. They are strips of leather wrapped with threaded glass beads. The feather ornaments are secured in metal cones. *Lengths 41 cm and 40 cm.*

This hair ornament is made of horse hair, small feathers, glass beads, and spent cartridges. *Length 92 cm, width 32 cm.*

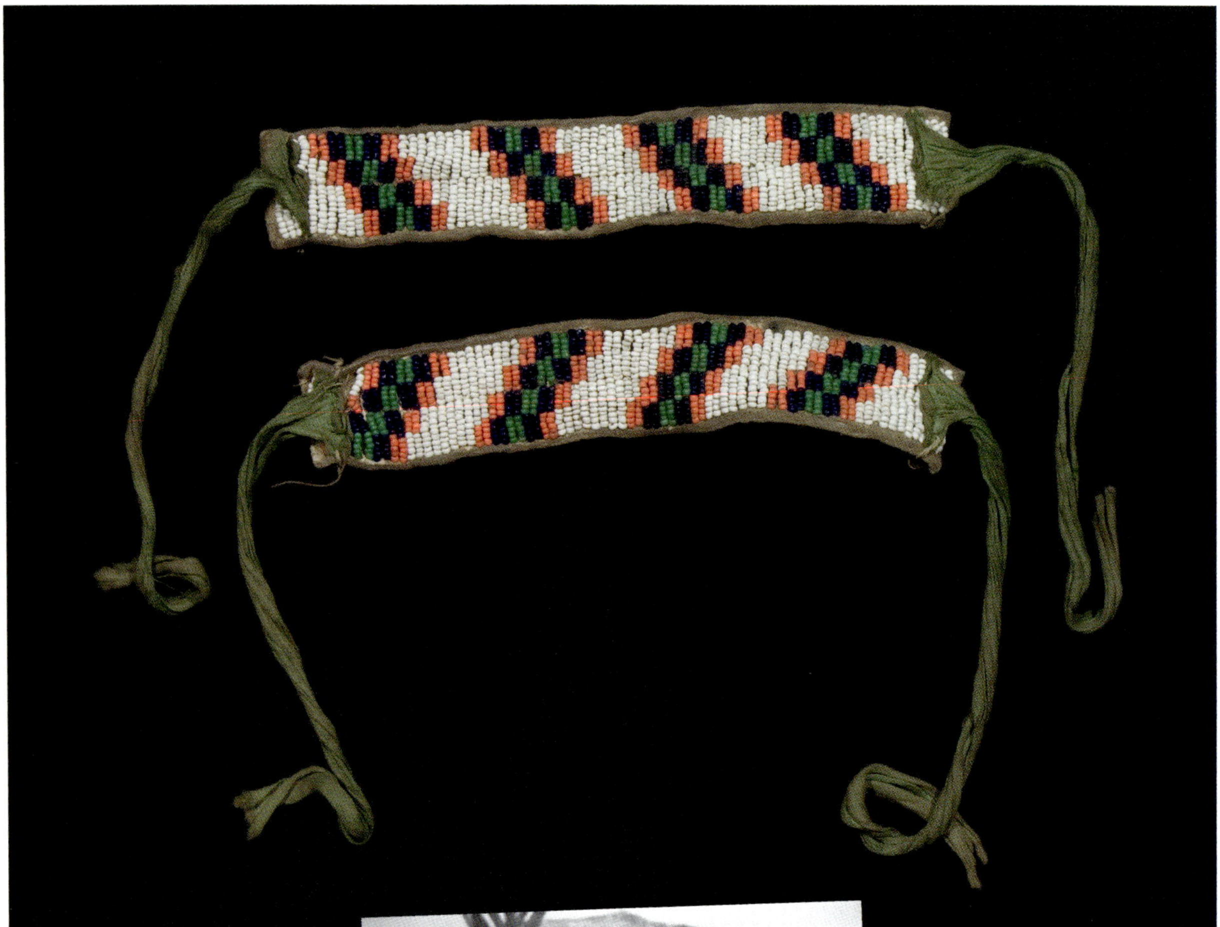

Armbands worn by Francis Little Moon, although Hermans mistakenly calls him Herbert on the tag for the artifacts. The tag reads, "Pair of armbands (hide and bcads) from lillle Herbert Little Moon. (White, orange, blue, green, blue, orange, white). Purchased November 3rd 1935." The armbands are visible in a photo of Francis and his siblings with Sam Lone Bear. Top: *length 18.5 cm, width 3 cm.* Bottom: *length 18 cm, width 3 cm.*

These brass bracelets belonged to Lucy Little Elk. Inside, each bears a different patent mark: H. W. Hayden, Dec. 16, 1851, and Miller & Company, 1870. Hermans' tag reads, "Pair of brass armbands from A Sioux squaw. Belonged to Lucy Little Elk who wore these for more than 25 years. Purchased October 27th 1935, striped brass. There is a mark inside." *Diameter 7.5 cm, width 6 cm.*

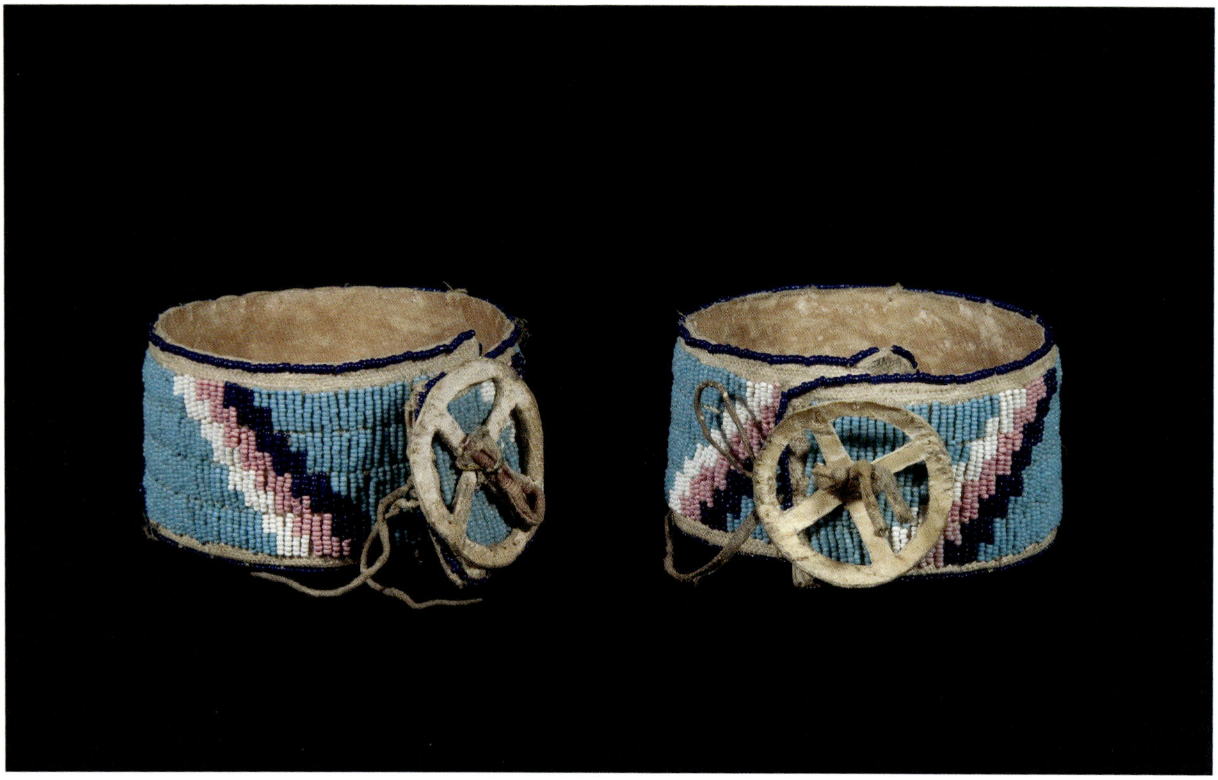

Armbands worn by John Little Elk. Hermans' tag reads, "A Pair of armbands from John Little Elk. . . . Made in 1930. The circles are made from hide and quills. Purchased November 3rd 1935. Quills come from porcupine. They are crushed and dyed." Little Elk can be seen wearing them on his upper arms in several photographs of the 1935 performers, such as the one shown. *Diameter 9.5 cm, width 5.5 cm.*

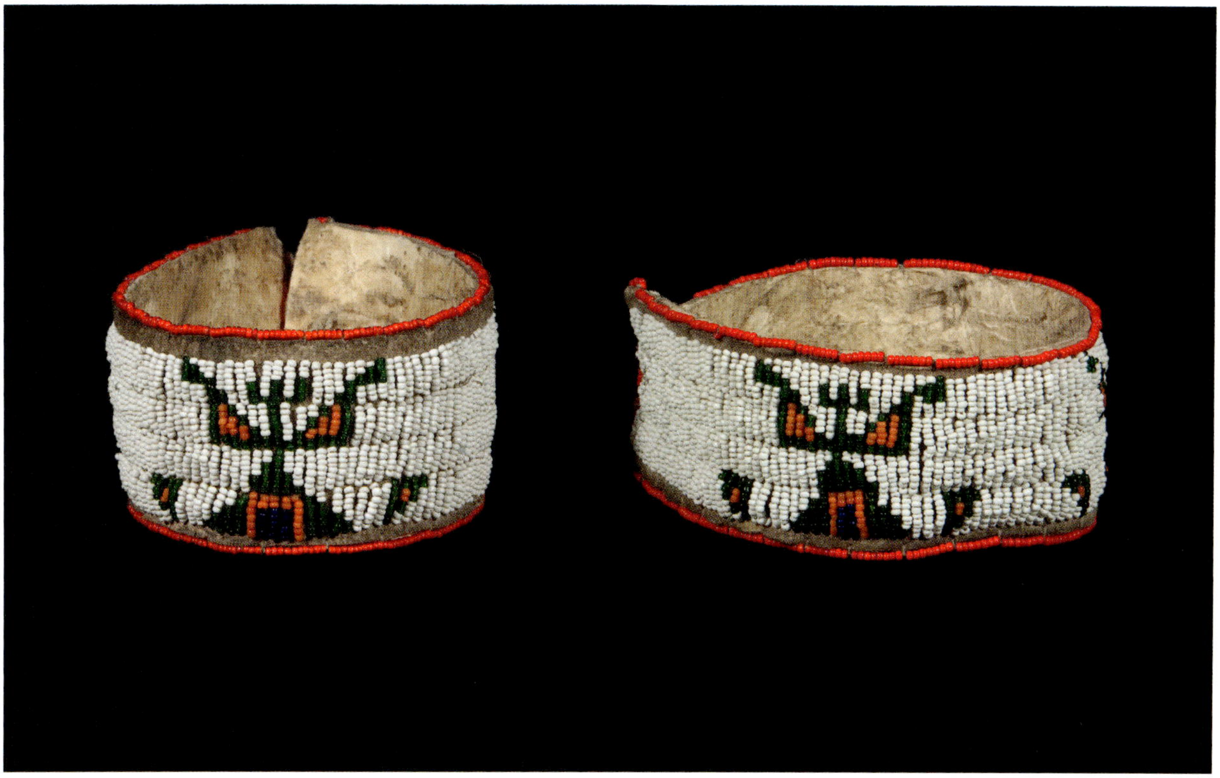

These armbands can be seen on Joshua Spotted Owl's upper arms in several photographs of the Lakota performers in Brussels, such as in the photo shown here. *Diameter 10 cm, width 5 cm.*

Cuffs worn on John Little Elk's forearms in addition to armbands on his upper arms. Both cuffs and armbands are visible in several photographs of the Lakota performers, including the photo of Little Elk shown here. Hermans' tag for the cuffs reads, "Pair of cuffs from John Little Elk (Sioux Indian). Hide and beads. Made in 1915. Purchased November 3rd 1935." *Diameter 8 cm, width 10 cm and 9.5 cm.*

Cuffs worn by White Buffalo Man (aka Tom Stabber) and visible on his forearms in a dance scene in the Indian village arena. *Width 14.5 cm, diameter 10 cm.*

Cuffs (*opposite*) and armbands (*above*) worn by Joshua Spotted Owl and visible in several photographs taken of the performers, including the photo shown here. Hermans' tag reads, "Pair of cuffs from Joshua Spotted Owl (Medicine Man from the tribe) Deerskin and beads. Made by his wife 24 years ago. (Purchased November 3rd 1935)." Cuff (*top*): *length 25.5 cm, width 15 cm.* Cuff (*bottom*): *length 26 cm, width 14.5 cm.* Armbands: *diameter 10 cm, width 6 cm.*

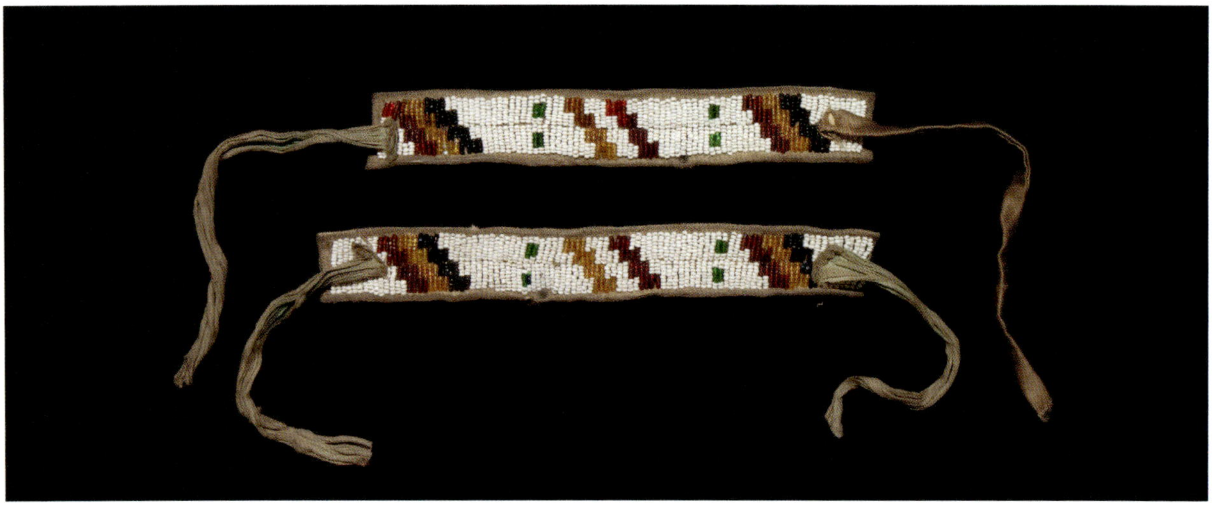

Cuffs (*right*) and armbands (*above*) worn by Al Little Moon. They are visible on his upper arms and forearms in several candid photographs taken with Sam Lone Bear. Cuff (*top*): *length 27.5 cm, width 13 cm.* Cuff (*bottom*): *length 26.5 cm, width 12.5 cm.* Armband (*top*): *length 21 cm, width 3 cm.* Armband (*bottom*): *length 22.5 cm, width 3 cm.*

Above: Bracelet worn by Virginia Little Elk. Hermans' tag for it reads, "Little brass bracelet American made for Virginia Little Elk. Purchased from Lucy Little Elk October 27th 1935. Brass bracelets are very popular by Sioux Indians." The bracelet is actually copper, as revealed by the softness of the metal and the verdigris on the inside. *Diameter 4 cm, width 2.2 cm.*

Left: Brass bracelets. *Diameter 8 cm, width 8.5 cm.*

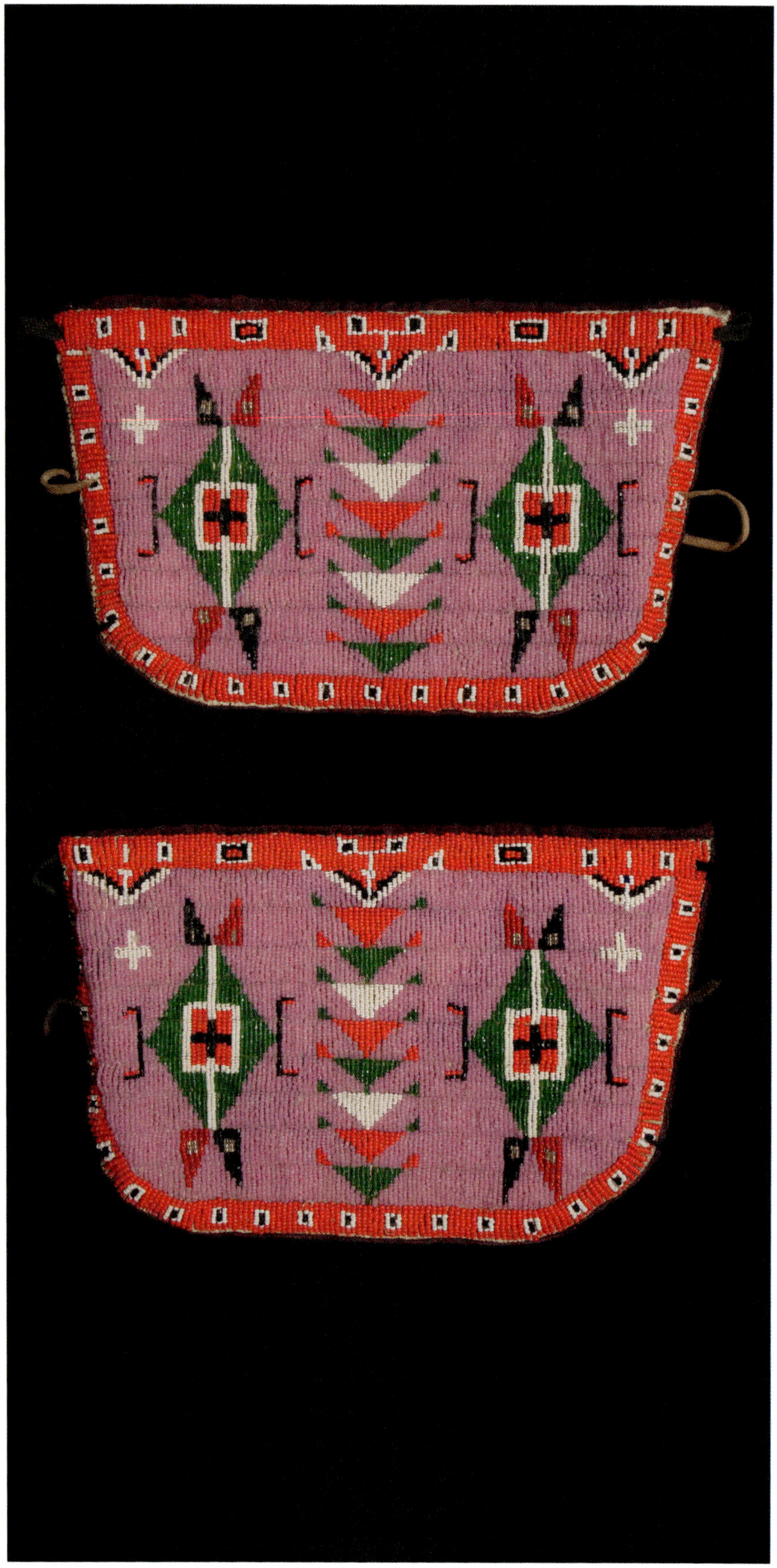

A pair of cuffs with leather ties.
Length 26.5 cm, width 16 cm.

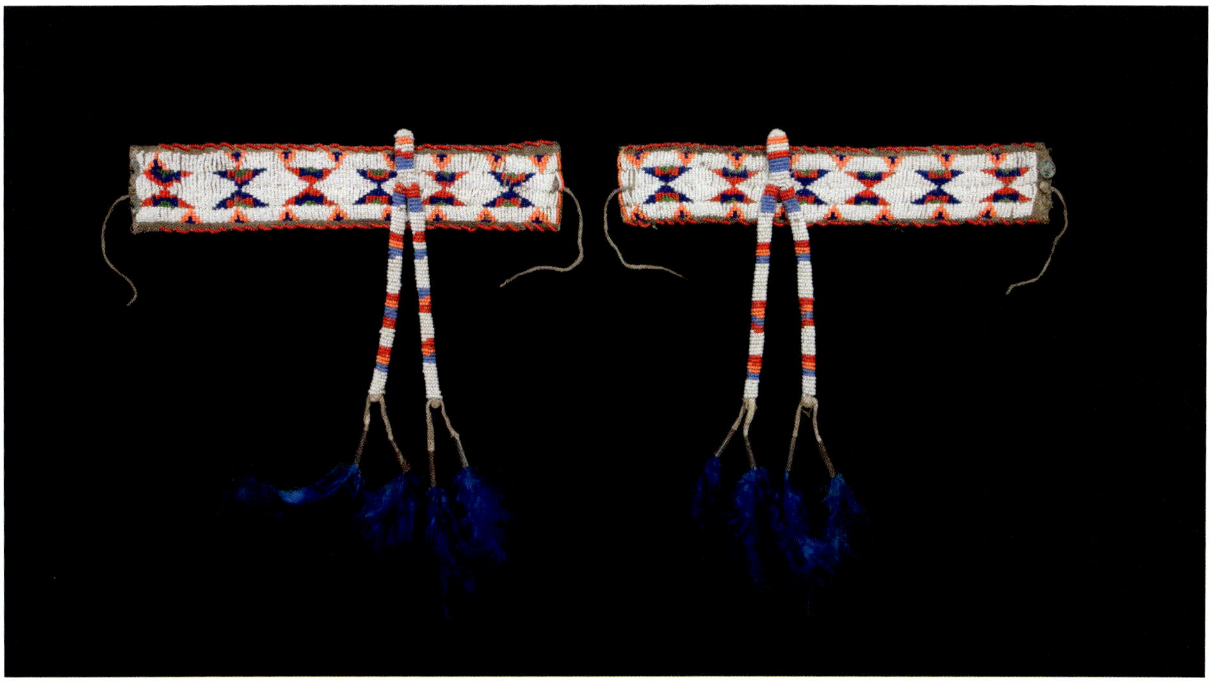

Above: Armbands with beaded decorative fringes and secured with leather ties. The ends of the fringe have feathers enclosed in metal cones. Armbands: *length 29.5 cm, width 5.5 cm.* Fringes: *length 33 cm and 32 cm.*

Left, middle: Child-sized cuffs, typically worn on the forearm, with glass beading and leather fringes. Left: *diameter 4 cm, width 8 cm.* Right: *diameter 4 cm, width 7 cm.*

Left: Armbands of rawhide and glass beads. *Diameter 12 cm, width 4.5 cm.*

Above: Armbands with tie closures and leather fringes decorated with glass beads and metal cones. Armbands: *diameter 12 cm, width 4.5 cm.* Fringes: *length 16 cm.*

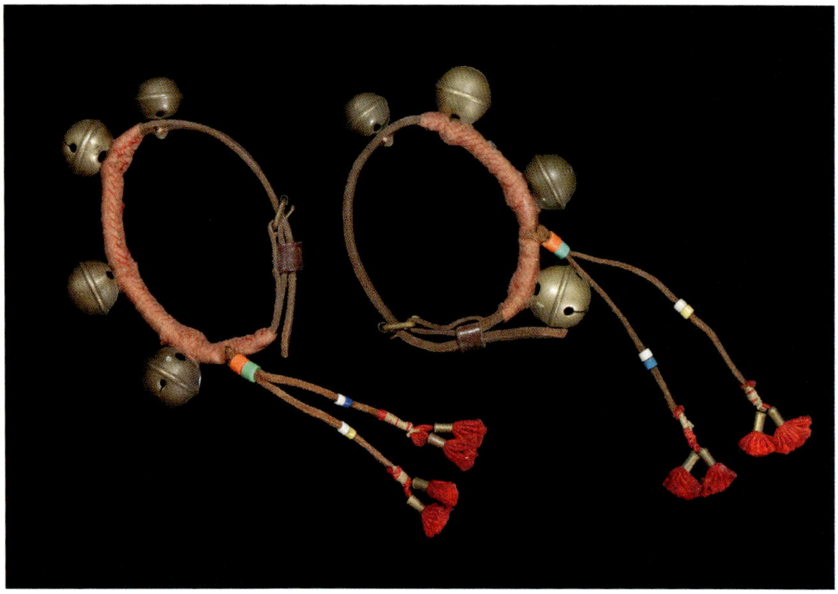

Right, middle: Dancer's legbands with jingle bells. They are made of wrapped leather decorated with brass bells, beads, and wool tassels in spent cartridge cases. *Diameter 31 cm and 32 cm, width 4 cm.*

Right: Three beaded bracelets. As pictured from top to bottom: *length 24.5 cm, width 2.5 cm; length 20.5 cm, width 4 cm; length 18.5 cm, width 2 cm.*

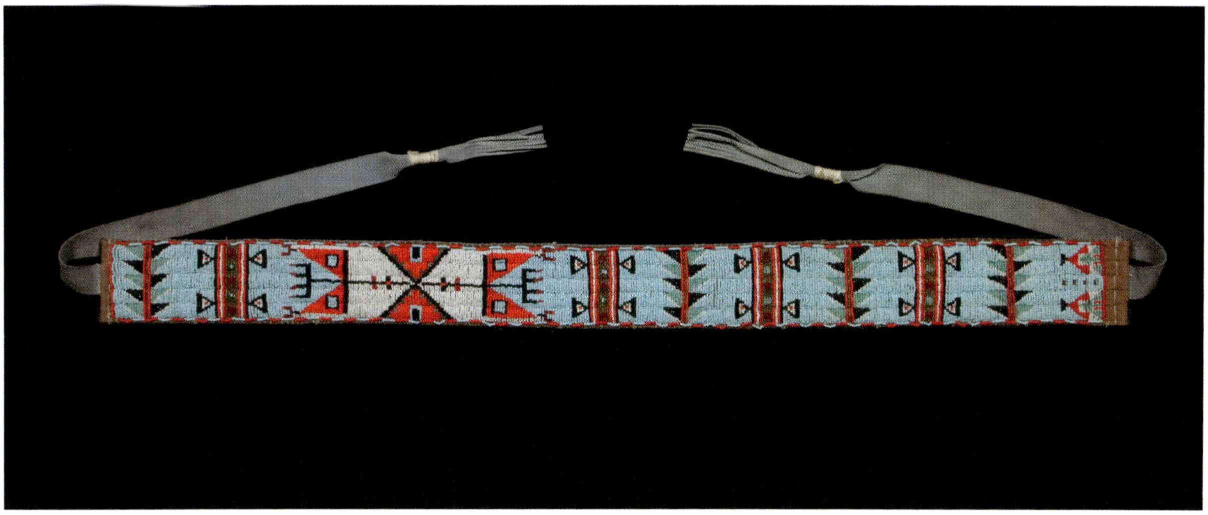

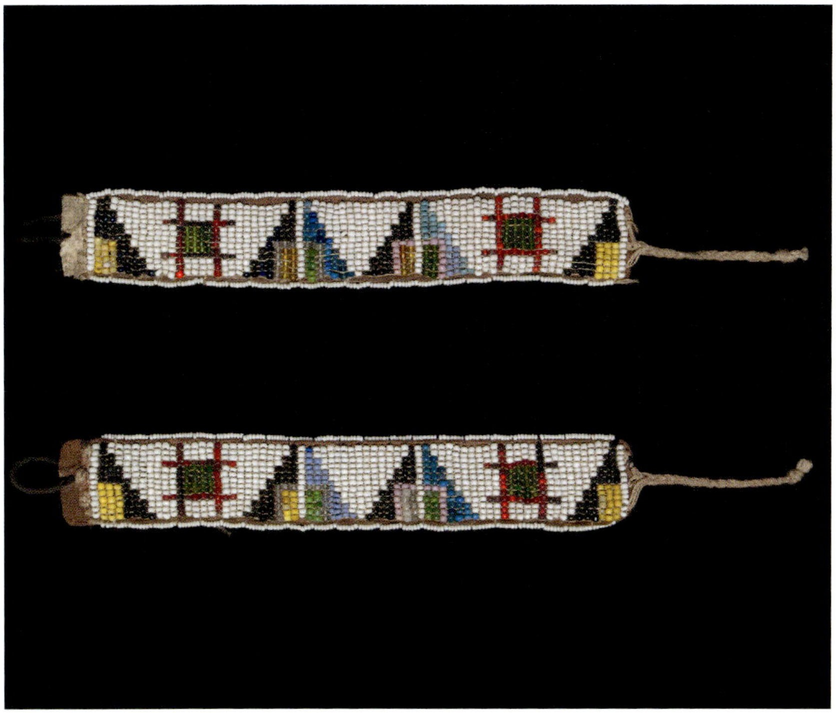

Above, top: Beaded belt with leather ties. *Length 84 cm, width 4 cm.*

Above, middle: Beaded belt with leather ties. *Length 186 cm, width 7 cm.*

Left: Armbands of rawhide and glass beads. *Length 26 cm, width 4.5 cm.*

Above: Armbands of rawhide and glass beads. Armband (*left*): *length 28.5 cm, width 6.5 cm*. Armband (*right*): *length 27 cm, width 6.5 cm*. Beaded rosettes with pendants: *lengths 41 cm and 40 cm*.

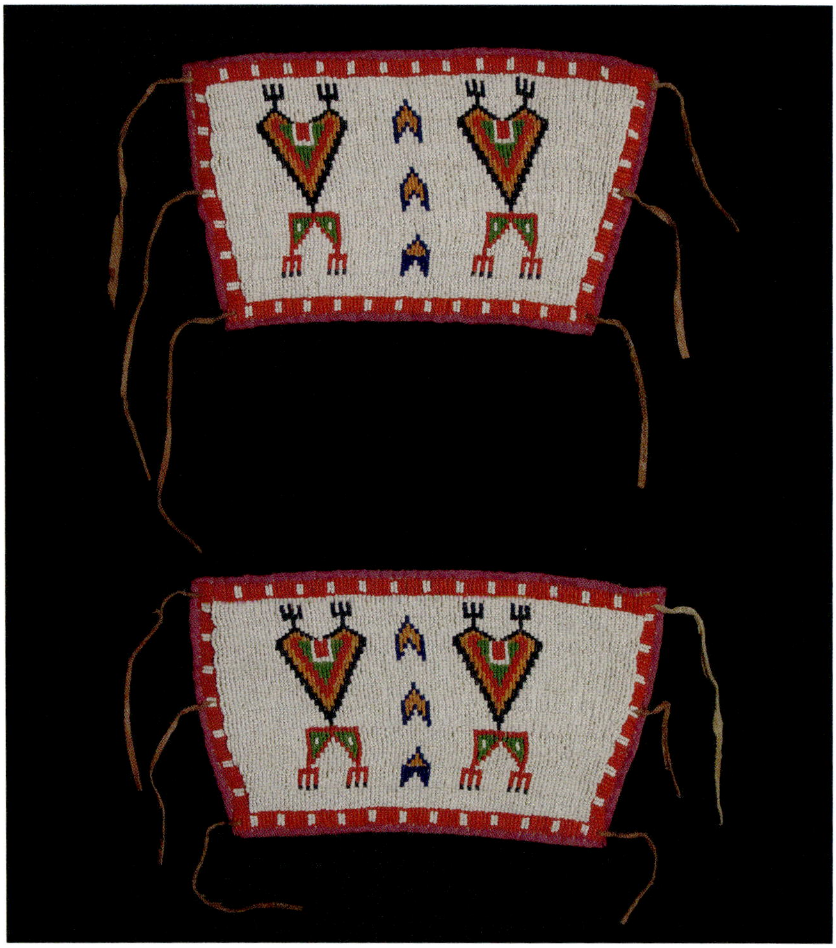

Right: Cuffs of hide, glass beads, and cloth. *Length 27.5 cm, width 15 cm*.

This porcupine quill breastplate was worn by Joshua Spotted Owl during performances at the exposition. The round raffia medallions appear to have been added later, perhaps by August Hermans. The tag by Hermans reads, "Wampum Breast Plate from Sioux Oglala Indians (Interesting work) Belonged to Joshua Spotted Owl. Made of Quills on rawhide." Hermans' choice of the word "wampum" to describe this breastplate is misleading, since it bears none of the seashell beads traditionally called wampum. *Length 84 cm, width 35 cm.*

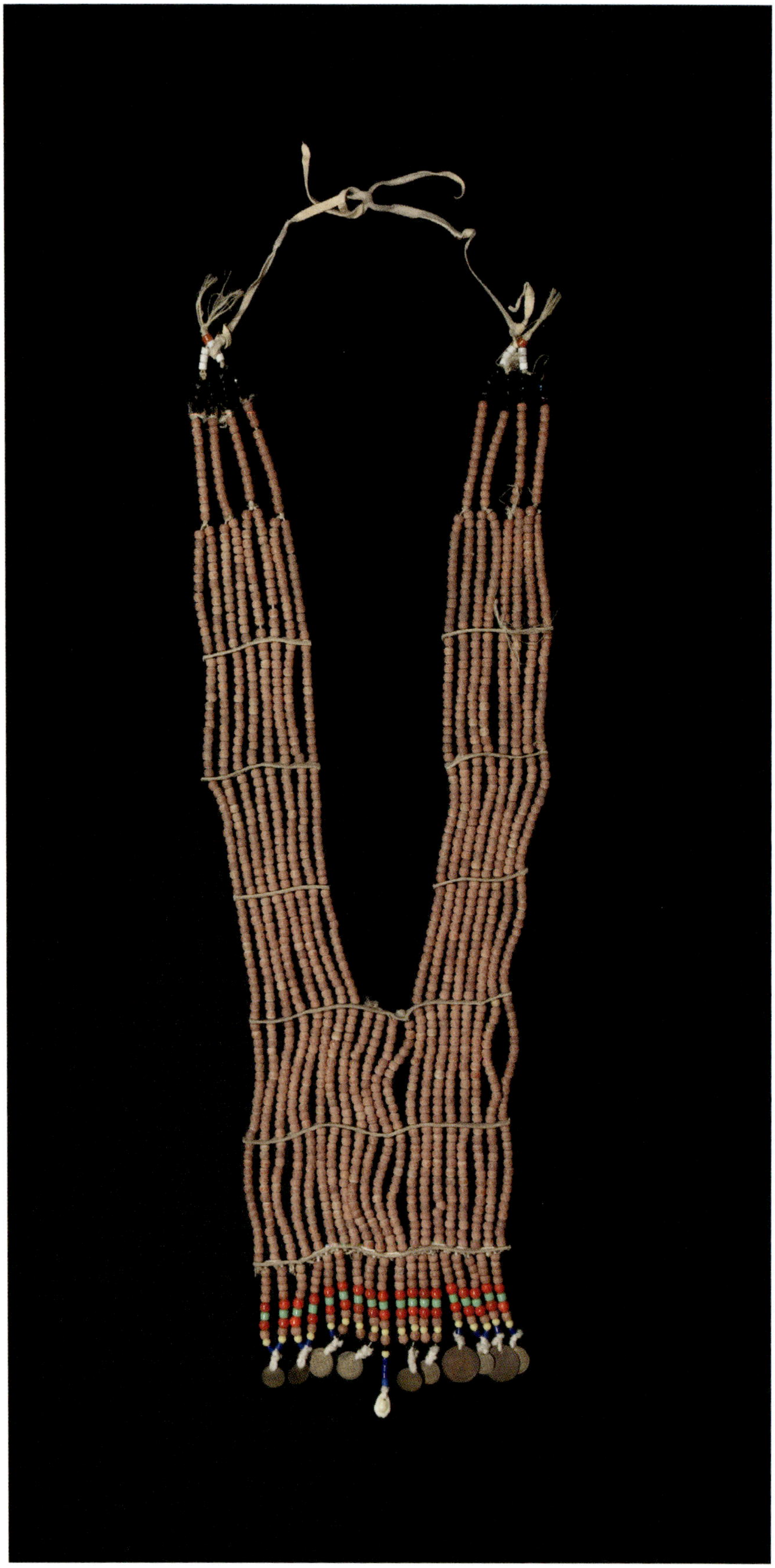

Breastplate-like necklace worn by Virginia Little Elk. Hermans' tag reads, "A Necklace from a small Sioux girl. The brown beads are terra cotta ended with shells (wampum). Purchased October 16th 1935. Imported in America and sold to the Indians. A few European black beads fixed with TAKAN (animal fibre). Brown beads very old and mounted in 1933. Belonged to Virginia Little Elk 3 years and 3 months. Very rare." *Length 62 cm, width 14 cm.*

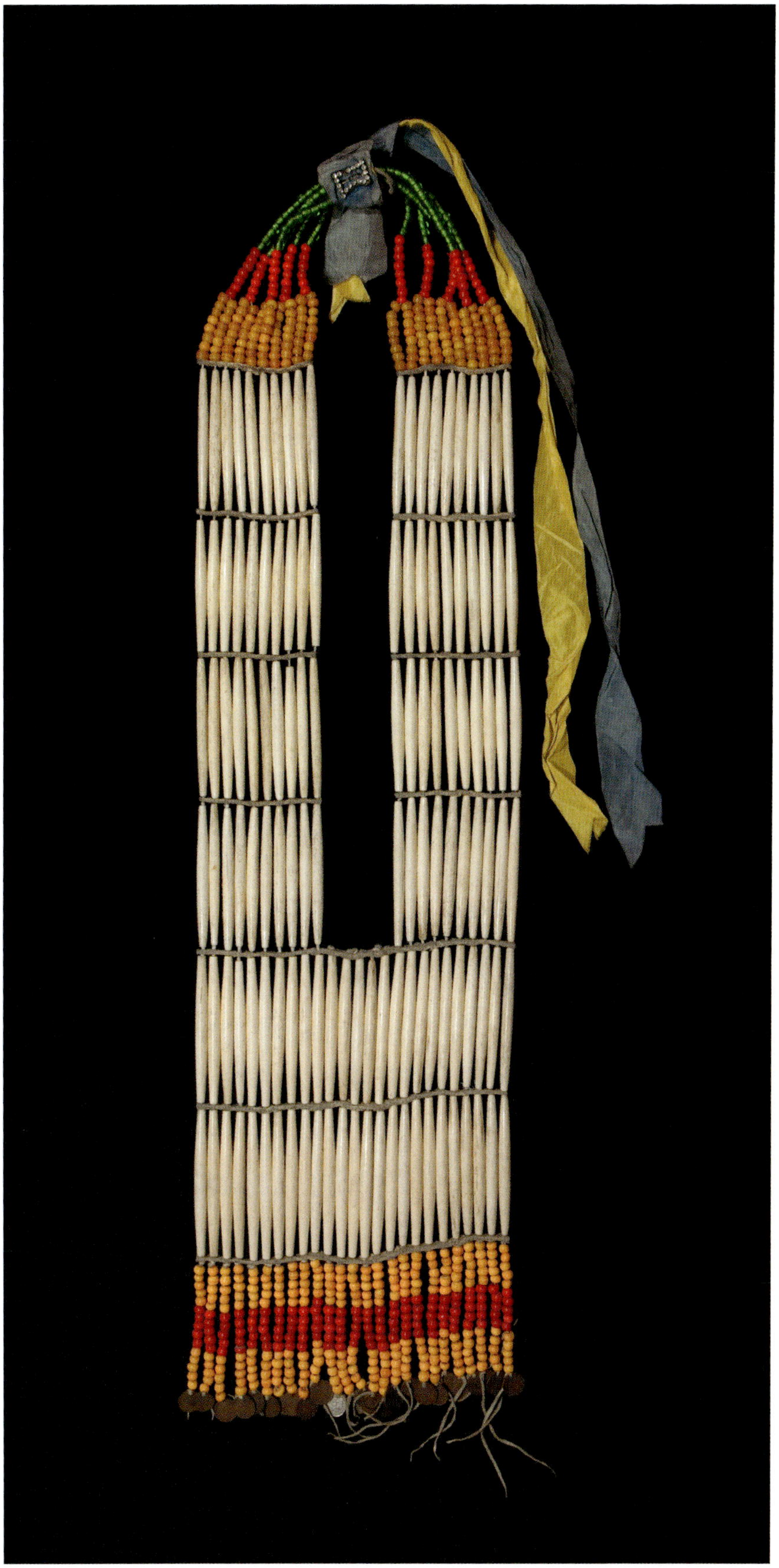

This breastplate-like necklace is made of bone hairpipe, with beaded decorations at the top and bottom. These were typically worn by Lakota women. Secured to the beads at the bottom are twenty-three U.S. pennies dated 1910 and one silver groszy coin from Poland. *Length 100 cm, width 28 cm.*

This breastplate was used by White Buffalo Man, as indicated by a typewritten note from Hermans. The note, loose in the same trunk as this breastplate, states that a breastplate with coins and a beaded star design came from White Buffalo Man. At the bottom the artifact bears a collection of twenty-one coins and tokens (traded for beer in Germany). These were from the United States, Austria, Turkey, Switzerland, and Germany. They all date between 1910 and 1929. *Length 90 cm, width 30 cm.*

This beaded necktie imitated the neckties Lakotas saw being worn by show visitors and was probably created as a souvenir for them. *Length 28 cm, width 14.5 cm.*

Opposite: The necktie represents a melding of Lakota beadwork and symbols with an item of European culture in order to create something that might appeal as a souvenir to exposition visitors. *Length 30 cm, width 14 cm.*

In the latter nineteenth century, American Indian beadworkers began to copy the American flag as a decorative motif, a practice that continued into the twentieth century. This particular necktie, probably made specifically to sell at the exposition, captured that decorative motif and symbolized the country that the Lakotas represented. *Length 23 cm, width 6 cm.*

The male performers at the exposition did not wear the beaded neckties they sold. Instead they wore beaded chokers with fabric decorations that hung down as a necktie did. This choker was worn by Joshua Spotted Owl while at the exposition, as seen in the photograph (he is on the left). August Hermans' tag reads, "Sioux necklace. Red wooden beads, round Shell and red stone and ribbon. Was worn by Joshua Spotted Owl until August 2nd 1935. The shell belonged to his late son and he kept it as a souvenir. Gift from J Spotted Owl on August 2nd 1935." *Length 89 cm, width 48.5 cm.*

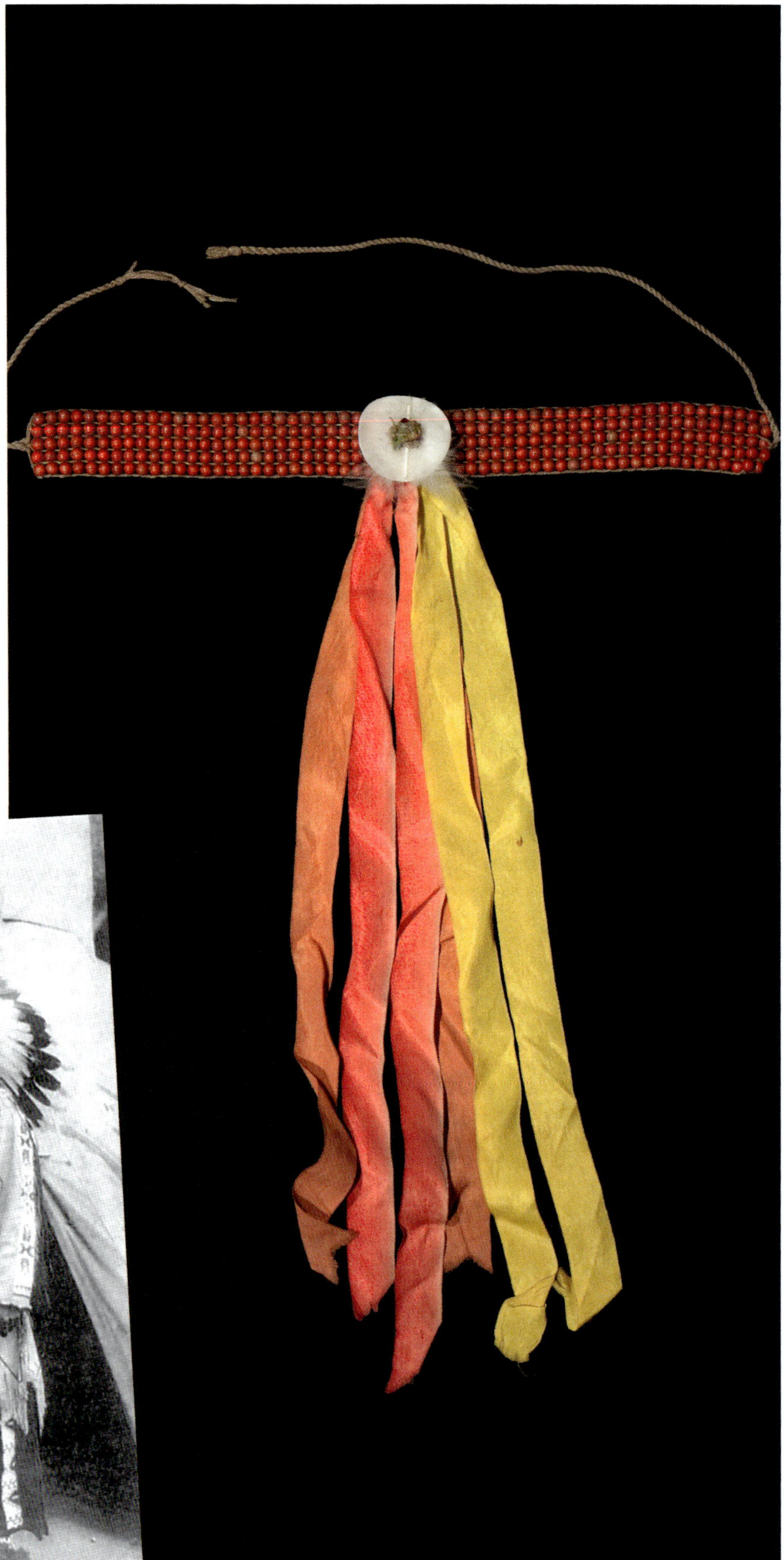

Although the adult males with the Brussels exposition group did not wear the beaded neckties that the group sold, seven-year-old Gilbert Little Moon did wear this bowtie, which can be seen in several photographs taken by visitors to the exposition, such as the one shown here. *Length 10.5 cm, width 5.5 cm.*

This beaded necklace was made on a small loom. Unlike the other artifacts in the collection, it has been damaged. *Length 46 cm, width 4 cm.*

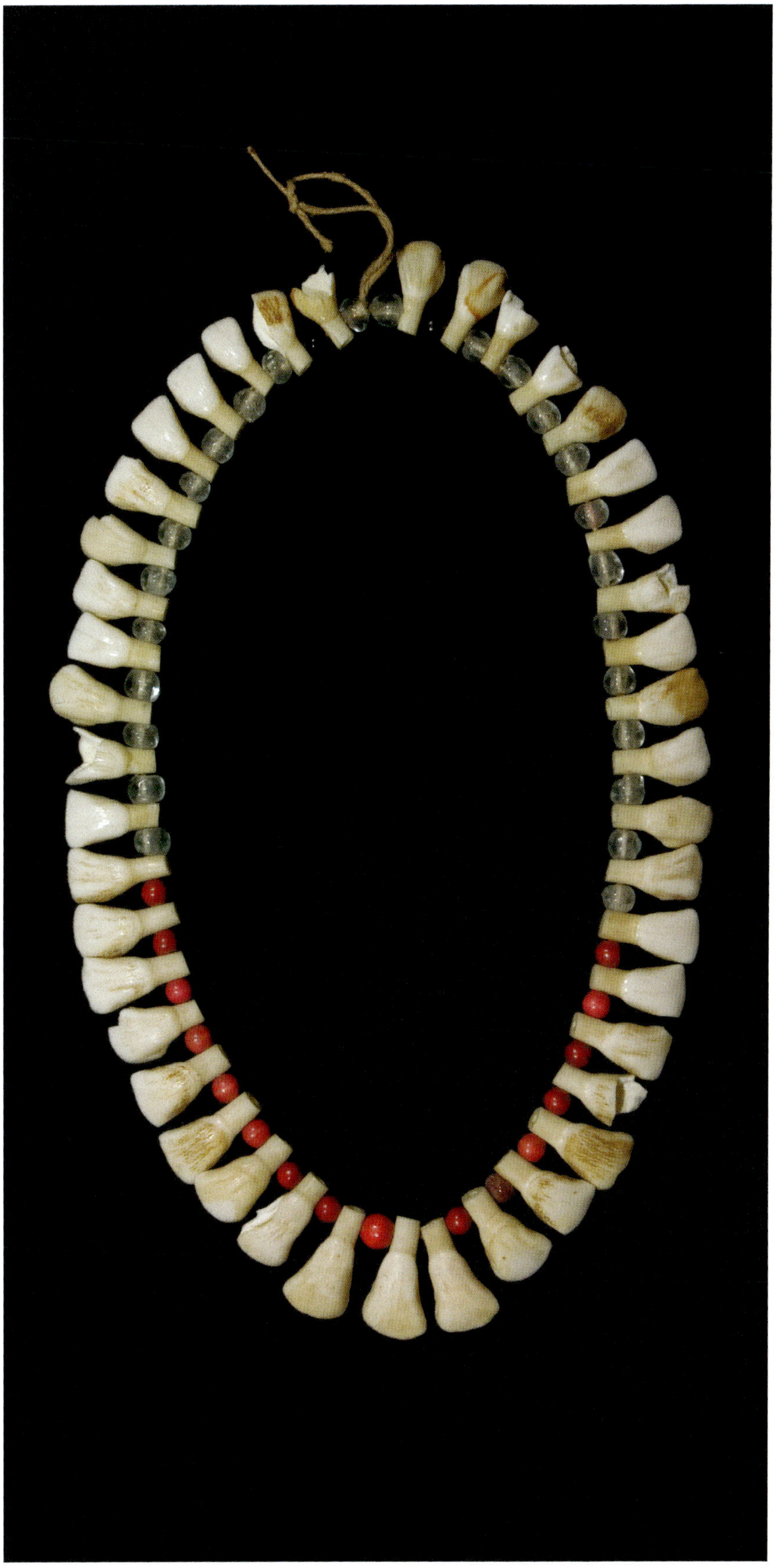

This necklace is made of semitransparent green glass beads, red wooden beads, and animal teeth. *Length 60 cm, width 3.5 cm.*

Moccasins worn by Francis Little Moon, as shown in the photo and detail of Pauline, Gilbert, and Francis Little Moon, with Sam Lone Bear. *Length 17.5 cm, width 7.5 cm, height 7 cm.*

Moccasins worn by Virginia Little Elk. *Length 15 cm, width 6.5 cm, height 7 cm.*

Moccasins worn by Virginia Little Elk. *Length 14.5 cm, width 7 cm, height 7 cm.*

Moccasins worn by Charles Little Boy, as shown in the photo of Francis, Joe, and Gilbert Little Moon posing on one side of a visitor, with Charles Little Boy on the other side, wearing the moccasins (*detail*). *Length 29.5 cm, width 11 cm, height 10 cm.*

Moccasins worn by Sam Lone Bear. *Length 28 cm, width 10.5 cm, height 9.5 cm.*

Moccasins worn by Joshua Spotted Owl. Hermans' tag for them reads, "Pair of Indian Sioux Oglala mocassins [*sic*] (Pine Ridge South Dakota). Deer skin and beads. Gift from Joshua Spotted Owl. May 20th 1935." *Length 28 cm, width 10.5 cm, height 10 cm.*

Moccasins worn by Gilbert Little Moon. In the photo, Gilbert poses with young visitors to the Indian village while wearing the moccasins. *Length 21.5 cm, width 9.5 cm, height 10 cm.*

Moccasins worn by Pauline Little Moon. *Length 19 cm, width 7.5 cm, height 6 cm.*

Moccasins worn by Rosa Little Moon. In the photo, Rosa Little Moon wears the moccasins while holding baby Wilson. Joe Little Moon's back is to the camera, while Francis stands in front of his mother. *Length 27 cm, width 10 cm, height 10 cm.*

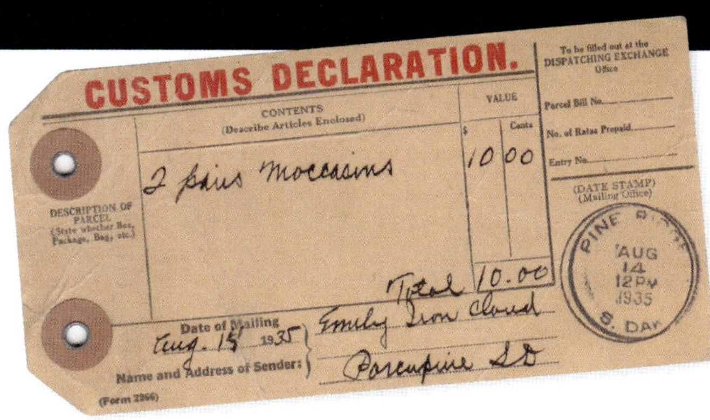

CUSTOMS DECLARATION.

CONTENTS (Describe Articles Enclosed)

DESCRIPTION OF PARCEL (State whether Box, Package, Bag, etc.)

2 pairs moccasins

VALUE $	Cents
10	00
Total 10.00	

Date of Mailing Aug. 15 1935

Name and Address of Sender: Emily Iron Cloud, Porcupine SD

To be filled out at the DISPATCHING EXCHANGE Office

Parcel Bill No.

No. of Rates Prepaid

Entry No.

(DATE STAMP) (Mailing Office)

PINE RIDGE AUG 14 12PM 1935 S. DAK.

(Form 2966)

Moccasins worn by Daniel Black Horn. These are identified by the typewritten slip packed with them in the trunk. Their good condition compared with the moccasins worn by the other performers suggests that this was one of the pairs of moccasins sent to Black Horn from Pine Ridge in August 1935. *Length 28.5 cm, width 11.5 cm, height 10 cm.*

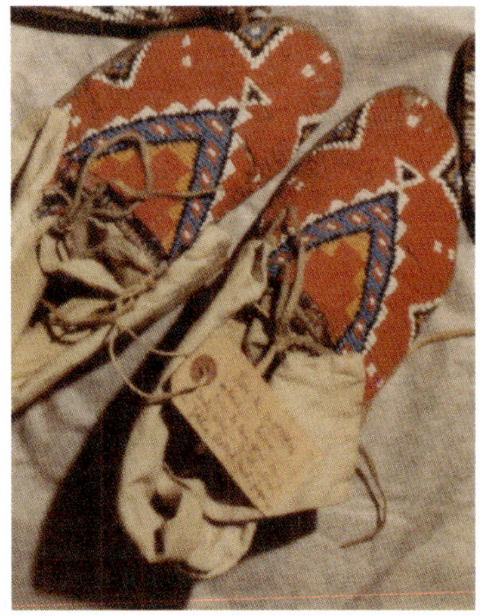

Moccasins worn by Joshua Spotted Owl. Hermans' tag for them was missing from the artifacts but can be seen in one of the color photographs (*at right*) from the trunks. Enlarged, the photo identifies the moccasins as belonging to Spotted Owl. *Length 26.5 cm, width 11 cm, height 10 cm.*

Moccasins worn by Joshua Spotted Owl. Hermans' tag for them reads, "Pair of mocassins [*sic*] from Joshua Spotted Owl Who wore these until November 3rd 1935. Purchased November 3rd 1935. Very worn out. Royal blue." The tag can be seen on the moccasins in one of the color photographs (*at right*) found in the trunks. *Length 27 cm, width 10 cm, height 9 cm.*

Moccasins worn by Wilson Little Moon. Hermans' tag reads, "Pair of Sioux mocassins [*sic*] from Wilson Little Moon (the youngest son of Joe Little Moon) deer skin and beads. Purchased October 6th 1935 from Joe Little Moon his father." *Length 13.5 cm, width 6 cm, height 6 cm.*

Moccasins worn by White Buffalo Man (Thomas Stabber), identified by a typewritten note in the trunk. *Length 28.5 cm, width 10.5 cm, height 10 cm.*

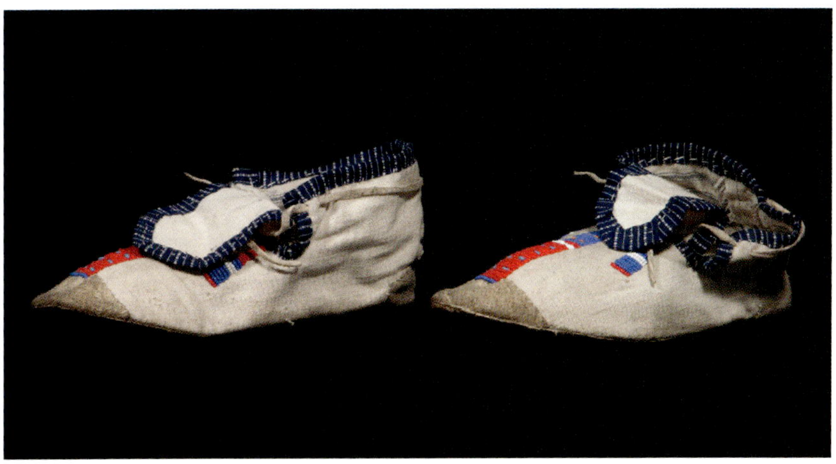

Moccasins worn by Sallie White Buffalo (Sallie Stabber), identified by a typewritten note in the trunk. *Length 25 cm, width 8.5 cm, height 9.5 cm.*

Moccasins worn by White Buffalo Man (Thomas Stabber). *Length 28.5 cm, width 11 cm, height 9 cm.*

Moccasins worn by John Little Elk. Identified by a typewritten note in the trunk. *Length 26.5 cm, width 9.5 cm, height 11 cm.*

Pair of moccasins. *Length 23.5. cm, width 10 cm, height 9.5 cm.*

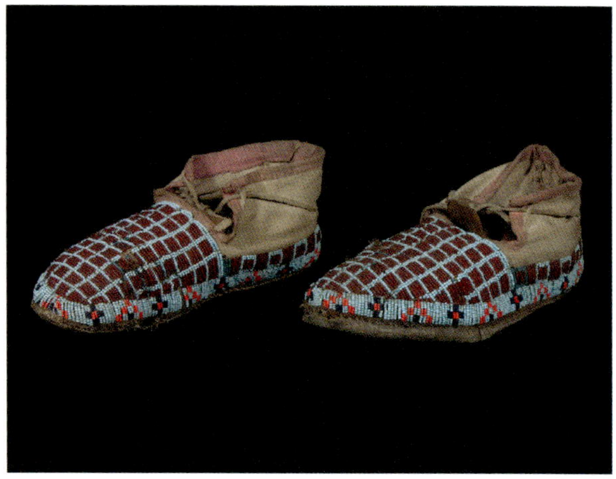

Pair of moccasins. *Length 26.5 cm, width 10 cm, height 10 cm.*

Pair of moccasins. *Length 29 cm, width 10 cm, height 9 cm.*

Pair of moccasins. *Length 27 cm, width 10 cm, height 11 cm.*

Pair of moccasins. *Length 27 cm, width 11 cm, height 10 cm.*

Pair of moccasins. *Length 28 cm, width 10.5 cm, height 12 cm.*

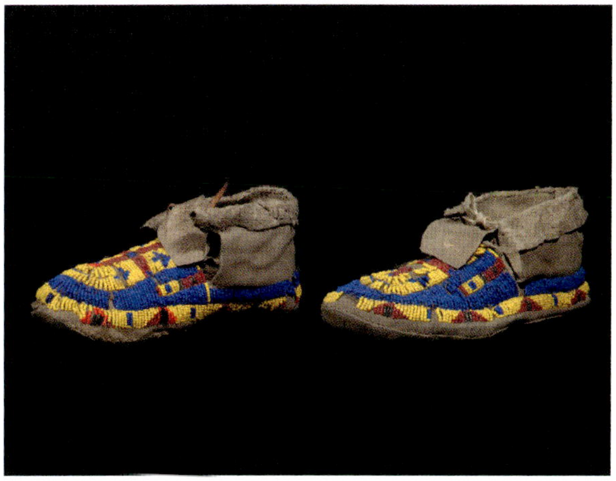

Pair of moccasins. *Length 24.5 cm, width 9 cm, height 9 cm.*

Pair of moccasins. *Length 23 cm, width 9.5 cm, height 9 cm.*

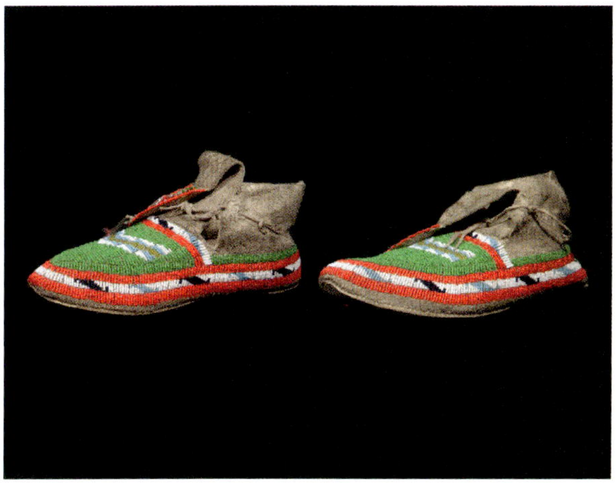

Pair of moccasins. *Length 26 cm, width 9.5 cm, height 9.5 cm.*

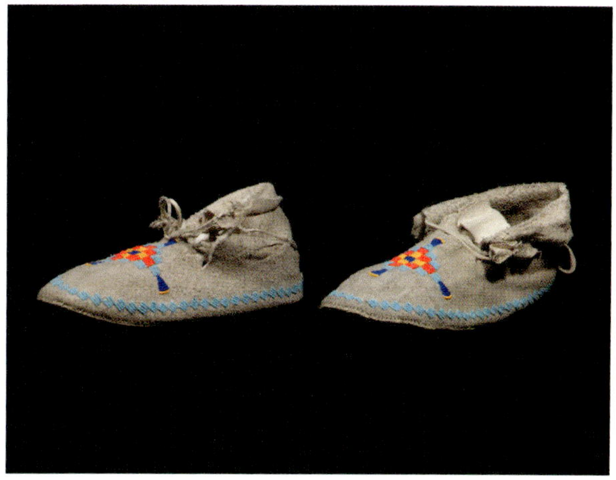

Pair of moccasins. *Length 27 cm, width 10 cm, height 9.5 cm.*

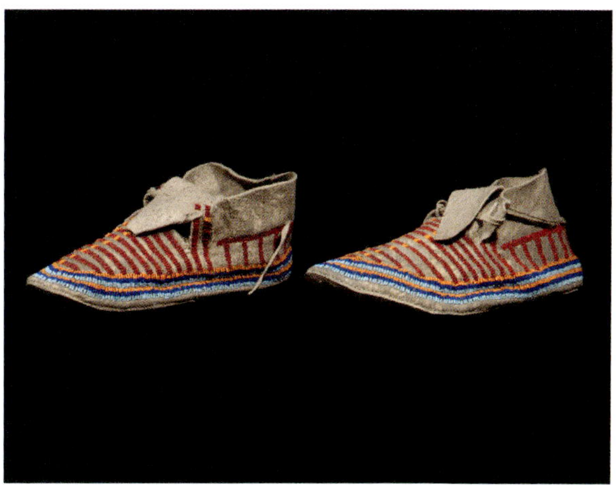

Pair of moccasins. *Length 28.5 cm, width 11 cm, height 11 cm.*

The bowl for this pipe is made of catlinite inlaid with lead for decoration. The end of the bowl appears to be the head of some animal, perhaps a snake. The pipe probably dates to the late nineteenth century. This may have been the pipe that Hermans acquired from Black Horn and that was mentioned in the 1955 article about the organization called Wigwam to which he and Eric Wansart belonged. Pipe with stem: *length 53 cm.* Bowl: *height 8 cm, diameter 5.5 cm.*

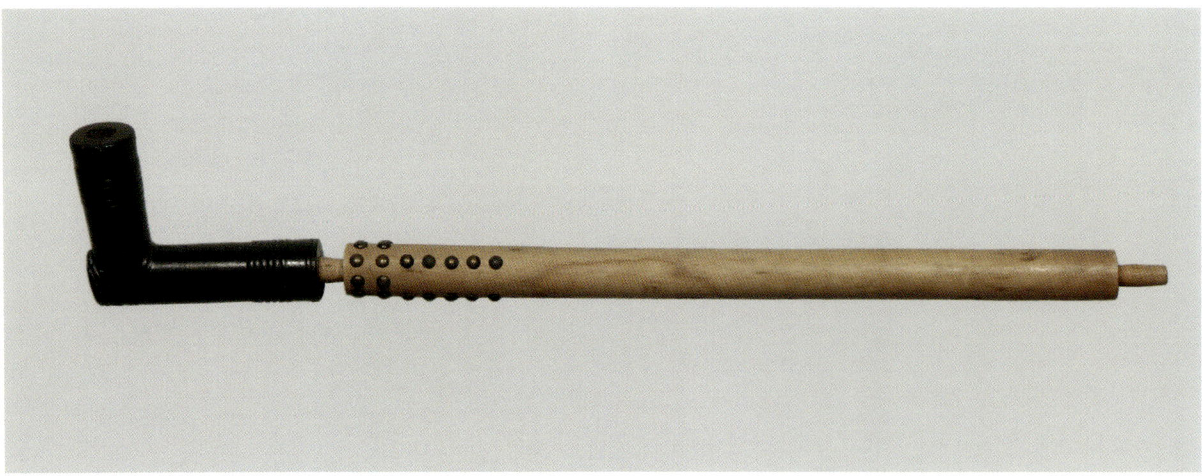

The bowl of this pipe is made of steatite, or black pipestone, a soapstone that was easily carved and sometimes used as a less expensive alternative to catlinite, the red pipestone. Pipe with stem: *length 55.5 cm.* Bowl: *height 9 cm, diameter 3 cm.*

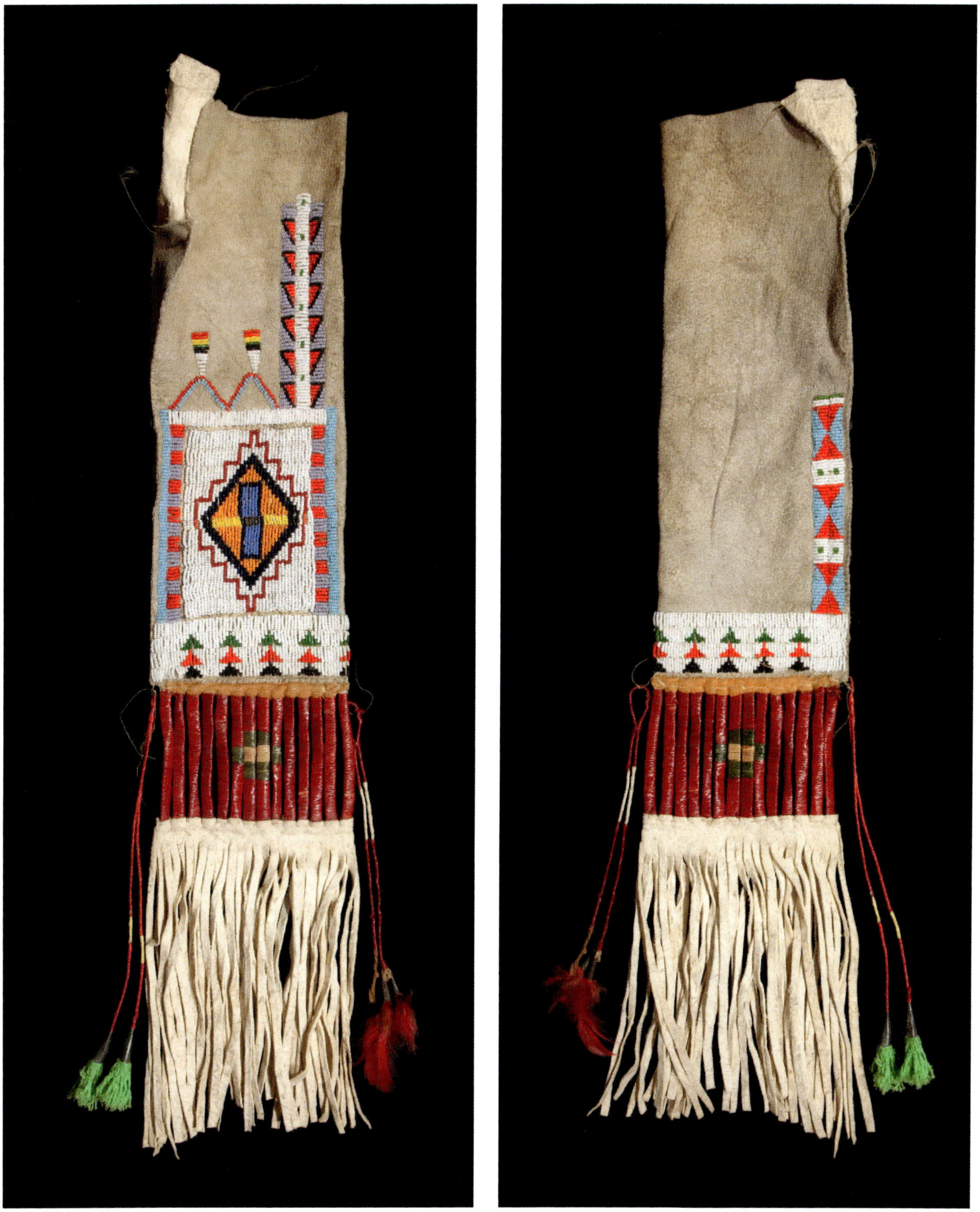

This pipe bag is decorated with a combination of dyed porcupine quills, beads, and small metal cones holding tassels of feather and frayed wool. *Length 73 cm, width 19 cm.*

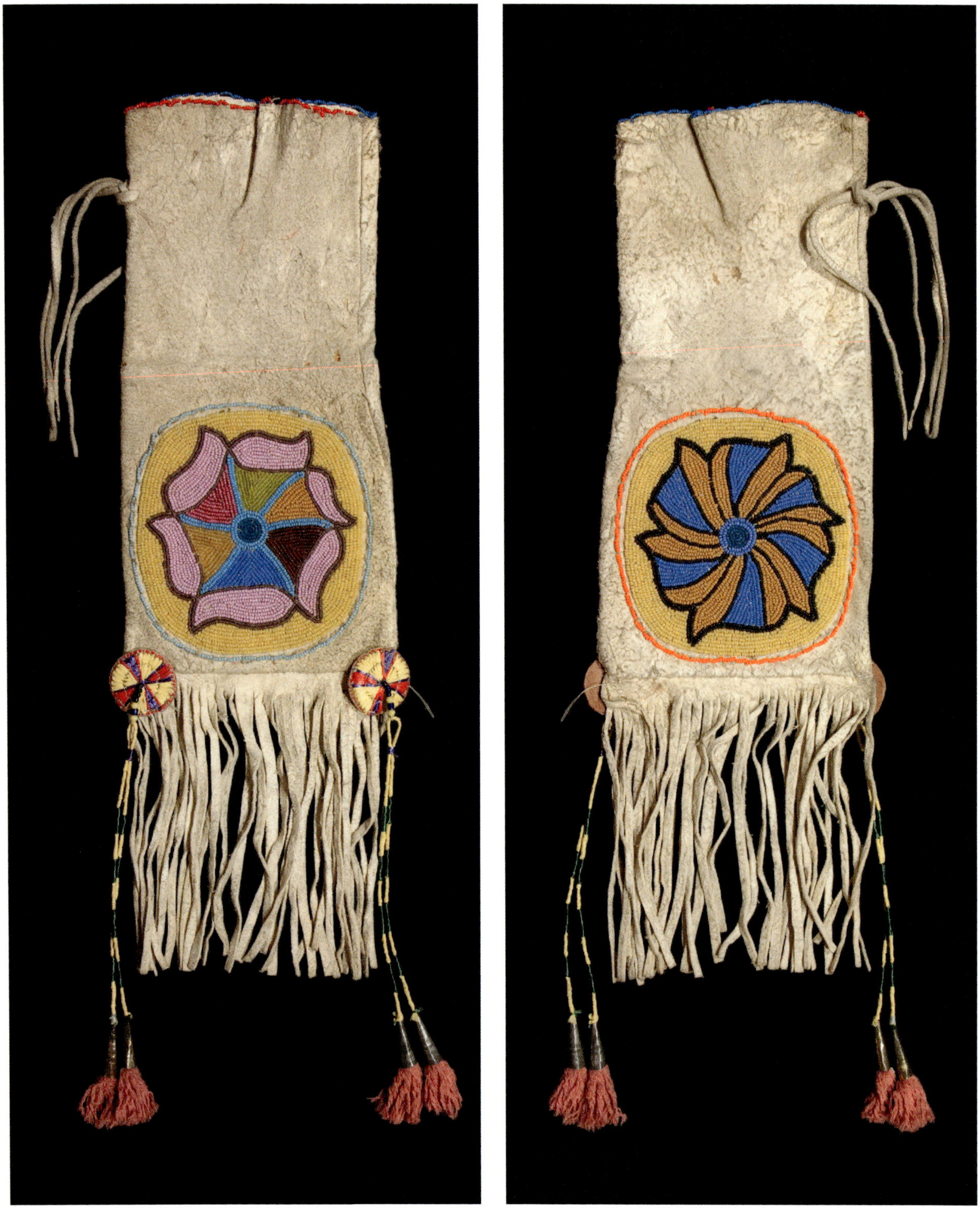

This pipe bag is decorated with beads and metal cones holding frayed wool tassels. The medallions that hold the tassels are made of raffia and are very similar to the raffia medallions on a breastplate in the Hermans collection. It is possible that the medallions on both artifacts were added by Hermans. *Length 57 cm, width 17 cm.*

This pipe bag is decorated with dyed porcupine quills, glass beads, and frayed wool tassels secured with both metal cones and spent rifle cartridges. One side has two animal teeth as additional decoration. *Length 58 cm, width 13 cm.*

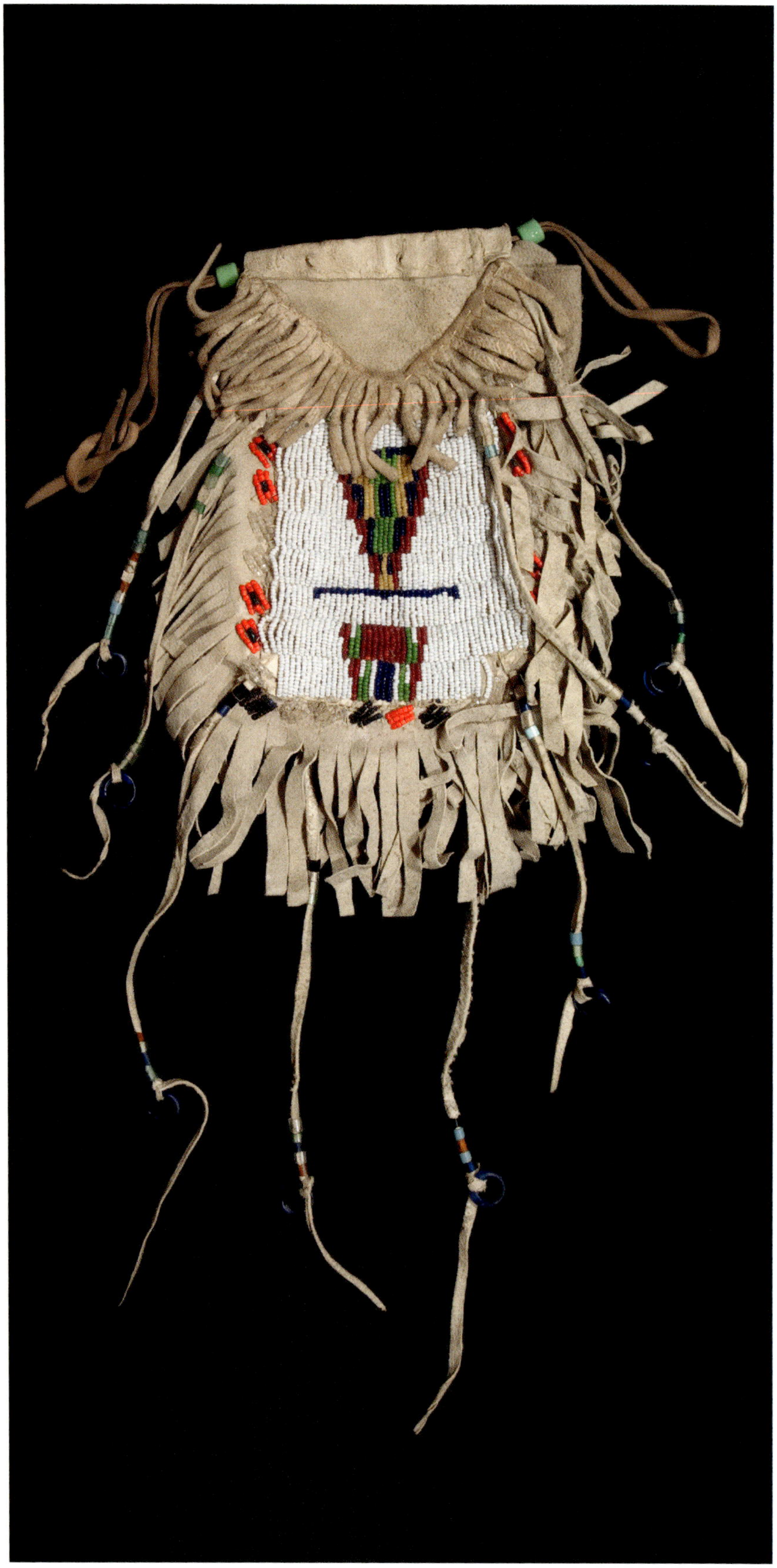

Although Lakotas had used similar bags, or pouches, with beads and/or porcupine quills at an earlier period, the design and ornamentation on this bag suggest that it was made to be sold as a souvenir at the exposition. *Length 58 cm, width 13 cm.*

This leather-handled knife and beaded sheath are clearly handmade. They might have belonged to Chief Black Horn, who wore hand symbols on one of his shirts. The hands on his shirt (shown in chapter 7) stood for "many handshakes" and represented the many people with whom he had shaken hands on his trips to Europe. *Length 47 cm, width 10 cm.*

This knife sheath has no accompanying knife, which suggests that it might have been made with the intent of selling it to an exposition visitor. *Length 53.5 cm, width 8.5 cm.*

This knife and sheath belonged to Chief Black Horn. August Hermans' tag for the set reads, "American knife (scalp knife) with horn handle. Deerskin covered with beads. Fringed suede. Belonged to the big Indian Sioux Chief Black Horn who gave it to me as a sign of our great friendship. The knife is from 1872. The knife sheath is not so old. Nice souvenir August 13th 1935." *Length 41 cm, width 11 cm.*

War club used by Joshua Spotted Owl. It is beaded and wrapped with rawhide and has a rawhide strap for carrying. Although there was no tag for the item and no photograph with him holding it, a typewritten sheet in the trunk from Hermans establishes its connection to Spotted Owl. *Length 49 cm, width 6.5 cm.*

War club, mostly ceremonial, that was probably used by the performers while dancing. It is wrapped with rawhide and bears two horns on one end. This might have been the club acquired by Hermans from Black Horn and mentioned in the 1955 article about the organization called Wigwam, to which he and Eric Wansart belonged. *Length 61 cm, width 19 cm.*

War club made by Joshua Spotted Owl. Hermans' tag for this reads, "Prehistoric flint. Wooden handle covered by horse hair red and black. Eagle feather original model. Sioux tomahawk made by Joshua Spotted Owl. Purchased September 30th 1935." *Length 81 cm, width 13.5 cm.*

Hermans' tag for this artifact, which is just above it, reads, "Piece of the American flag from Joshua Spotted Owl (Pine Ridge South Dakota) May 1935." *Length 38 cm, width 24 cm.*

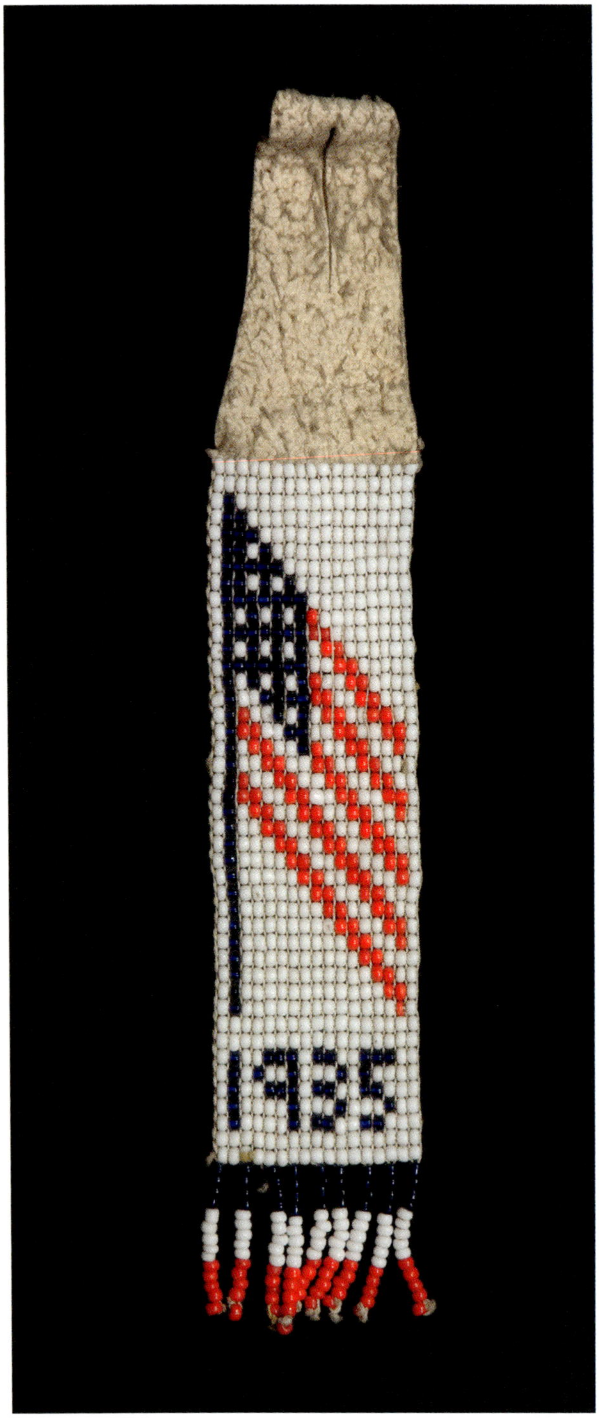

When Buffalo Bill's Wild West was first in Europe, Lakotas made beaded watch fobs to sell to visitors. This fob was made in 1935 specifically for sale at the Brussels exposition, where Hermans acquired it. *Length 17.5 cm, width 3 cm.*

Like a watch fob, this pendant with a representation of a warrior had no real precedent in Lakota culture and was probably created specifically for sale as a souvenir to exposition visitors. *Length 30 cm, width 9 cm.*

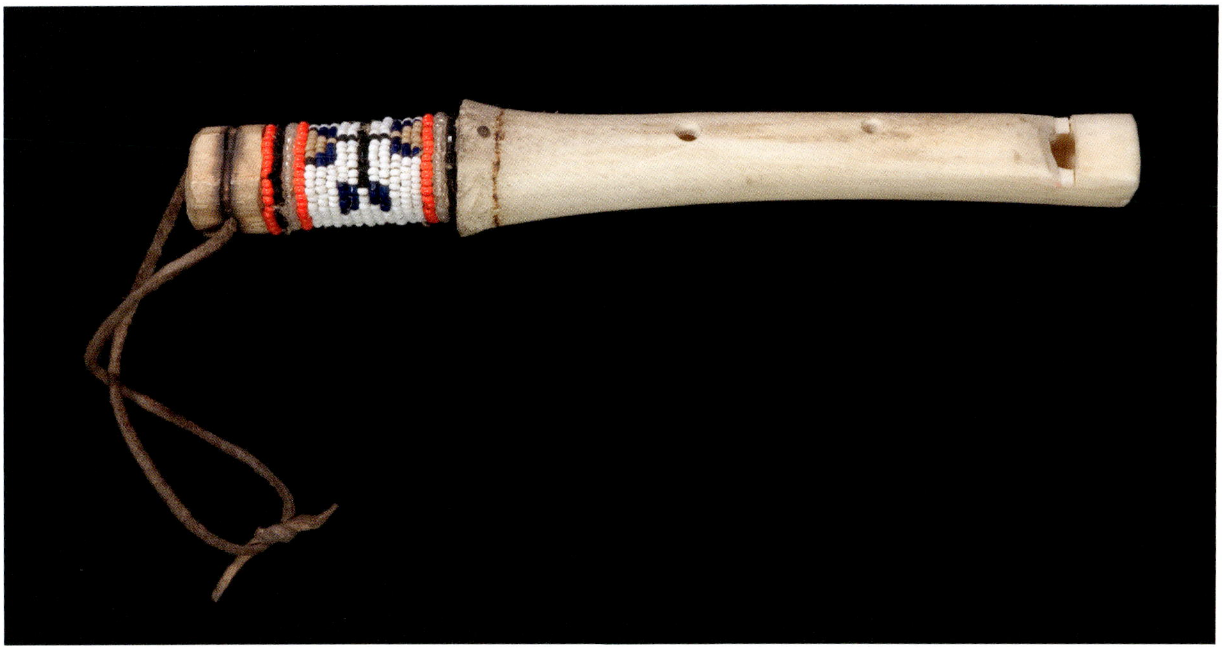

Whistles, traditionally made from eagle wing bones, were important parts of Lakota ceremonies and dances. This whistle was made from bone and would have been used during the dances performed at the exposition. *Length 26 cm, diameter 2.5 cm.*

Like whistles, flutes were used by Lakotas in ceremonies and dances. They were also called love flutes because they were used to play love songs while courting. *Length 51.5 cm, diameter 6 cm.*

This shoe horn made of buffalo horn belonged to Black Horn, according to a typewritten note from Hermans tucked in with the artifacts. By 1935 the Lakotas were wearing street shoes when not performing, so Black Horn probably used the horn with those shoes rather than with moccasins. Though Hermans would not have been interested in an ordinary shoe horn, this piece made of buffalo horn clearly attracted him. *Length 21.5 cm, width 4.5 cm.*

Like watch fobs, picture frames were not within the Lakota tradition, but they appealed to show visitors. *Length 19.5 cm, width 16 cm.*

Hermans' tag for this item reads, "Fan from Chief Black Horn, Sioux name HESAPA, American eagle wing with at the end a grass smelling plait." In Lakota *hé* means horn and *sapa* means black. As the chief of the group in the Indian village, Black Horn would have carried this fan as a mark of his rank and for use in ceremonies. *Length 60 cm, width 14 cm, depth 2.5 cm.*

These pieces of sinew and knives were used by Lucy Little Elk for sewing. Hermans' tag for them reads, "Dry muscle (sinew). Used by the Indians as yarn to sew mocassins [*sic*] and to thread beads. This is sinew (very strong). Lucy Little Elk, June 3rd 1935." Tendons: *length 51 cm.* Knife (*bottom*): *length 17 cm, width 2 cm.* Knife (*top*): *length 12.5 cm, width 1.5 cm.*

Hermans' tag with this group of feathers reads, "Indian head ornament. Belonged to Joshua Spotted Owl. Given by him on June 20th 1935." These are not complete feathers but have been cut down with colored tufts attached. They probably did not come from a headdress. The holes in the bottom of the quills suggest that these feathers were woven directly into Spotted Owl's hair. *Length 20 cm.*

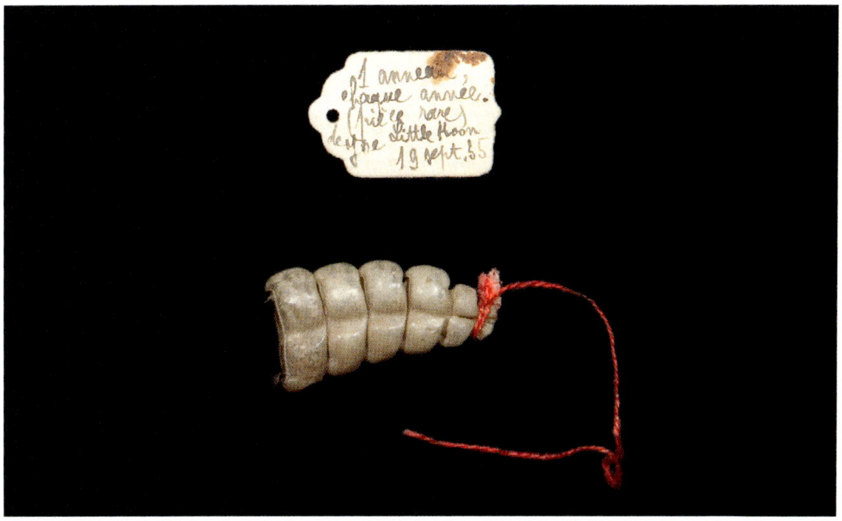

Hermans' tag with this item reads, "A rattle of a rattle snake from 1930. One ring every year (rare piece) from Joe Little Moon September 19th 1935." Although rattlesnakes are fairly common in the United States, particularly in the West, they are not indigenous to Europe. Thus this rattle would have been quite unusual and "rare" to August Hermans. *Length 3 cm, width 1.5 cm.*

Hermans' tag with these eight cowrie shells reads, "Shells pierced with a little hole (done by Indians). They were on the vest of Joshua Spotted Owl. (Oglala Sioux Indian) Given by him on June 1st 1935. The Indians use to decorate their vest with shells. Others did it with teeth. Very original." Each shell: *length 2 cm, width 1.5 cm.*

Hermans' tag with these thirteen cowrie shells reads, "Sea shells (13). In English WAMPUM, In Indian WANNURA. Used by the Sioux to decorate men's vests and women dresses. Come from the dress from little Virginia Little Elk (Three years and six months old) October 11th 1935. These shells are used from generation to generation." Each shell: *length 1.8 cm, width 1.3 cm.*

Leather strips with beaded designs on them were one of the building blocks of decorated clothing for Lakotas. They could be added to moccasins, vests, shirts, and leggings. For the performers in 1935, the strips could also be sold as souvenirs to visitors, who might want to use them as bookmarks or for other purposes. *Length 33 cm to 63 cm, width 4.5 cm to 7 cm.*

A pair of decorative leather strips that could be applied to clothing. Note the broken cross, or "whirling log" symbol, popular among some American Indians until it was adopted by the Nazis as the swastika. Left: *length 64 cm, width 4 cm*. Right: *length 65 cm, width 4 cm*.

Photo of Joe and Rosa Little Moon, taken in a photo booth at the 1935 Exposition Universelle in Brussels. It had been the only photograph that Moses and Walter Littlemoon had had of their parents until François Chladiuk met them in 2006. *From the family album of Walter Littlemoon*

EPILOGUE

Once Chladiuk had pieced together information about the Lakotas who had owned the artifacts, he decided he must find their descendants. With the information he had about the Little Moon family, he made his first visit to Pine Ridge in 2006. There he met Moses Littlemoon. Moses had been born after the family returned from Brussels in 1935. By the time Chladiuk met him, the family name had been changed from Little Moon to Littlemoon. Chladiuk showed him the postcard of the family he had acquired and asked, "Who are these people?" Moses replied, "My father Joe and mother Rosa." He also identified the children in the image. Then Moses left the room for a moment and returned with a photograph of his father and mother. All the other family photographs had been destroyed by a fire in their home, and this was the only photograph he had of his parents. It was labeled "Exposition de Bruxelles 1935."

The family's connection to Hermans' collection was firmly established. When François got home from the visit, he sent copies of the photographs and cards he had gathered, as replacements for those destroyed in the fire. Not long after that visit, François received an e-mail from Moses' younger brother Walter, who told him that Moses had died. Chladiuk also learned that Walter had additional family photographs. Walter and François continued to correspond, establishing a friendship. Chladiuk observes, "The beaded vests, moccasins, and armbands in my collection from that family are the ones I treasure most because of the beautiful story and the good friendship I developed with Walter."

Pair of adult-sized moccasins given by Gilbert Little Moon to Claude Misraki. The moccasins rejoined the other items from the "time capsule" in 2010. *Length 28 cm, height 8 cm.*

Chladiuk met with Guy Huygens and Guy Missian, both of whom had been friends of Hermans and who gave him more information.[1] As Chladiuk continued his research, word spread about his unusual collection of Indian items. Claude Misraki, whose father built the large curving bridge that led to the Indian Village, had been ten at the time of the exposition. He had developed a friendship with seven-year-old Gilbert Aloysius "Al" Little Moon, who had

Claude Misraki's father built a bridge that provided one of the access points to the Indian village at the exposition. In the process young Claude became friends with Gilbert Little Moon, who gave him a pair of moccasins. In 2010 those moccasins were returned to Walter Littlemoon, who asked Chladiuk to keep them with the collection.
François Chladiuk Collection

given him a pair of moccasins. Misraki's grandson contacted Chladiuk and asked him to return the moccasins to Walter Littlemoon, Gilbert's youngest brother. On a visit to Pine Ridge in 2010, François took the moccasins to Walter Littlemoon, but Walter asked François to keep the moccasins because he felt it was more important that the moccasins stay with the other materials. He also thought they would be seen and enjoyed by more people in the collection than if they were at his home.

More people would indeed see the Lakota artifacts. Unlike Hermans, Chladiuk was happy to share the items in the collection. Working with Sergio Purini in 2006, he put together a special exhibit at the Royal Museums of Art and History, which included a small illustrated catalog written by Purini. On Chladiuk's way to Pine Ridge in 2006, he stopped at the Buffalo Bill Museum and Grave near Denver, Colorado, to explore the connections of this group of Lakotas to those who had performed in Buffalo Bill's Wild West. It soon became clear that several of the performers in Brussels had indeed been in Buffalo Bill's Wild West. The result of this visit was an exhibit at the museum in 2009. François Chladiuk, Brussels

François Chladiuk shows the 1935 Lakota materials exhibited in his shop to visitor Monta Lee Dakin. *Steve Friesen Collection*

mayor Freddy Thielemans, and Walter Littlemoon all traveled to Denver for the exhibit opening on February 26, declared Brussels Day by Denver mayor John Hickenlooper. It was Walter Littlemoon's first opportunity to see the artifacts that his family had used and left behind in Brussels. In 2010 Chladiuk created a special exhibit area on the third floor of his shop, open to visitors by request. The grand opening of the exhibit was attended by Mayor Thielemans and other dignitaries.

Today, the artifacts can be seen on exhibit in downtown Brussels, in the third-floor exhibit at Western Shop. But the exhibit is not complete as far as Chladiuk is concerned; he continues his research efforts. And word continues to spread about the collection, bringing new leads. In 2014 François' old friend André Lesire dropped by with a family photograph album from the 1935 exposition.

This family album of photographs taken at the 1935 Exposition Universelle, containing a page of images of the Indian village, was given to Chladiuk by his old friend André Lesire when Lesire learned of Chladiuk's quest. *François Chladiuk Collection*

One of the 1935 headdresses in Chladiuk's collection inspired custom bootmaker Lisa Sorrel to create this pair of boots. *Lisa Sorrel Collection*

On the last page were six photographs of the Lakotas performing and wearing items that were in the collection. Word has also spread about the exhibit in Western Shop, with visitors from Europe and America dropping in to see the artifacts. Chladiuk shares the collection in other ways as well. One of the headdresses appeared at a special exhibit of Indian art at Florence's Pitti Palace in 2012. Another headdress inspired renowned bootmaker Lisa Sorrel to make an award-winning pair of custom cowboy boots.

August Hermans rarely shared his collection of Lakota artifacts. They slumbered, hidden away in his house, for most of his lifetime and for the twenty years following his death. But once discovered, like the objects in a time capsule, they became the keys to unlocking stories of the past, stories that had begun before the artifacts came into being and stories that would continue even after the objects were stored away in their metal trunks. The stories are those of Red Shirt, who was an honored guest of British Parliament; of Jennie LaPoint, a single woman who journeyed to a strange continent not just once but five times; of Sam Lone Bear, who spoke four languages; and of many other Lakota performers. The artifacts represent a cultural patrimony that extended from the nineteenth century through the 1935 Exposition Universelle et Internationale Bruxelles and the waning days of the wild west shows. Today, after being preserved in a Belgian house for nearly seventy years, they symbolize a vibrant and valid heritage. Walter Littlemoon, son of those performers in Europe, can look at his people's history and say with dignity, as he did when he saw his family's artifacts for the first time, "I am not a savage." This, then, is the greater story . . . a message of cultural resilience and survival, of collective and individual worth, and of the pride of a people.

NOTES

CHAPTER 1

1. Carolyn Thomas Foreman, *Indians Abroad: 1493–1938* (Norman: University of Oklahoma Press, 1943), 122–23.

2. Ibid., 138–40.

3. Paul Reddin, *Wild West Shows* (Urbana: University of Illinois Press, 1999), 38–46; Foreman, *Indians Abroad*, 194–95.

4. Don Russell, *The Wild West: A History of the Wild West Shows* (Fort Worth: Amon Carter Museum of Western Art, 1970), 2–3.

5. Mark Twain to Bill Cody, September 10, 1884, Mark Twain Papers, Bancroft Library, University of California at Berkeley.

6. H. Glenn Penny, *Kindred by Choice* (Chapel Hill: University of North Carolina Press, 2013), 57; Miklos Letay, "'Redskins at the Zoo': Sioux Indians in Budapest, 1886," in *Indians and Europe*, ed. Christian F. Feest (Lincoln: University of Nebraska Press, 1989), 375–79.

7. Advertisement in St. George Casino Program, July 16, 1886, Staten Island, Buffalo Bill Museum and Grave Archives, Golden, Colorado; "Buffalo Bill's 'Wild West,'" *Brooklyn Daily Eagle*, August 15, 1886.

8. Buffalo Bill Wild West advertisement, *New Orleans Picayune*, December 16, 1884; American Exhibition flyer, Earl's Court, 1887, Buffalo Bill Papers, Western History Collection, Denver Public Library. Joe Starita, *The Dull Knifes of Pine Ridge* (New York: Putnam, 1995), 150. Joan Carpenter Troccoli, "The Sketchbooks of Emil Lenders: Down to the Soles of the Moccasins," *Gilcrease Journal* 1, no. 1 (Spring 1993): 35. Luther Standing Bear and E. A. Brininstool, *My People the Sioux* (Cambridge, Mass.: Riverside Press, 1928), 255.

9. Steamship *State of Nebraska* passenger list, March 31, 1887, Buffalo Bill Museum and Grave Archives. Linda Scarangella, "Spectacular Native Performances from the Wild West to the Tourist Site, Nineteenth Century to the Present" (Ph.D. diss., McMaster University, 2008), 100.

CHAPTER 2

1. Stanley Vestal, *Sitting Bull: Champion of the Sioux* (Norman: University of Oklahoma Press, 1957), 145.

2. "Indians at Erastina," *New York Times*, June 26, 1886; Linda Scarangella McNenly, *Native Performers in Wild West Shows* (Norman: University of Oklahoma Press, 2012), 69.

3. Lakota tribal information provided by Ehanamani (Dr. Allen Ross) in an interview by the author, March 13, 2014; Waterloo Monument guest register, 1889–1894, Waterloo Battlefield Archives, Waterloo, Belgium; Photograph in Buffalo Bill Museum and Grave Archives.

4. Russell, *Wild West*, 52, 121–27; Marc Lauwens and Sergio Purini, *Indians in Brussels: World Fair 1935*, exhibition catalog (Brussels: Royal Museums of Art and History, 2006), 15; R. V. Belt, Commissioner of the Office of Indian Affairs, to Dr. W. F. Carver and Fred C. Whitney, May 10, 1889, box 165, 047, Records of the Bureau of Indian Affairs, Record Group 75, National Archives and Records Administration, Kansas City, Missouri (hereafter RG 75, NARA, Kansas City).

5. "Indians Complain to the Commissioner," *Washington Post*, October 4, 1895; Peter Nabokov, ed., *Native American Testimony: A Chronicle of Indian-White Relations from Prophecy to the Present, 1492–1992* (New York: Viking Penguin, 1991), 261. Black Heart quoted in L. G. Moses, *Wild West Shows and the Images of American Indians, 1883–1933* (Albuquerque: University of New Mexico Press, 1996), 103. Standing Bear and Brininstool, *My People the Sioux*, 270.

6. Standing Bear and Brininstool, *My People the Sioux*, 259; Sam Lone Bear to Mrs. Alfred Angell, October 24, 1936, private family collection of Kristi Angell, Denver, Colorado; Penny, *Kindred by Choice*, 258.

7. William A. Jones, Commissioner of Indian Affairs, to Colonel William A. Clapp, July 13, 1899, box 22, Letters Received from the Office of Indian Affairs, Indian Warehouses, and Special Agents, 1871–1907 (NAID 598889), RG 75, NARA, Kansas City; financial record from Jule Keen, Buffalo Bill's Wild West treasurer, June 6, 1891 (NAID 285586), box 162, 047, RG 75, NARA, Kansas City.

8. David Bull Bear and Sam Lone Bear business cards, Buffalo Bill Museum and Grave Archives. Reference to David Bull Bear as translator made by Billy McGinty in Jim Filbright and Albert Stehno, eds., *Oklahoma Rough*

Rider: Billy McGinty's Own Story (Norman: University of Oklahoma Press, 2008), 106. H. M. Tidwell, Agent at Pine Ridge, to Charles Cole, March 26, 1921, box 165, 047, RG 75, NARA, Kansas City.

9. E. W. Jermark, Pine Ridge Superintendent, to Frank Goings, a show Indian who was performing with the Sells-Floto Circus, May 22, 1928, box 165, 047, RG 75, NARA, Kansas City; letterhead in M-407, box 5, FF1, Western History Collection, University of Oklahoma Norman; James Hawkins passport, box 9, Buffalo Bill Papers, Western History Collection, Denver Public Library.

10. The Rau photographs are in the collection of the Buffalo Bill Museum and Grave, Golden, Colorado. Calvin Jumping Bull quoted in Alice J. Hall, "Buffalo Bill and the Enduring West," *National Geographic*, July 1981, 84–88. Direct translation of Lakota to English is difficult since there are fewer words in Lakota and they can hold several meanings, depending upon how they are used and in what combinations. Oskate means a "show" or a "fair," and wicasa means "man." Since there were women and children who performed as well, the term oskate wicasa applied to more than adult men. Juti A. Winchester, "Buffalo Bill and the Indians: Pine Ridge Remembers William F. Cody" (paper presented at Western History Association Annual Meeting, October 12, 2000, San Antonio, Texas), 6; Severt Young Bear and R. D. Theisz, *Standing in the Light* (Lincoln: University of Nebraska Press, 1994), 97.

11. Starita, *Dull Knifes*, 142–43; Hall, "Buffalo Bill," 84–88; Winchester, "Buffalo Bill," 6–7; John R. Brennan, Superintendent of Pine Ridge, to W. F. Cody, June 18, 1914, box 160, 047, RG 75, NARA, Kansas City.

12. Standing Bear and Brininstool, *My People the Sioux*, 278.

CHAPTER 3

1. Moses, *Wild West Shows*, 182–83.

2. David Wallace Adams, *Education for Extinction: American Indians and the Boarding School Experience* (Lawrence: University Press of Kansas, 1995), 15, 48; Edmund Jefferson Danzinger Jr., "United States Indian Policy During the Late Nineteenth Century: Change and Continuity," *Hayes Historical Journal* 12, nos. 1/2 (Fall 1992/Winter 1993), accessed online at the Rutherford B. Hayes Presidential Center, http://www.rbhayes.org/hayes/onlinepubs.

3. Advertisement in Buffalo Bill's personal scrapbook for the 1907 season, McCracken Research Library, Buffalo Bill Center of the West, Cody, Wyoming.

4. *Indian Helper*, Carlisle Indian School, March 18, 1898.

5. "Iron Tail," *Indian Helper*, August 13, 1897; Iron Tail to Major Brennan, Pine Ridge Indian Agent, May 27, 1904, box 162, 047, RG 75, NARA, Kansas City; "Indians Die in a Wreck," *Omaha Daily Bee*, April 8, 1904, 1.

6. Adams, *Education for Extinction*, 21. William F. Cody, *True Tales of the Plains* (New York: Cupples and Leon, 1908), 247; William F. Cody to Pine Ridge Agent Charles Penny, May 28, 1891, box 28, 047, RG 75 NARA, Kansas City; Moses, *Wild West Shows*, 116.

7. Louis S. Warren, *Buffalo Bill's America: William Cody and the Wild West Show* (New York: Knopf, 2005), 412–13; *Screenland's First Americans*, booklet, Indian Actors Association, ca. 1935, Buffalo Bill Museum and Grave Archives.

8. "Indians in the Wild West Show," *New York Times*, February 21, 1901; Starita, *Dull Knifes*, 143; Young Bear and Theisz, *Standing in the Light*, 55.

9. Thomas Jefferson Morgan report to Congress, September 5, 1890, cited in Robert Lewis, *From Traveling Show to Vaudeville* (Baltimore, Md.: Johns Hopkins University Press, 2003), 277.

10. "No More Wild West Shows," *New York Times*, December 23, 1899; Moses, *Wild West Shows*, 95–103; Standing Bear and Brininstool, *My People the Sioux*, 261.

11. "At Pine Ridge," *Brooklyn Daily Eagle*, November 22, 1890, 6. "As Narrated by Short Bull," handwritten document, Buffalo Bill Museum and Grave Archives.

12. W. F. Cody to John R. Brennan, Agent, Pine Ridge, June 10, 1903, box 22, Letters Received from the Office of Indian Affairs, Indian Warehouses, and Special Agents, 1871–1907 (NAID 598889), RG 75, NARA, Kansas City.

13. Moses, *Wild West Shows*, 259. Commissioner of Indian Affairs Francis E. Leupp to John R. Brennan, Pine Ridge Superintendent, February 10, 1909, box 164, 047, RG 75, NARA, Kansas City.

14. William House diary, 1898–1899, Buffalo Bill Museum and Grave Archives.

15. Charles Eldridge Griffin, *Four Years in Europe with Buffalo Bill* (Albia, Iowa: Stage Publishing, 1908), 55; postcard of Iron Tail, Buffalo Bill Museum and Grave Archives; House diary.

16. "A Visit to Paris: Graphic Description of the Great Exhibition," *Brooklyn Daily Eagle*, September 13, 1889; "Indians in the Wild West Show," *New York Times*, February 21, 1901.

17. McNenly, *Native Performers*, 58.

18. Chauncey Yellow Robe, "The Menace of the Wild West Shows," *Quarterly Journal of the Society of American Indians* (July–September, 1914), cited in Lewis, *From Traveling Show*, 276–77.

CHAPTER 4

1. Most of the area in eastern Europe was part of the Austro-Hungarian Empire at the time, the countries are referenced here by their twenty-first-century names. Griffin, *Four Years in Europe*, 137–53.

2. Ibid., 55, 127–30; Buffalo Bill's Wild West and Rough Riders of the World program, Olympia, London, 1903, Buffalo Bill Museum and Grave Archives; "Buffalo Bill's Wild West Show Center of Local Interest Today," *Atlanta Constitution*, October 7, 1907.

3. Russell, *Wild West*, 124. Moses, *Wild West Shows*, 189, 321n61. Show Indian Database, based on BBWW contracts, compiled by Jason Heppler, University of Nebraska, Lincoln, available at *"Self-sustaining and a good citizen": William F. Cody and the Progressive Wild West*, http://www.codystudies.org/showindians/database.

4. Russell, *Wild West*, 64–65.

5. McNenly, *Native Performers*, 115. Souvenir postcards from the 1905 exhibition depict Lakota and Ojibway performers in nearly identical costumes.

6. Red Man's Syndicate draft agreement, 1908; "List of 37 Indians Examined by the Pine Ridge Agency physician and declared in good health," March 27, 1909, both in box 164, 047, RG 75, NARA, Kansas City. Names from a list of more than five hundred Indians who performed with Buffalo Bill's Wild West, compiled in 2013, were used in *Oskate Wicasa: One Who Performs*, a 2013 exhibit at the Buffalo Bill Museum and Grave.

7. Robert Wynne, American Consulate General's Office, London, to Francis E. Leupp, Commissioner of Indian Affairs, January 18, 1909, box 164, 047, RG 75, NARA, Kansas City.

8. Commissioner of Indian Affairs Francis E. Leupp to John R. Brennan, Pine Ridge Superintendent, February 10, 1909, box 164, 047, RG 75, NARA, Kansas City.

9. Contract between Frank C. Goings and John R. Brennan, Pine Ridge Superintendent, March 24, 1909, box 164, 047, RG 75, NARA, Kansas City.

10. Indian performers for the Red Man's Syndicate at Earl's Court to Earle B. Gandy, May 22, 1909, box 164, 047, RG 75, NARA, Kansas City; Earle B. Gandy to John R. Brennan, Pine Ridge Superintendent, October 18, 1909, box 164, 047, RG 75, NARA, Kansas City.

11. Moses, *Wild West Shows*, 200.

12. The American Wild West Show program, Brussels, 1910, Buffalo Bill Museum and Grave Archives.

13. Ibid.

14. Earle Gandy to Mr. Valentine, the Indian Commissioner in Washington, and to John R. Brennan, Pine Ridge Agent, June 2, 1910; F. C. Goings to J. R. Brennan, Superintendent Pine Ridge, June 33, 1910, box 164, 047, RG 75, NARA, Kansas City; Moses, *Wild West Shows*, 202.

15. Lauwens and Purini, *Indians in Brussels*, 3.

16. Alex Gates, "Paris' 'Human Zoo'—the Legacy of the Jardin d'Acclimatation," *Paris History Guide*, February 2013, http://parishistoryguide.blogspot.com/2013/02/paris-human-zoo-legacy-of-jardin.html; agreement between Frank C. Goings and John R. Brennan, Superintendent of Pine Ridge, April 10, 1911, box 163, 047, RG 75, NARA, Kansas City.

17. List of Indians to go to Paris, attached to Goings/Brennan agreement, April 10, 1911; Moses, *Wild West Shows*, 215.

18. Contract between Jennie LaPoint and Fernand A. Akoun and Company, April 5, 1911, box 163, 047, RG 75, NARA, Kansas City; Moses, *Wild West Shows*, 202–3.

19. Wolfgang Haberland, "Adrian Jacobsen on Pine Ridge Reservation, 1910," *European Review of Native American Studies* 2, no. 1 (1988): 11–12, 15; Peter Bolz, "Life Among the 'Hunkpapas': A Case Study in German Indian Lore," *Indians and Europe*, ed. Christian F. Feest (Lincoln: University of Nebraska Press, 1989), 483.

20. "Buffalo Bill's Wild West Show Center of Local Interest."

21. Pioneer Scouts program for Buffalo Bill's Wild West and Pawnee Bill's Far East, 1912 and 1913 seasons, Buffalo Bill Museum and Grave Archives.

22. Sells-Floto program, 1923 season, Buffalo Bill Museum and Grave Archives.

23. Russell, *Wild West*, 82.

24. Michael Wallis, *The Real Wild West* (New York: St. Martin's Press, 1999), 260; Moses, *Wild West Shows*, 184–85; John R. Brennan to Sarrasani's Wild West Show, listing Lakota performers, May 19, 1914, box 165, 047, RG 75, NARA, Kansas City; *101 Ranch Real Wild West Souvenir Program*, Anglo-American Exposition, Buffalo Bill Museum and Grave Archives.

25. Two Two's grave has been cared for by Indian hobbyists ever since and is frequently visited by Lakotas traveling in Europe. Wallis, *Real Wild West*, 420–25; Moses, *Wild West Shows*, 186–88.

26. Wallis, *Real Wild West*, 498–99, 510.

CHAPTER 5

1. Clarence O. Shultz, regarding Stanley Adams, to James McGregor, Pine Ridge Superintendent, July 28, 1932, box 165, 047, RG 75, NARA, Kansas City; Moses, *Wild West Shows*, 264; Circus Sarrasani program, box 165, 047, RG 75, NARA, Kansas City.

2. H. M. Tidwell, Agent at Pine Ridge, to the Commissioner of Indian Affairs, April 12, 1919, box 165, 047; Commissioner of Indian Affairs Francis E. Leupp to John R. Brennan, Pine Ridge Superintendent, February 10, 1909, box 164, 047, RG 75, NARA, Kansas City.

3. H. M. Tidwell, Superintendent of Pine Ridge, to Colonel W. F. Fleming, October 21, 1922; H. M. Tidwell, Superintendent of Pine Ridge, to Charles H. Burke, Commissioner of Indian Affairs, August 7, 1923, box 160, 047, RG 75, NARA, Kansas City; Moses, *Wild West Shows*, 258; E. W. Jermark to Charles Burke, [undated] 1924; Charles Burke to E. W. Jermark, Superintendent of Pine Ridge, August 23, 1924, box 161, 047, RG 75, NARA, Kansas City.

4. Eight reservation superintendents to fair associations, February 1, 1925, box 161, 047, RG 75, NARA, Kansas City.

5. Charles Burke to P. H. Marshall, June 18, 1924, box 161, 047, RG 75, NARA, Kansas City.

6. Moses, *Wild West Shows*, 261; contract between the Miller Brothers and sundry Indians, November 15, 1925, box 164, 047, RG 75, NARA, Kansas City.

7. Chief Black Horn and his wife, Bessie; James Grass Sr.; Marshall Hand; William Big Charge; and William Ghost Dog from Dresden, Germany, to E. W. Jermark, Pine Ridge Superintendent, February 13, 1926; James Grass to E. W. Jermark, Pine Ridge Superintendent, September 14, 1926; William Ghost Dog to E. W. Jermark, Pine Ridge Superintendent, September 23, 1926; William Ghost Dog to E. W. Jermark, Pine Ridge Superintendent, received October 9, 1926, all in box 164, 047, RG 75, NARA, Kansas City.

8. Ghost Dog to Jermark, September 23, 1926.

9. Joe Miller to E. W. Jermark, Pine Ridge Superintendent, January 31, 1927, box 164, 047, RG 75, NARA, Kansas City.

10. A. T. Haeberle, American Consul in Charge, Dresden, Germany, to the Secretary of State, Washington, D.C., February 1, 1928, box 165, 047, RG 75, NARA, Kansas City; Wallis, *Real Wild West*, 432; J. C. Miller of 101 Ranch to E. W. Jermark, Pine Ridge Agent, May 10, 1927, box 165; list of performers in Miller Brothers 101 Ranch Real Wild West and Great Far East, 1928 season, box 166, 047, RG 75, NARA, Kansas City.

11. Wallis, *Real Wild West*, 502; Haeberle to Secretary of State, February 1, 1928; Pine Ridge Superintendent E. W. Jermark to George Miller of the Miller Brothers Real Wild West and Great Far East Shows, February 29, 1928, box 166; Clarence Shultz to E. W. Jermark, Pine Ridge Agent, April 1, 1928, box 165; Mr. and Mrs. C. O. Shultz to E. W. Jermark, Pine Ridge Superintendent, June 17, 1928, box 165, 047, RG 75, NARA, Kansas City.

12. C. O. Shultz to E. W. Jermark, April 1, May 1, June 1, July 1, August 1, September 1, October 1, November 1, and December 1, 1928, box 165, 047, RG 75, NARA, Kansas City.

13. Karl Marcus Kreis, "Indians Playing; Indians Praying: Native Americans in Wild West Shows and Catholic Missions," in *Germans and Indians: Fantasies, Encounters, Projections*, ed. Colin G. Calloway, Gerd Gemünden, and Susanne Zantop (Lincoln: University of Nebraska Press, 2002), 202–3. Lother Drager, Rolf Krusche, and Klau Hoffman, *Indianer Nordamerikas* (Radebeul, Germany: Karl May Museum, 1992), 89.

14. John Milk to E. W. Jermark, Pine Ridge Superintendent, September 14, 1928. Originally written in Lakota, the letter was translated into English as well; both copies are in box 165, 047, RG 75, NARA, Kansas City. C. O. Shultz to E. W. Jermark, Pine Ridge Superintendent, December 9, 1928; copy of Milk letter with handwritten note and signatures, box 165, 047, RG 75, NARA, Kansas City; passenger list from the S.S. *Cleveland*, January 20, 1929, accessed through Ancestry.com.

15. Contract between E. W. Jermark, Superintendent of the Pine Ridge Reservation, and C. O. Shultz of Marland, Oklahoma, on behalf of the Sarrasani Circus, February 26, 1929; letters of agreement between C. O. Shultz on behalf of the Sarrasani Circus and Indians who were hired from Pine Ridge, March 1, 1929, box 165, 047, RG 75, NARA, Kansas City.

16. Shultz/Sarrasani Circus and Pine Ridge Indians agreement, March 1, 1929; "Names of Indians from Porcupine that Mr. Shultz Wishes to Take with Show, 1929–1930," box 165, 047, RG 75, NARA, Kansas City; passenger list for the S.S. *Albert Ballin*, March 29, 1930, accessed through Ancestry.com.

17. Hamburg-American Line to E. W. Jermark concerning transportation for the Indians, May 8, 1930; list of performers with Sarrasani Circus for 1930–31 season; agreement between C. O. Shultz and Sam Lone Bear, May 3, 1930; C. O. Shultz to E. W. Jermark, Superintendent of Pine Ridge, June 19, 1930, all in box 165, 047, RG 75, NARA, Kansas City; passenger list for the S.S. *Deutschland*, January 30, 1931, accessed through Ancestry.com. Telegram from Shultz to J. H. McGregor, Superintendent of Pine Ridge, January 31, 1931, box 165, 047, RG 75, NARA, Kansas City.

18. Clarence O. Shultz to James McGregor, Superintendent of Pine Ridge, March 20, 1931; Hans Stosch-Sarrasani to Superintendent of the Pine Ridge

Reservation, March 16, 1931, box 165, 047, RG 75, NARA, Kansas City.

19. Telegram from Captain Henning to Sarrasani, May 1, 1931, box 165, 047, RG 75, NARA, Kansas City; B. G. Courtwright, Field Agent at Pine Ridge, to Commissioner of Indian Affairs, June 19, 1931, box 165, 047, RG 75, NARA, Kansas City.

20. C. A. Henning to Hans Stosch-Sarrasani, May 8, 1931; telegram from Sarrasani to Captain Henning, en route to Pine Ridge, April 30, 1931, box 165, 047, RG 75, NARA, Kansas City.

21. Thomas Stabber to the Pine Ridge Superintendent, April 13, 1931, box 165, 047, RG 75, NARA, Kansas City.

22. Henning to Sarrasani, May 8, 1931.

23. Telegram from Hans Stosch-Sarrasani to Pine Ridge Superintendent Courtwright, June 23, 1931; Henning in Rushville to Bertram W. Mills in London, July 10, 1931, box 165, 047, RG 75, NARA, Kansas City.

24. James McGregor to the Commissioner of Indian Affairs, August 31, 1931; agreement between Clarence Shultz and Mark Spider, September 1, 1931; list of Sarrasani performers' names entitled "Indians 1931," box 165; contract between Charley High Hawk and Buffalo Bill's Wild West for 1912 and 1913, box 162, 047, RG 75, NARA, Kansas City.

25. Don Russell, *Lives and Legends of Buffalo Bill* (Norman: University of Oklahoma Press, 1960), 352.

26. Articles and photos in City Archives, s-Hertogenbosch, Netherlands, accessed March 15, 2014, http://bosschebabbels.nl/lakota-indianen-1926-1931.

27. Lauwens and Purini, *Indians in Brussels*, 16. Oscar Chapman to the Secretary of State in response to an inquiry from Belgium, April 30, 1934, box 165, 047, NARA, Kansas City.

28. Sarrasani company history (in German), https://www.sarrasani.de/unternehmen/historie.

29. Clarence Shultz to James McGregor, Pine Ridge Superintendent, July 30, 1933, box 165, 047, RG 75, NARA, Kansas City. "How to Enjoy this Week at the Fair, Week ending July 29," *Official World's Fair Weekly*, printed by the Cuneo Press for the Century of Progress, July 23, 1933, private collection of Steve Friesen; Moses, *Wild West Shows*, 269–70.

30. "How to Enjoy this Week at the Fair"; Shultz to McGregor, July 30, 1933; Moses, *Wild West Shows*, 271–72; Starita, *Dull Knifes*, 136.

31. James McGregor to Lew Wright, with a list of Indians who will perform at the Century of Progress, June 23, 1933; Clarence Shultz to James McGregor, Pine Ridge Superintendent, October 26, 1933, box 165, 047, RG 75, NARA, Kansas City.

CHAPTER 6

1. Oscar L. Chapman to the Secretary of State, April 30, 1934, box 165, 047, RG 75, NARA, Kansas City. Letterhead of the Associated American Indian Group, private collection of François Chladiuk.

2. "Redskins Block Paris Traffic," UP release, July 5, 1935, *Hammond (Ind.) Times*; "Indians Bound for Brussels," *New York Times*, April 26, 1935.

3. "Redskins Block Paris Traffic"; "Indians Bound for Brussels." Lone Bear's name appears in performer lists and contracts associated with six European appearances by Buffalo Bill's Wild West and the Sarrasani Circus. In a letter written to Mrs. Alfred Angell on October 24, 1936 (Angell collection), he wrote, "I was eight times across ocean."

4. *Le Livre d'Or de l'Exposition Universelle et Internationale—Bruxelles 1935* (*The Golden Book of the Brussels World Fair, 1935*), undated newspaper clipping from 1935, and AAIG letterhead, all in Chladiuk collection.

5. McNeil Island Penitentiary Records of Prisoners Received, 1887–1951, M1619, roll 3, NARA, Washington, D.C.; letter of agreement between C. O. Shultz and Sam Lone Bear, April 13, 1935, box 165, 047, RG 75, NARA, Kansas City.

6. Indian census records 1894, 1895, 1896, 1897, 1898, 1899, 1900, NARA, accessed through Ancestry.com; information associated with Sam Lone Bear's pencil drawing, which appears in Michelle Delaney, *Buffalo Bill's Wild West Warriors* (New York: Harper Collins, 2007), 70–71; Paul Stewart, unpublished biography of Sam Lone Bear, based on personal interview, ca. 1935, presented in 1972 to the Colorado Historical Society Archives, Denver.

7. Delaney, *Wild West Warriors*, 69; William Rau photographs and Lone Bear business card, Buffalo Bill Museum and Grave Archives; Stewart, Sam Lone Bear biography.

8. Sandra Sagala, *Buffalo Bill on the Silver Screen: The Films of William F. Cody* (Norman: University of Oklahoma Press, 2013), 106. Stewart, Sam Lone Bear biography. On October 15, 1923, Marthe Antoine Gerardin drew a portrait of Sam Lone Bear in Paris while he was appearing there with the *Covered Wagon* party. It was dated by Gerardin with the number 15, followed by an X and 1923. The words "Covered Wagon" were also written on the portrait. This information was provided by Christian Sturgis of Sturgis Auctions on June 3, 2015. Sturgis sold the drawing, for which he has documentation.

9. Indian census record 1900 and United States censuses 1910 and 1930, NARA, accessed through Ancestry.com;

Buffalo Bill to Major John R. Brennan, regarding Sam Lone Bear's wife's illness, June 20, 1907, Buffalo Bill Museum and Grave Archives; Sam Lone Bear to Mrs. Alfred Angell, December 1, 1936, Angell collection.

10. Omer C. Stewart, *Peyote Religion: A History* (Norman: University of Oklahoma Press, 1987), 178.

11. Ibid., 178, 185–87, 195–201, 265–67.

12. Ibid., 180, 200, 274. Indian censuses from Pine Ridge 1894–1902 and 1915–1937; Indian censuses from Uncompaghre 1922–1929; United States censuses 1900, 1910; Record of Prisoners at McNeil Penitentiary, 1887–1951, NARA, all accessed through Ancestry.com.

13. Lone Bear to Angell, December 1, 1936; United States census 1930, NARA, accessed through Ancestry.com.

14. Indian census 1896, NARA, accessed through Ancestry.com; draft registration card for Thomas Stabber, September 18, 1917, NARA, accessed through Ancestry.com; list of Indians with Buffalo Bill's Wild West, April 12, 1895, box 162, Main Decimal Files, 1900–1965, RG 75, NARA, Kansas City; route books and staff lists for Buffalo Bill Wild West, season 1899 and season 1900, Buffalo Bill Museum and Grave Archives.

15. Griffin, *Four Years in Europe*, 21–28; passenger list for the S.S. *Etruria*, May 16, 1903, accessed through Ancestry.com.

16. "Le Petit 'Vingtième' Chez les Peaux-Rouges," *Le Petit Vingtième*, supplement to *Le Vingtième Siècle*, February 25, 1932, Chladiuk collection.

17. Standing Bear and Brininstool, *My People the Sioux*, 246–49.

18. Ibid., 270–71, 283–85.

19. Meghan Backhouse, accession details for Newton Turvey Collection, Pitt Rivers Museum, University of Oxford, England.

20. Passenger lists for the R.M.S. *Majestic*, December 11, 1925; the S.S. *Albert Ballin*, January 10, 1927; and the S.S. *Deutschland*, June 24, 1932, all accessed through Ancestry.com; performers' list, Miller Brothers 101 Ranch Real Wild West and Great Far East, 1928 season, box 166, 047, RG 75, NARA, Kansas City.

21. Interview by the author with Stella Iron Cloud, great-granddaughter of Daniel Black Horn, August 8, 2016; passenger list for the S.S. *Deutschland*, December 8, 1935, accessed through Ancestry.com.

22. Lakota Tribal Council information from "Tribal Council Members (Indian Reorganization Act)," last updated July 14, 2016, http://freepages.genealogy.rootsweb.ancestry.com/~mikestevens/ira_councils.htm; Heppler, Indian Performers Database; James McGregor to Lew Wright, with a list of Indians who will perform at the Century of Progress, June 23, 1933, box 165, 047, RG 75, NARA, Kansas City; United States census 1910, accessed through Ancestry.com.

23. Heppler, Indian Performers Database; Indian censuses 1902, 1915, 1925, accessed through Ancestry.com; United States census 1910; Belle Fouche performers' lists, 1925 and 1928, box 161, 047, RG 75, NARA, Kansas City; S.S. *Deutschland* passenger list, December 8, 1935.

24. Indian censuses 1899, 1934, accessed through Ancestry.com; contract between John Little Elk and John Robinson Combined Ten Big Shows, April 17, 1905, box 163, 047, RG 75, NARA, Kansas City; Heppler, Indian Performers Database; United States census 1910; S.S. *Deutschland* passenger list, December 8, 1935. Information on Little Elk's first visit to Europe in 1929 in a scrapbook in the archives of the Munich Cowboy Club, shown to me during a visit on May 9, 2015.

25. S.S. *Deutschland* passenger list, December 8, 1935; United States census 1910; Heppler, Indian Performers Database.

26. Littlemoon (also Little Moon) family tree as provided to François Chladiuk by Walter Littlemoon; Indian census 1934, accessed through Ancestry.com; my survey of wild west and circus programs from 1883 to 1935; Scarangella, "Spectacular Native Performances," 105–7.

27. Contract between Little Moon and the Young Buffalo Wild West Co., box 166, 047, RG 75, NARA, Kansas City; Russell, *Wild West*, 85–86.

28. Contracts between C. O. Shultz and Lakota performers, April 15, 1935, box 165, 047, RG 75, NARA, Kansas City.

29. "Surprise for Belgians," *Lowell Sun*, May 20, 1935.

CHAPTER 7

1. *Miller Brothers 101 Ranch Real Wild West and Great Far East Official Program*, 1926, Buffalo Bill Museum and Grave Archives.

2. *Buffalo Bill Wild West Courier*, 1898, 27, Buffalo Bill Museum and Grave Archives.

3. *Pawnee Bill's Historic Wild West Program*, ca. 1900. *Buffalo Bill's Wild West and Pawnee Bill's Far East Program*, 1909, Buffalo Bill Museum and Grave Archives.

4. Souvenir program, Wonderland, Revere Beach, Mass., featuring Pawnee Bill's Great Wild West, 1908, Buffalo Bill Museum and Grave Archives; "Indians in the Wild West Show," *New York Times*, February 21, 1901.

5. Contract used by the Red Man's Syndicate for the performances at Earl's Court in 1909, box 164, 047, RG 75, NARA, Kansas City.

6. Haberland, "Adrian Jacobsen," 13.

7. Julian Ralph, "Behind the 'Wild West' Scenes," *Harper's Weekly*, August 1894. McNenly, *Native Performers*, 92–97.

8. *Le Petit Vingtième*, February 28, 1932.

9. Tina Koeppe, "Omaha Charley and the Bristol Collection of Native American Artifacts," *Nebraska History* (Winter 2009): 183; Troccoli, "Sketchbooks of Emil Lenders," 37.

10. Standing Bear and Brininstool, *My People the Sioux*, 246.

11. Moses, *Wild West Shows*, 171–75.

12. Henning to Mills in London, July 10, 1931.

13. Ray Lyon to Pine Ridge Superintendent Jermark on Lyon Curio Store letterhead, [undated] 1927, box 161; C. A. Henning to Hans Stosch-Sarrasani, May 8, 1931, box 165, 047, RG 75, NARA, Kansas City.

14. C. O. Shultz to Pine Ridge Superintendent McGregor on Lyon Curio Store letterhead, May 23, 1933; note from Clarence Shultz regarding Strong Talk's account, sent to the Pine Ridge Agency, arrived September 8, 1933; James McGregor, Pine Ridge Superintendent, to Clarence Shultz, September 29, 1933, all in box 165, 047, RG 75, NARA, Kansas City.

15. *Pawnee Bill's Indian Trading Post Catalog*, no. 5 and no. 6, ca. 1935, Chladiuk collection.

16. Henning to Sarrasani, May 8, 1931.

17. Record of provenance for Black Horn "Many Handshakes" shirt (#11450) in Denver Museum of Nature and Science collection. In 1940 the shirt was sold by Black Horn to Drew Bax, from whom the museum acquired it. Photographs of Lakotas shaking hands in the Buffalo Bill Museum and Grave Archives; customs tags for two pairs of moccasins sent to Brussels in the Chladiuk collection.

18. Clarence O. Shultz to James McGregor, Pine Ridge Superintendent, July 28, 1932, box 165, 047, RG 75, NARA, Kansas City; *Pawnee Bill's Indian Trading Post Catalog*, no. 5.

CHAPTER 8

1. "Le Livre d'Or de l'Exposition Universelle et Internationale—Bruxelles 1935."

2. Ibid.

3. Lauwens and Purini, *Indians in Brussels*, 3–4.

4. Jane Turner, ed., *The Dictionary of Art* (London: Macmillan, 1996), 852. Wansart artwork and information from the Chladiuk collection, including Eric Wansart 1910 sketchbook, drawing of White Buffalo Man.

5. Lauwens and Purini, *Indians in Brussels*, 3; Theo Tassencourt, "Le Soir Illustré," November 10, 1955, Chladiuk collection; François Chladiuk interview with August Hermans' friend Guy Huygens, August 2004, Chladiuk collection.

CHAPTER 9

1. S.S. *Deutschland* passenger list, December 8, 1935.

2. William F. Cody, "Mobilizing a Mimic Army," *Collier's Weekly*, April 13, 1901, 20; *Buffalo Bill's Wild West and Pawnee Bill's Far East Program*, 1909, Buffalo Bill Museum and Grave Archives.

3. Matthew Krystal, *Indigenous Dance and Dancing Indian* (Boulder: University Press of Colorado, 2012), 98; John William Troutman, *Indian Blues: American Indians and the Politics of Music, 1879–1934* (Norman: University of Oklahoma Press, 2009), 36; Moses, *Wild West Shows*, 275; "Indian Tribes to Pow Wow at Rapid City," undated news clipping, box 161, 047, RG 75, NARA, Kansas City.

4. Troutman, *Indian Blues*, 257.

5. *Oglala Sioux Fair and Festival Program*, August 14–16, 1941, box 161, 047, RG 75, NARA, Kansas City.

6. Russell, *Wild West*, 110–12.

7. List of performers at Nebraska event in 1936, box 161, 047, RG 75, NARA, Kansas City; Russell, *Wild West*, 112–14; bankruptcy papers for Tim McCoy Circus, box 163, 047, RG 75, NARA, Kansas City; Stella Iron Cloud interview; Pine Ridge Superintendent O. R. Sande to George Comer of the Sheridan County Fair, box 161, 047, RG 75, NARA, Kansas City; Walter Littlemoon, *They Called Me Uncivilized* (Bloomington, Ind.: iUniverse, 2009), 18–19.

8. Penny, *Kindred by Choice*, 136–37, 150–51. Penny's citations include correspondence between Stabber and Eber, in the possession of Max Oliv, Munich; United States census 1940, NARA, accessed through Ancestry.com.

9. Correspondence between Sam Lone Bear and Mrs. Alfred Angell, October 24, December 1, and December 27, 1936, Angell collection.

10. United States census 1940; list of performers at Nebraska event in 1936, box 161, 047, RG 75, NARA, Kansas City; "Eagles Will Watch," *Indian Sentinel* (published by the Bureau of Catholic Indian Missions) 27, no. 7 (1947): 110; "Indians Protest at Paleface Legislation," *Syracuse Herald*, April, 23, 1937; Starita, *Dull Knifes*, 140–41.

11. Death records for Pine Ridge, NARA, accessed through Archives.com; Littlemoon, *They Called Me Uncivilized*, 17, 37–46, 55.

CHAPTER 10

1. Joe McNeill, "Heil Hitler Away," *True West*, June 2010, 24; Hartmut Lutz, "German Indianthusiasm," in Calloway, Gemünden, and Zantop, *Germans and Indians*, 178–79.

2. Advertising postcard for 1940 program at Rathen, Friesen collection; Signe O. Wegener, "Not Really the Last Mohican: Chingachgook and the Curious Case of East Germany's Indian Movement, 1956–1989," in *James Fenimore Cooper: His Country and His Art*, Papers from the 2009 Cooper Seminar, ed. Hugh C. MacDougall (Oneonta: State University of New York College at Oneonta, 2009), 77–81.

3. Lutz, "German Indianthusiasm," 177; Kenneth William Townsend, *World War II and the American Indian* (Albuquerque: University of New Mexico Press, 2000), 32–36.

4. Colin G. Calloway, "Historical Encounters Across Five Centuries," in Calloway, Gemünden, and Zantop, *Germans and Indians*, 73; R. D. Theisz, "The Bad Speakers and the Long Braids: References to Foreign Enemies in Lakota Song Texts," in Feest, *Indians and Europe*, 429–32.

5. Burnel Hershey, "Indians on the Warpath" (from *American Mercury*), *Evening Bulletin, Providence*, October 11, 1944; Herman J. Viola, *Warriors in Uniform: The Legacy of American Indian Heroism* (Washington, D.C.: National Geographic, 2008), 99.

6. Calloway, "Historical Encounters," 74–75; Townsend, *World War II*, 72.

7. Russell, *Wild West*, 121–27; American Wild West Show and Rodeo program, Chladiuk collection.

8. Bolz, "Life Among the 'Hunkpapas,'" 480, 484; Wegener, "Not Really the Last Mohican," 77–81.

9. Bolz, "Life Among the 'Hunkpapas,'" 480, 484.

10. Christian F. Feest, "Germany's Indians in a European Perspective," in Calloway, Gemünden, and Zantop, *Germans and Indians*, 36–37. Information furnished to François Chladiuk by the Royal Museums of Art and History.

11. Information gathered by François Chladiuk from employee records at the Royal Museums of Art and History.

12. Jules Piteraerens to Eric Wansart, November 30, 1943, Chladiuk collection; Tassencourt, "Le Soir Illustré." Martougin Chocolate sticker books, Chladiuk collection.

13. Tassencourt, "Le Soir Illustré."

14. John Plompen, Brussels Section Chief, U.S. Information Service, to August Hermans, March 9, 1962, Chladiuk collection.

15. Philip Burnham, *Song of Dewey Beard* (Lincoln: University of Nebraska Press, 2014), 95–96; programs and photographs from the 1958 World's Fair, Chladiuk collection.

16. Paul Pattengale, Cooperative Extension Service, Fort Collins, Colorado, to August Hermans, December 30, 1959; letters from Southern Colorado Land and Livestock Company, Walsenburg, Colorado; and "Colorado Ranch," *Western Gazette* (a western enthusiast magazine in France), 1966, all in the Chladiuk collection.

17. Chladiuk interview with Huygens; François Chladiuk interview with August Hermans' friend Guy Missian, 2006; notation of death on Certificat de Residence & D'Inscription for August Joseph Hermans, Administration Communale de Schaerbeek, all in Chladiuk collection.

CHAPTER 11

1. All François Chladiuk quotations and paraphrases in this chapter are from multiple conversations over ten years of friendship, including during our collaboration on this book.

EPILOGUE

1. Chladiuk interview with Huygens; Chladiuk interview with Missian.

BIBLIOGRAPHY

ARCHIVES AND MANUSCRIPT COLLECTIONS

Angell, Kristi. Private family collection, Denver, Colorado.

Buffalo Bill Museum and Grave Archives, Golden, Colorado.

Buffalo Bill. Papers. Western History Collection, Denver Public Library.

Chladiuk, François. Private collection, Brussels, Belgium.

Colorado Historical Society Archives, Denver.

Friesen, Steve. Private collection, Littleton, Colorado.

McCracken Research Library. Buffalo Bill Center of the West, Cody, Wyoming.

Munich Cowboy Club Archives, Munich, Germany.

Records of the Bureau of Indian Affairs. Record Group 75. National Archives and Records Administration, Kansas City, Missouri.

Sturgis, Christian. Private collection, Sturgis Antiques, Baltimore, Maryland.

Twain, Mark. Papers. Bancroft Library, University of California at Berkeley.

Waterloo Battlefield Archives, Waterloo, Belgium.

Western History Collection. University of Oklahoma, Norman.

BOOKS, ARTICLES, AND PAPERS

Adams, David Wallace. *Education for Extinction: American Indians and the Boarding School Experience.* Lawrence: University Press of Kansas, 1995.

Bolz, Peter. "Life Among the 'Hunkpapas': A Case Study in German Indian Lore." In *Indians and Europe*, edited by Christian F. Feest, 483. Lincoln: University of Nebraska Press, 1989.

Burnham, Philip. *Song of Dewey Beard.* Lincoln: University of Nebraska Press, 2014.

Calloway, Colin G. "Historical Encounters Across Five Centuries." In *Germans and Indians: Fantasies, Encounters, Projections*, edited by Colin G. Calloway, Gerd Gemünden, and Susanne Zantop, 73. Lincoln: University of Nebraska Press, 2002.

Calloway, Colin G., Gerd Gemünden, and Susanne Zantop. *Germans and Indians: Fantasies, Encounters, Projections.* Lincoln: University of Nebraska Press, 2002.

Cody, William F. "Mobilizing a Mimic Army." *Collier's Weekly*, April 13, 1901, 20.

———. *True Tales of the Plains.* New York: Cupples and Leon, 1908.

Danzinger, Edmund Jefferson, Jr. "United States Indian Policy During the Late Nineteenth Century: Change and Continuity." *Hayes Historical Journal* 12, nos. 1/2 (Fall 1992/Winter 1993), accessed online at the Rutherford B. Hayes Presidential Center, http://www.rbhayes.org/hayes/onlinepubs.

Delaney, Michelle. *Buffalo Bill's Wild West Warriors.* New York: Harper Collins, 2007.

Deloria, Philip J. *Indians in Unexpected Places.* Lawrence: University Press of Kansas, 2004.

———. *Playing Indian.* New Haven, Conn.: Yale University Press, 1999.

Drager, Lother, Rolf Krusche, and Klau Hoffman. *Indianer Nordamerikas.* Radebeul, Germany: Karl May Museum, 1992.

Feest, Christian F. "Germany's Indians in a European Perspective." In *Germans and Indians: Fantasies, Encounters, Projections*, edited by Colin G. Calloway, Gerd Gemünden, and Susanne Zantop, 36–37. Lincoln: University of Nebraska Press, 2002.

———, ed. *Indians and Europe.* Lincoln: University of Nebraska Press, 1989

Filbright, Jim, and Albert Stehno, eds. *Oklahoma Rough Rider: Billy McGinty's Own Story.* Norman: University of Oklahoma Press, 2008.

Foreman, Carolyn Thomas. *Indians Abroad: 1493–1938.* Norman: University of Oklahoma Press, 1943.

Gates, Alex. "Paris' 'Human Zoo'—the Legacy of the Jardin d'Acclimatation." *Paris History Guide*, February 2013. http://parishistoryguide.blogspot.com/2013/02/paris-human-zoo-legacy-of-jardin.html.

Griffin, Charles Eldridge. *Four Years in Europe with Buffalo Bill.* Albia, Iowa: Stage Publishing, 1908.

Haberland, Wolfgang. "Adrian Jacobsen on Pine Ridge Reservation, 1910." *European Review of Native American Studies* 2, no. 1 (1988): 11–12, 15.

Hall, Alice J. "Buffalo Bill and the Enduring West." *National Geographic*, July 1981, 84–88.

Hoxie, Frederick E. *A Final Promise: The Campaign to Assimilate the Indians, 1890–1920*. Lincoln: University of Nebraska Press, 1984.

Koeppe, Tina. "Omaha Charley and the Bristol Collection of Native American Artifacts." *Nebraska History* (Winter 2009): 183.

Kreis, Karl Marcus. "Indians Playing; Indians Praying: Native Americans in Wild West Shows and Catholic Missions." In *Germans and Indians: Fantasies, Encounters, Projections*, edited by Colin G. Calloway, Gerd Gemünden, and Susanne Zantop, 202–3. Lincoln: University of Nebraska Press, 2002.

Krystal, Matthew. *Indigenous Dance and Dancing Indian*. Boulder: University Press of Colorado, 2012.

Lauwens, Marc, and Sergio Purini. *Indians in Brussels: World Fair 1935*. Brussels: Royal Museums of Art and History, 2006. Exhibition catalog.

Letay, Miklos. "'Redskins at the Zoo': Sioux Indians in Budapest, 1886." In *Indians and Europe*, edited by Christian F. Feest, 375–79. Lincoln: University of Nebraska Press, 1989.

Lewis, Robert. *From Traveling Show to Vaudeville*. Baltimore, Md.: Johns Hopkins University Press, 2003.

Littlemoon, Walter. *They Called Me Uncivilized*. Bloomington, Ind.: iUniverse, 2009.

Lutz, Hartmut. "German Indianthusiasm." In *Germans and Indians: Fantasies, Encounters, Projections*, edited by Colin G. Calloway, Gerd Gemünden, and Susanne Zantop, 178–79. Lincoln: University of Nebraska Press, 2002.

MacDougall, Hugh C., ed. *James Fenimore Cooper: His Country and His Art*. Papers from the 2009 Cooper Seminar. Oneonta: State University of New York College of Oneonta, 2009.

Madra, Sam. *Hostiles: The Lakota Ghost Dance and Buffalo Bill's Wild West*. Norman: University of Oklahoma Press, 2006.

McNeill, Joe. "Heil Hitler Away." *True West*, June 2010, 24.

McNenly, Linda Scarangella. *Native Performers in Wild West Shows*. Norman: University of Oklahoma Press, 2012.

Moses, L. G. *Wild West Shows and the Images of American Indians, 1883–1933*. Albuquerque: University of New Mexico Press, 1996.

Nabokov, Peter, ed. *Native American Testimony: A Chronicle of Indian-White Relations from Prophecy to the Present, 1492–1992*. New York: Viking Penguin, 1991.

Penny, H. Glenn. *Kindred by Choice*. Chapel Hill: University of North Carolina Press, 2013.

Ralph, Julian. "Behind the 'Wild West' Scenes." *Harper's Weekly*, August 1894, 775–76.

Reddin, Paul. *Wild West Shows*. Urbana: University of Illinois Press, 1999.

Russell, Don. *Lives and Legends of Buffalo Bill*. Norman: University of Oklahoma Press, 1960.

———. *The Wild West: A History of the Wild West Shows*. Fort Worth: Amon Carter Museum of Western Art, 1970.

Sagala, Sandra. *Buffalo Bill on the Silver Screen: The Films of William F. Cody*. Norman: University of Oklahoma Press, 2013.

Scarangella, Linda. "Spectacular Native Performances from the Wild West to the Tourist Site, Nineteenth Century to the Present." Ph.D. diss., McMaster University, 2008.

Standing Bear, Luther, and E. A. Brininstool. *My People the Sioux*. Cambridge, Mass.: Riverside Press, 1928.

Starita, Joe. *The Dull Knifes of Pine Ridge*. New York: Putnam, 1995.

Stewart, Omer C. *Peyote Religion: A History*. Norman: University of Oklahoma Press, 1987.

Theisz, R. D. "The Bad Speakers and the Long Braids: References to Foreign Enemies in Lakota Song Texts." In *Indians and Europe*, edited by Christian F. Feest, 429–32. Lincoln: University of Nebraska Press, 1989.

Townsend, Kenneth William. *World War II and the American Indian*. Albuquerque: University of New Mexico Press, 2000.

Troccoli, Joan Carpenter. "The Sketchbooks of Emil Lenders: Down to the Soles of the Moccasins." *Gilcrease Journal* 1, no. 1 (Spring 1993): 35.

Troutman, John William. *Indian Blues: American Indians and the Politics of Music, 1879–1934*. Norman: University of Oklahoma Press, 2009.

Turner, Jane, ed. *The Dictionary of Art*. London: Macmillan, 1996.

Vestal, Stanley. *Sitting Bull: Champion of the Sioux*. Norman: University of Oklahoma Press, 1957.

Viola, Herman J. *Warriors in Uniform: The Legacy of American Indian Heroism.* Washington, D.C.: National Geographic, 2008.

Wallis, Michael. *The Real Wild West.* New York: St. Martin's Press, 1999.

Warren, Louis S. *Buffalo Bill's America: William Cody and the Wild West Show.* New York: Knopf, 2005.

Wegener, Signe O. "Not Really the Last Mohican: Chingachgook and the Curious Case of East Germany's Indian Movement, 1956–1989." In *James Fenimore Cooper: His Country and His Art*, Papers from the 2009 Cooper Seminar, edited by Hugh C. MacDougall, 77–81. Oneonta: State University of New York College at Oneonta, 2009.

Winchester, Juti A. "Buffalo Bill and the Indians: Pine Ridge Remembers William F. Cody." Paper presented at Western History Association Annual Meeting, October 12, 2000, San Antonio, Texas.

Young Bear, Severt, and R. D. Theisz. *Standing in the Light.* Lincoln: University of Nebraska Press, 1994.

INDEX

Page numbers in italic *type refer to illustrations.*